Freedom, Redemption and Communion

D1567997

Freedom, Redemption and Communion

Studies in Christian Doctrine

Oliver D. Crisp

t&tclark

LONDON • NEW YORK • OXFORD • NEW DELHI • SYDNEY

T&T CLARK
Bloomsbury Publishing Plc
50 Bedford Square, London, WC1B 3DP, UK
1385 Broadway, New York, NY 10018, USA
29 Earlsfort Terrace, Dublin 2, Ireland

BLOOMSBURY, T&T CLARK and the T&T Clark logo are trademarks
of Bloomsbury Publishing Plc

First published in Great Britain 2021

Cover design: Terry Woodley
Cover image: "Negative Sky" by Oliver D. Crisp, acrylic on canvas, March 2021.
Used with permission of the artist.

A catalogue record for this book is available from the British Library.

Names: Crisp, Oliver, author.
Title: Freedom, redemption and communion: studies in Christian doctrine /
by Oliver D. Crisp, University of St Andrews.
Description: London ; New York: T&T Clark, 2021. | Includes bibliographical references
and index. | Identifiers: LCCN 2020045661 (print) | LCCN 2020045662 (ebook) |
ISBN 9780567698704 (hb) | ISBN 9780567698711 (epdf) | ISBN 9780567698735 (epub)
Subjects: LCSH: Reformed Church—Doctrines.
Classification: LCC BX9422.3 .C745 2021 (print) | LCC BX9422.3 (ebook) | DDC 230/.42–dc23
LC record available at https://lccn.loc.gov/2020045661
LC ebook record available at https://lccn.loc.gov/2020045662

ISBN: HB: 978-0-5676-9835-3
PB: 978-0-5676-9834-6
ePDF: 978-0-5676-9838-4
ePUB: 978-0-5676-9836-0

Typeset by Deanta Global Publishing Services, Chennai, India
Printed and bound in Great Britain

To find out more about our authors and books visit www.bloomsbury.com
and sign up for our newsletters.

To my soul mate:
A thousand words cannot express
how grateful I am for you every single day

CONTENTS

Acknowledgements viii
Preface x

PART ONE: FREEDOM AND SIN 1

1   Providence and Libertarian Calvinism 3
2   Sin in Reformed Theology 24

PART TWO: PERSON OF CHRIST 51

3   Andrew Loke's Preconscious Christ 53
4   Colin Gunton's Christology 64

PART THREE: APPLIED SALVATION 85

5   Anglican Hypothetical Universalism 87
6   T. F. Torrance and Universal Salvation 112
7   Regeneration Reconsidered 134

PART FOUR: CHRISTIAN LIFE 161

8   Eucharistic Presence 163
9   Prayer as Complaint 182

Bibliography 201
Name Index 213
Subject Index 215
Scripture Index 219

ACKNOWLEDGEMENTS

I would like to thank the following scholars and friends who have helped in the writing of the studies contained in this volume: Revd Dr James Arcadi, Dr Joshua Cockayne, Jesse Gentile, Revd Dr Myk Habets, Revd Dr Scott Harrower, Revd Dr Stephen Holmes, Revd Dr Matt Jenson, Dr Kimberley Kroll, Dr T. J. Lang, Dr Joanna Leidenhag, Dr Darian Lockett, Dr Andrew Loke, Professor Tom McCall, Steven Nemes, Professor Michael Rea, Revd Professor Christoph Schwoebel, Revd Professor Alan Torrance, Dr Andrew Torrance, Dr Kevin Timpe, Dr J. T. Turner Jr., Revd Dr Olli-Pekka Vainio, Revd Dr Leigh Vicens, Dr Aku Visala, Dr Jordan Wessling, Professor Judith Wolfe and Dr Christopher Woznicki. I am sure to have missed some people out. I offer my apologies to anyone I may have inadvertently overlooked.

Although members of St Mary's College have heard many of these chapters in research seminars, a number of them were first given as papers in academic contexts beyond the bounds of St Andrews. Chapter 3 was an invited paper at a panel on Andrew Loke's monograph, *A Kryptic Model of the Incarnation* (2014) at the American Academy of Religion Conference in 2018. Chapter 6 was an invited paper at a meeting of the T. F. Torrance Fellowship at the American Academy of Religion Conference in November 2019. Chapter 7 was originally presented as an invited plenary paper at the HEAT (Helsinki Analytic Theology) Conference in February 2020. Some of the chapters have appeared elsewhere. An earlier version of Chapter 2 was first published in a textbook on Christian dogmatics. Chapter 4 saw the light of day in the *T&T Clark Companion to Colin Gunton*. Chapter 5 was a contribution to a symposium on Amyraldism. Chapter 9 was an essay in a symposium on prayer published with Oxford University Press. All are reprinted here with permission and have been revised for publication in this volume.

My editor, Anna Turton, has been very supportive and helpful. I am, as ever, profoundly thankful for the assistance of my family who have buoyed me up during the writing of this work, much of which was composed in a period of great upheavals, including the Covid-19 pandemic of 2020.

PREFACE

Q. What is your only comfort in life and in death?

A. That I am not my own, but belong – body and soul, in life and in death – to my faithful Saviour, Jesus Christ

– HEIDELBERG CATECHISM, 1563

When faced with matters of life and death, we must ask the hard questions. We are compelled to consider our own mortality and our place in the world in which we live. What sort of people will we be? What stories, values and ideas will shape our lives? The chapters collected together in this volume were written over the last six years. They are a sequel to my earlier work, entitled *God, Creation, and Salvation: Studies in Reformed Theology* (2020). As with its predecessor, this volume is a snapshot of theology seen from a particular vantage at a particular time. Many of these studies were composed during a pandemic unprecedented in my lifetime, which continues even as I write these lines. It has been a time for asking hard questions – including hard theological questions.

Turn back the clock 500 years to the great upheavals of the Protestant Reformation in Europe. The divines responsible for drafting the great confessions of the sixteenth and seventeenth centuries were alive to such concerns. They lived in times of great disruption, distress and uncertainty about the future. (The Swiss Reformer Huldrych Zwingli even lived through an outbreak of the plague, survived infection and wrote a hymn about the different stages of his experience.) They thought deeply about what sort of people they would be, and about what stories, values and ideas would shape their lives. It should be no surprise, then, that the confessional records of this period should reflect this sense of urgency. And that is just what we find. Consider the first question of the Heidelberg Catechism, which is the epigraph to this Preface. It cuts straight to the heart of the matter. *What is our only comfort in life and death?* The answer is a heartfelt affirmation of the central truth of the gospel: *That I am not my own but belong – body and soul, in life and death – to my faithful saviour, Jesus Christ.*

What hope does the Christian faith offer? Our Protestant forebears would surely have replied with the answer of the Heidelberg Catechism: *the hope of the gospel.* Often, we think of theology as a purely intellectual concern, divorced from the vicissitudes of life, occupying some lofty perch above the social and political concerns of the day. That is a mistake. Writing at the height of National Socialism in 1930s Germany, the authors of the Barmen Declaration – which included Karl Barth – proclaimed: 'The church's commission, upon which its freedom is founded, consists in delivering the message of the free grace of God to all people in Christ's stead, and therefore in the ministry of his own Word and work through sermon and Sacrament.'[1] This is confessional theology that affirms eternal truths while addressing pressing social and political concerns.

Doctrine matters. Reformed theology is a tradition with significant investment in the discussion of right doctrine. The studies collected together in this volume represent the rumination of one Reformed theologian in conversation with his theological forebears, and in the hope of articulating something of the great things of the gospel to which the framers of the Heidelberg Catechism and the Barmen Declaration bear witness. For Christian theology ought to be confessional. It ought to be something to which we cleave 'in life and death'. And it ought to speak of the freedom we find in Christ, of the redemption he offers, and of the communion of the saints in the church and in participation in the divine life, of which Scripture and the Christian tradition speak so eloquently.

With this in mind, the chapters that follow focus on four central themes of Christian theology. These are human freedom in relation to God; the person of Christ as the mediator of salvation; the shape

---

[1] *The Constitution of The Presbyterian Church (USA) Part I: Book of Confessions* (Louisville: Office of the General Assembly, 2004), 250.

and scope of redemption in Christ; and practical issues in the life
of faith in the celebration of the Eucharist, and in prayer. The four
parts of the book reflect these four themes.

We begin with the part on human freedom and sin. In the
popular imagination, Reformed theology is usually associated
with unrelenting determinism: God ordains all that comes to pass.
However, in recent scholarship this story has been nuanced and
developed by research being done on early Reformed theology.
In previous work I have also argued that there may be Reformed
theologians who have a much more robust doctrine of human free
will, such as John Girardeau.[2] Perhaps there is even conceptual
space for a kind of *libertarian Calvinism*.[3] In this previous work
I was concerned with the broadening what we think of as within
the bounds of Reformed theology in the direction of the debate
about human free will. In this chapter, I focus on a problem with
libertarian Calvinism, namely that it implies human beings are the
ultimate source of their actions, which is contrary to traditional
Reformed theological anthropology. I call this *the sourcehood
problem*. I give some conceptual framework for the problem,
provide a brief recapitulation of libertarian Calvinism, and then
tackle the sourcehood problem with reference to the structural
similarities that libertarian Calvinism has to Thomist doctrines of
concurrence. Concurrence is roughly the doctrine that God concurs
with creaturely actions so that they have a human source and a
divine source. If it turns out that concurrence is able to make room
for both divine meticulous providence and human freedom, then
maybe the same can be said to be true, the relevant changes having
been made, with respect to libertarian Calvinism. I argue that this
is indeed the case, and that this helps address some of the concerns
raised by the sourcehood problem.[4]

---

[2]See Oliver D. Crisp, *God, Creation, and Salvation: Studies in Reformed Theology*
(London: T&T Clark, 2020), ch. 4.
[3]See Oliver D. Crisp, *Deviant Calvinism: Broadening Reformed Theology*
(Minneapolis: Fortress Press, 2014), ch. 3.
[4]For discussion of the relation between meticulous providence, traditional Reformed
thought, and Thomism, see Oliver D. Crisp, 'Meticulous Providence', in Oliver
D. Crisp and Fred Sanders, eds, *Divine Action and Providence: Explorations
in Constructive Dogmatics*. Proceedings of the Seventh Los Angeles Theology
Conference, 2019 (Grand Rapids: Zondervan Academic, 2019), 21–40.

Chapter 2 considers the broad sweep of Reformed theological accounts of sin. Elsewhere, I have argued in favour of a broadly Zwinglian understanding of sin as a vitiated condition with which we are generated, a view that is hinted at here as well.[5] But this chapter is more concerned with a broader theological context, offering some account of live options in the Reformed tradition that also intimates my preference for the Zwinglian view. It is a kind of dogmatic overview of the main issues in Reformed ways of thinking about this doctrine.

Part Two is focused on the person of Christ as mediator of salvation. Chapter 3 kicks off the part. It is a critical response to the Christology of Andrew Loke. Building on recent work in analytic theology that deals with the metaphysics of the incarnation, Loke presents what he calls the divine preconscious model of incarnation.[6] He claims that Christ has a conscious human mental life and something like a divine preconscious mental life, in an attempt to provide some account of the psychology of Christ. This is similar to some earlier attempts to account for the complex and mysterious mental life of a divine-human person in the work of the twentieth-century Anglican theologian, William Sanday.[7] The chapter is a sustained critique of this position, and in favour of a more traditional two-natures doctrine of the incarnation.

Chapter 4 is focused on the Christology of the English Reformed theologian, Colin E. Gunton. He is widely thought to be one of the most important recent Anglophone divines, and is particular associated with the project of Trinitarian theology, which he pursued vigorously in his long tenure at Kings College, London.[8] The chapter considers some central themes in Gunton's Christology, arguing that although he sought to stay within the broad remit of

---

[5]See Crisp, *God, Creation, and Salvation*, ch. 5.
[6]Andrew Ter Ern Loke, *A Kryptic Model of the Incarnation*. Ashgate New Critical Thinking in Religion, Theology and Biblical Studies (Aldershot: Ashgate, 2014).
[7]See William Sanday, *Christology and Personality, Containing I. Christologies Ancient and Modern II. Personality in Christ and in Ourselves* (Oxford: Oxford University Press, 1911).
[8]Full disclosure: I was a graduate student at King's College, London, in the late 1990s, knew and admired Gunton and his work, and was a regular participant in the Research Institute for Systematic Theology (RIST), which Gunton co-founded with Christoph Schwoebel.

traditional, orthodox Christology, his sensibilities as a dissenting minister and theologian led him to be more revisionist in his thinking than the unwary reader might suppose. The net result is that his Christology has some elements that push him beyond the bounds of orthodoxy, in an attempt to restate what he took to be a properly biblical understanding of the full humanity of God incarnate.

Part Three of the book concerns the shape and scope of Christ's redemptive act. Chapter 5 deals with the scope of the atonement. Reformed theology is particularist in its view about the redemption of Christ. In other words, Reformed theologians presume that Christ's reconciling work atones for the sin of a particular number of fallen humanity. Disagreement arises in Reformed thought on the question of the mechanism by which this occurs and on issue of the particular number of those saved. How narrow or expansive is this particularism about redemption? Hypothetical universalism is one underappreciated Reformed response to this issue. It turns on what is sometimes called *the sufficiency-efficiency distinction*. This is the distinction that Christ's reconciling work is sufficient in principle for the salvation of all humanity, but efficient or effectual only for those to whom God gives the gift of faith. I provide a contemporary restatement of this view and defend it against several well-known objections.[9]

Chapter 6 continues the theme of the scope of atonement but with reference to the work of the modern Scottish Reformed theologian, Thomas F. Torrance, on theosis and universal salvation. The chapter looks at some central themes in his theology which provide keys with which to unlock some persistence tensions in Torrance's work on these interrelated topics. For Torrance defended a Reformed version of theosis, and – despite himself – held views that imply the doctrine of universal salvation. In this chapter I give an account of key themes in Torrance's work and show how his views do, indeed, imply universalism not just the possibility of universal salvation.

Chapter 7 deals with the doctrine of regeneration. What does it mean to be transformed by divine grace in salvation? Among Reformed theologians, Jonathan Edwards had some interesting and

---

[9]Although it can be read independent of my previous forays into this area, the argument of this chapter does build on previous work on this topic in *Deviant Calvinism*.

illuminating things to say on this topic. He spoke of regeneration as a 'new sense of things' granted by the supernatural working of the Holy Spirit in the heart of fallen human beings. Using him as a foil, I develop a version of an *infusion account of regeneration*, according to which the Holy Spirit is infused into the believer at the moment of regeneration. This position has been the subject of some dispute in recent analytic theology (and has been contentious among Edwards scholars as well[10]). Drawing on the work of Ray Yeo and Kimberley Kroll, I defend the infusion account against some of the most serious problems it faces.

The fourth and final part deals with two contested practical issues in the Christian life. These are the Eucharist and the prayer. In keeping with the attempt to reflect the breadth of the Reformed tradition in previous chapters, Chapter 8 focuses on the notion of the presence of Christ in the sacrament. What, if anything, occurs to the eucharistic elements of bread and wine when they are blessed during the liturgy of the sacrament, and taken by members of the congregation? How is Christ present in the eating of these sacramental elements? This issue has been a topic of energetic theological controversy down the centuries. Recent work in this area in analytic and postliberal theology has raised a cluster of issues that make revisiting these questions opportune. Drawing on studies by James Arcadi, George Hunsinger and Marilyn Adams, the chapter offers a taxonomy of different views on eucharistic presence, before focusing in on whether it is possible to have a Reformed understanding of eucharistic presence that implies the real corporeality of God the Son in the eucharistic elements. Surprising though it may initially seem, it seems to me that it is feasible. I give an initial account of what this might look like in the final section of the chapter as a piece of constructive analytic theology in the Reformed tradition.

Chapter 9 is the final chapter in the volume. It tackles a thorny question with respect to another central Christian practice, namely prayer. In analytic theology, much attention has been paid to the

---

[10]See, for example, Anri Morimoto, *Jonathan Edwards and the Catholic View of Salvation* (University Park: Pennsylvania State University Press, 1995).

right analysis of petitionary prayer.[11] Can our prayers change God's mind? Can they affect the outcome of events? Often in popular piety, the assumption is that petitionary prayer is about changing God's mind and the outcome of particular circumstances. The classic example of this is prayers for the sick. Rather than deal with this issue head on, the chapter comes to it in a roundabout way, by focusing on a different sort of prayer. This is prayer as complaint. There are many prayerful complaints in Scripture, such as the woes expressed by Job and in the Psalms. How are we to understand these prayers? Is it appropriate to rail against God, and to complain about our lot if God is in control of all things? I offer an account of complaint-prayers and their relation to lament in Scripture. I then connect this to prayers of petition. The argument is that what we think we are doing in complaint-prayers (and perhaps lament prayers as well) may give us some insight into how we should think about petitionary prayer too.

* * * *

In the Preface to *God, Creation, and Salvation*, I said that theology is always *in via*. There is no final statement of dogmatics, just dogmatics from the time and vantage at which we find ourselves. Events of this last year with the pandemic that is sweeping the globe only underline that claim. Nevertheless, like the theological remains of the Magisterial Reformers, theological edifices built in a particular time and place may speak beyond those times and places to others in different situations. Sometimes the most urgent and most contemporary theology can also, somewhat, paradoxically, produce the most timeless restatement of the Gospel. The Barmen Declaration is surely an example of this. The studies in this volume are written along the way – they are examples of theology *in via* in dialogue with theology of the past in order to forge theology for the present and the future. It is not for an author to say whether her or

---

[11]See, for example, Vincent Brümmer, *What Are We Doing When We Pray? On Prayer and the Nature of Faith* (Aldershot: Ashgate, 2008); Scott A. Davison, *Petitionary Prayer: A Philosophical Investigation* (Oxford: Oxford University Press, 2017); and Christopher G. Woznicki, 'Peter Martyr Vermigli's Account of Petitionary Prayer: A Reformation Alternative to Comtemporary Two-Way Contingency Accounts', *Philosophia Christi* 20.1 (2018): 119–37.

his outputs will stand the test of time in the way that the Barmen Declaration has done. But the studies within the covers of this volume are about central dogmatic themes in Christian theology *today*. The hope is that they may also help in some small way to shape the discussion of these themes for the Christian theology of *tomorrow*.

PART ONE

Freedom and Sin

1

Providence and
Libertarian Calvinism

It is commonly assumed that Calvinism implies some version
of theological determinism – usually some version of 'soft'
determinism or compatibilism, according to which human free
will is consistent with divine ordination.[1] However, this picture of
Calvinism has recently been contested by a number of historical
theologians, who have argued that historic Reformed theology
does not imply or entail determinism, and may even be consistent
with something like a version of libertarianism.[2] In previous
work in this area I have argued that the Reformed confessions
are metaphysically underdetermined, and consistent with a
broader range of views than those that fall under the description
of theological compatibilism. Specifically, the claim in this earlier
work is that confessional Calvinism is commensurate with a kind
of 'mixed' or 'complex' understanding of human free will and
moral responsibility, which assumes that incompatibilism is true;

---

[1]For instance, James N. Anderson and Paul Manata write, 'It is commonly held that
Calvinism is committed to theological determinism'. In 'Determined to Come Most
Freely: Some Challenges for Libertarian Calvinism', *Journal of Reformed Theology*
11 (2017): 272.
[2]See, for example, Richard A. Muller, *Divine Will and Human Choice: Freedom,
Contingency, and Necessity in Early Modern Reformed Thought* (Grand Rapids:
Baker Academic, 2017), and Willem J. Van Asselt, J. Martin Bac and Roelf T. te Velde,
eds, *Reformed Thought on Freedom: The Concept of Free Choice in Early Modern
Reformed Theology*. Texts and Studies in Reformation and Post-Reformation
Thought (Grand Rapids: Baker Academic, 2010). See also Crisp, *Deviant Calvinism*.

that a 'hard' version of theological determinism applies to certain actions that pertain to ensuring human salvation; and that a version of source libertarianism applies to some mundane human actions that fall outside the scope of the divine action of ensuring human salvation. This view I have characterized as *libertarian Calvinism*.[3]

This chapter follows on from this previous work. One worry about libertarian Calvinism that has recently been raised in the literature is that it seems inconsistent with a Reformed understanding of meticulous providence because it affirms that human agents are the ultimate source of their free choices.[4] However, accounts of divine concurrence often associated with Thomism are commonly thought to affirm both meticulous providence and libertarian creaturely freedom. I will argue that if concurrence accounts are consistent with meticulous providence, then something similar should be true of libertarian Calvinism, since both views share relevantly similar views about the relation between providence and human agency. This should not be all that surprising given that a number of historic Reformed thinkers thought of their own work in continuity with much of Thomism, and their views of providence as Protestant versions of something like a concurrence doctrine.

The argument proceeds as follows. In the first section I shall set out some important terminological distinctions. With these in hand, I shall turn in the second section to give a brief account of libertarian Calvinism. In the third section I deal with the problem for libertarian Calvinism raised by the question of the source of human free choices, which I call *the sourcehood problem*. Then, in the fourth section, I shall argue that there are structural similarities between libertarian

---

[3]Some philosophers think that Augustine was a source libertarian throughout his career, although he thought God ordained all that comes to pass. For discussion of this, see Eleonore Stump, 'Augustine on Free Will', in Stump and Norman Kretzmann, eds, *The Cambridge Companion to Augustine* (Cambridge: Cambridge University Press, 2001), ch. 10. Similar things can be said of Anselm, as we shall see. This is not insignificant given that Calvinism is usually thought to be a branch of Augustinianism. The technical terminology I am using here is explained in the next section of the chapter.

[4]See Anderson and Manata, 'Determined to Come Most Freely: Some Challenges for Libertarian Calvinism', and Michael Patrick Preciado, *A Reformed View of Freedom: The Compatibility of Guidance Control and Reformed Theology* (Eugene, OR: Pickwick Publications, 2019), ch. 3.

Calvinism and concurrence accounts of meticulous providence. If concurrence accounts can allow for libertarian creaturely actions in a world governed by meticulous providence, then (so it seems to me) libertarian Calvinism can as well. I conclude with a brief section on the theological upshot of this argument. As with my previous work in this area, the aim throughout is to explore and defend aspects of libertarian Calvinism, even though I am not committed to libertarian Calvinism, in order to test the extent to which it is a defensible form of Reformed theology.

Preliminary Conceptual Distinctions

Let us begin with the notion of meticulous providence. This is the view according to which the scope of divine preservation, concurrence and governance in creation encompasses all that comes to pass. Preservation, concurrence and governance are the three traditional dogmatic heads under which providence is usually discussed. They are not necessarily distinct divine actions, but more like different modes of the one divine act, or different aspects of the one action of divine providence. God is said to preserve the world he has created in existence by the immediate exercise of his power. For defenders of meticulous providence, without such an act of divine preservation the creation would immediately cease to exist. God also acts in concurrence or in 'agreement' with creaturely actions, without which no creaturely action would take place. So God's providence is necessary in order for creatures to act as well as continue to exist. And God governs his creatures by means of his constant oversight of the creation, ordering all things to the goal or consummation for which he has ordained the created order in the first place. Thus, there is nothing that obtains in creation without God's preservation of, concurrence with and government respecting that thing. Absent God's preservation of, concurrence with and government respecting that thing at each moment of its existence, it would not exist. In this way, according to the doctrine of meticulous providence, all that exists in creation is in some important sense *radically* dependent on God's preservation, concurrence and government. The idea is similar to the way in which a person's thoughts are radically dependent upon their continuing to think those things in order for the thoughts in question to continue to exist.

Now, meticulous providence so understood is often thought to be equivalent to determinism. I take it that determinism is, in the words of Peter van Inwagen, 'the thesis that the past *determines* a unique future'.[5] That is, the past determines *exactly one* future physical state of affairs. Put a bit more expansively, suppose that the past up to midday yesterday is summarized in the proposition *P*. To this, add a complete account of the laws of nature, summarized in the proposition *L*. Determinism is the view according to which the conjunction of *P* plus *L* entails a unique future state of affairs. In other words, *P* + *L* entails that you are reading this sentence right now rather than, say, basking in the sunshine on Manhattan Beach, or skiing at Big Bear, or whatever.[6]

Of course, there are different sorts of determinism. Usually, when analytic philosophers talk about determinism, they are interested in *physical* or *causal* determinism (I shall use these two terms interchangeably since I presume that causation is a relation that obtains between physical things). Philosophers are interested in the way in which one thing may causally affect another in the physical universe in which we live. So causal determinism is the thesis that a particular event, y, is causally necessitated by x; if x is some acting thing or some event, such that, given x, the unique event y *must* happen, because x *makes* it happen.[7]

By contrast, theologians like to talk about *theological* determinism. This is not the same thesis as causal determinism because the idea is that God, an immaterial agent, determines a unique future for the created order. This includes the physical creation, but does not comprise it. For presumably there are many things that are not physical in the created order, such as angels and demons, yet, on the theological determinist view God is said to determine their actions as well. What is more, some theological determinists seem to think that God's meticulous oversight of the creation, which involves his ordaining all that comes to pass, does

---

[5]Peter van Inwagen, *An Essay on Free Will* (Oxford: Oxford University Press, 1983), 2. Emphasis original.
[6]For discussion of this point, see Kevin Timpe, *Free Will: Sourcehood and Its Alternatives*, Second Edition (London: Bloomsbury Academic, 2013), 13–14.
[7]Adapted from Katherin A. Rogers, *Freedom and Self-Creation: Anselmian Libertarianism* (Oxford: Oxford University Press, 2015), 10–11.

not involve him physically or causally bringing things about in the world. His action is logically prior to physical causation, and is sometimes said to be what informs or gives rise to, such physical causation.[8]

Be that as it may, one clear difference between theological determinism and causal determinism is that according to theological determinism it is *God* that determines what comes to pass, whereas on causal determinism the idea is that physical events in the past plus the laws of nature determine a unique future physical state of affairs. Perhaps God utilizes physical events to bring about a unique future physical state of affairs. If that is right, then at least some versions of theological determinism imply some version of physical or causal determinism. Nevertheless, the two theses are conceptually distinct.

With this in mind, let us turn next to compatibilism and incompatibilism and how they bear upon meticulous providence. In this context, compatibilism is the thesis that determinism is compatible with human free will and moral responsibility. Notice that I use the term 'determinism' without qualification in the previous sentence. This is because the idea here is that whatever sort of determinism is in view, the issue is whether that form of determinism (whether causal, theological or whatever) is consistent with human free will and moral responsibility. We might also worry about the free will and moral responsibility of other non-human creatures such as angels and primates. But we need not trouble ourselves with such complications here. It is sufficient for our purposes to focus on the free will and moral responsibility of

---

[8]One historic example of this sort of idea can be found in idea of 'physical premotion'. This term of art was made famous in the *de auxiliis* controversy between Báñezians and Molinists in the sixteenth-century Iberian peninsula. It states that nothing in creation acts without the predetermination of God. Hence, there is what we might call a divine 'motion' or action that obtains prior to any physical action in creation – hence, a physical *pre*motion. For discussion of this, see the Introduction to Dennis Jowers, ed., *Four Views on Divine Providence* (Grand Rapids: Zondervan, 2011), 17, Thomas P. Flint, *Divine Providence: The Molinist Account* (Ithaca: Cornell University Press, 1998), the editorial introduction to Louis De Molina, *On Divine Foreknowledge: Part IV of the Concordia*, ed. and trans. Alfred J. Freddoso (Ithaca: Cornell University Press, 1988), and especially the excellent study of R. J. Matava, *Divine Causality and Human Free Choice: Domingo Báñez, Physical Premotion and the Controversy De Auxiliis Revisited. Studies in Intellectual History*, vol. 252 (Leiden: Brill, 2016).

human creatures irrespective of whether there are other rational creatures that also have free will and moral responsibility.

If compatibilism is the thesis that determinism is compatible with human free will and moral responsibility, incompatibilism is the thesis that determinism is incompatible with human free will and moral responsibility. Either determinism is true or human free will and moral responsibility is true, but not both.

Next, let me say something about libertarianism, since this will be important for the concurrence account. There are various ways of construing libertarianism. I will put it like this. Libertarianism is the view according to which incompatibilism is true, and determinism is false. That is, libertarianism states that determinism and the combination of human free will plus moral responsibility are not compossible, and, in addition, that determinism is false. To this we should add a claim about the fact that libertarians think that at least some human agents possess free choices on at least some occasions, so as to make clear that libertarian views give some conceptual content to the notion of free will, a matter to which we shall return in due course. Some people think that libertarianism also requires commitment to some form of the principle of alternative possibilities, according to which a person has free will only if she or he could have done otherwise.[9] But it is not clear to me that this is a *requirement* for libertarianism, though it is a common feature of much contemporary libertarianism. It seems to me that the following claims could all be true:

1. Incompatibilism
2. The denial of determinism
3. Agents are the source of actions that are free and
4. Those actions that are free actions are actions for which humans are morally responsible

In this respect, I am understanding free will as a kind of *control condition*, that is, some control upon action in virtue of which

---

[9]In its modern guise this principle derives from the work of the Princeton philosopher, Harry Frankfurt. See Frankfurt, *The Importance of What We Care About: Philosophical Essays* (Cambridge: Cambridge University Press, 1998), ch. 1. For a helpful recent discussion of the issues, see Timpe, *Free Will*, ch. 5.

human agents are held morally responsible.[10] It could be argued that although these four claims are consistent, each being a necessary condition for libertarianism, they are not sufficient. For, so it might be thought, one must add to this the principle of alternative possibilities in order to have a set of necessary and sufficient conditions for libertarianism. But perhaps not.

Consider, for example, the case of Anselm of Canterbury.[11] His view seems to be that human free will requires something like the four conditions stated earlier. But he also thinks that the truly free person is one who measures up to the standard set by God – to that rightness or rectitude of will (*rectitudio*) that involves acting in accordance with God's will. The truly free person, on Anselm's view, seems to be one who acts rightly, according to the rectitude of will *for its own sake* not as a means to some other end, so that the truly free agent rightly desires what she ought to desire.[12] Such a person is the source of her or his action, not God. Nevertheless, it is not obvious that such a position requires a principle of alternative possibilities or some similar idea of metaphysical wiggle room or *leeway*, in order for the action in question to be free and one for which the creature is morally responsible.[13] The alternative to such rectitude, for the Anselmian, is the dereliction of one's moral duty to follow divine commands. That, far from being an alternative

---

[10]See Kevin Timpe, *Free Will in Philosophical Theology* (London: Bloomsbury Academic, 2014), 7.

[11]See especially, Anselm's Three Dialogues comprising: *On Truth* (*De veritate*), *On Freedom of Choice* (*De libertate arbitrii*), *On the Fall of the Devil* (*De casu diaboli*), and his much more substantial piece, *On the Harmony of God's Foreknowledge, Predestination, and Grace with Free Choice* (*De Concordia*), all of which can be found in translation in *Anselm: Basic Writings*, trans. Thomas Williams (Indianapolis: Hackett Publishing, 2007). The Critical edition of Anselm's works I have consulted is *S. Anselmi, Cantuariensis Archepiscopi, Opera Omnia, Tomus Primus et Tomus Secundus*, ed. F. S. Schmit (Stutgart: Friedrich Frommann Verlag, 1984 [1968]). Useful discussion of Anselm's view can be found in Sandra Visser and Thomas Williams, *Anselm. Great Medieval Thinkers* (Oxford: Oxford University Press, 2008), ch. 11, an interpretation I find persuasive. For a rather different approach to Anselm, one that claims he does hold to a principle of alternative possibilities for free will tout court, see Katherin Rogers, *Anselm on Freedom* (Oxford: Oxford University Press, 2008), and idem, *Freedom and Self-Creation*.

[12]See Anselm, *On Freedom of Choice*, ch. 3, in *Anselm: Basic Writings*, 151.

[13]At least, not on all occasions. See discussion of this point in Visser and Williams, *Anselm*, ch. 11.

that is enjoyed by the truly free individual, is only a 'choice' in the Pickwickian sense of being the privation of some good state that ought to obtain. The truly free person, for the Anselmian, is the source of his or her choice and has rectitude of will for its own sake. Indeed, from an Anselmian point of view, it is possible to be in a state in which such rectitude is the only live option, as, presumably, is the case for those who are glorified, as well as elect angels and God himself. This, for the Anselmian, is a more morally exalted state than one in which there is the real prospect of some wiggle room or leeway to choose some alternative.

Of course, this analysis of libertarianism might be disputed. I raise the point about Anselm in order to show that there are theological cases where something like libertarianism seems to be in view, and where a principle of alternative possibilities or some other similar sense of metaphysical leeway does not appear to be a requirement of the analysis of such free will; instead, sourcehood is the fundamental issue. We can distinguish these two sorts of libertarianism by referring to them as *leeway libertarianism* and *sourcehood libertarianism*, respectively.[14]

The leeway libertarian thinks that in addition to the four components to libertarianism I have outlined thus far – namely, incompatibilism, the denial of determinism, the claim that agents are the source of actions that are free, and the claim that those actions that are free are actions for which humans are morally responsible – what is needed is some sort of principle of alternate possibilities in order for a creaturely action to count as one that is truly free and for which the person concerned is morally responsible.

By contrast, the sourcehood libertarian is like the Anselmian; she thinks that what is required for libertarian freedom is our four components: incompatibilism, the denial of determinism, the claim that agents are the source of actions that are free, and the claim that those actions that are free are actions for which humans are morally responsible. Add to this the claim about the possession of rectitude of will for its own sake, which is a kind of teleological claim about the right ordering of the will, and we have the major aspects of what

---

[14]There are also leeway and sourcehood versions of compatibilism, but we won't treat them here. Stump's account of Augustine is, of course, another account that has a similar pay-off. See 'Augustine on Free Will'.

the Anselmian thinks is needed in order for a creaturely action to count as one that is truly free and for which the person concerned is morally responsible. Unlike the leeway libertarian, what is most important here is that the creaturely agent is the source of her action.

We are now in possession of a rough-and-ready concept of meticulous providence. We also have in our possession several further distinctions relevant to our discussion. These are physical or causal determinism, and theological determinism; compatibilism and incompatibilism; and leeway and sourcehood versions of libertarianism. As I have already indicated, normally meticulous providence is thought to imply some sort of soft theological determinism or compatibilism. It is thought to be contrary to incompatibilism because the incompatibilist denies that meticulous providence and human free will are compossible, which is the very thing the defender of meticulous providence affirms. And meticulous providence is commonly thought to be contrary to libertarianism because God's meticulous oversight of all things is often thought to be antithetical to libertarian accounts of human agency.

Libertarian Calvinism and Meticulous Providence

The Scottish Reformed theologian David Fergusson gives a whole chapter over to meticulous accounts of providence and its problems in his recent monograph on the subject. He observes that 'notwithstanding its formidable intellectual weight, architectural beauty and baroque appeal', the sort of meticulous providence doctrine favoured by the Reformed orthodox account 'faces a range of modern anxieties, rendering it neither persuasive nor attractive to most Christian audiences today'. Among the reasons given for this modern disillusionment with the Reformed orthodox account of meticulous providence are 'its adequacy to the diverse materials of Scripture, a prioritising of divine control over love, a determinism that problematises human freedom, and a heavy stress on the will of God in relation to everything that happens'. He goes on to say that the 'caveats introduced by exponents of Reformed orthodoxy' and its doctrine of meticulous providence 'have done little to allay the cogency of these criticisms which, taken together, have generated something approaching a modern consensus against this position'.[15]

It may be asking too much to expect to turn back such a 'modern consensus' against meticulous providence. But it seems to me that libertarian Calvinism may provide resources from within the Reformed tradition that might assuage some of the worries motivating this modern consensus. For if one of the principal reasons for wariness of meticulous providence is, as Fergusson suggests, its prioritizing of the divine will, control and determinism over human freedom, then libertarian Calvinism offers an alternative worth considering.

The libertarian Calvinist version of meticulous providence can be easily stated. Recall our rough characterization of meticulous providence. This was as follows:

> METICULOUS PROVIDENCE: that species of doctrine which stipulates that the scope of divine preservation, concurrence, and governance, encompasses all that comes to pass.

Preservation, concurrence and governance are the three traditional dogmatic heads under which the one divine act of providence is usually considered. They are not necessarily discrete divine acts, but more like three aspects of one divine act in creation. God preserves the world in being at each moment, without which it would cease to exist; he concurs with creaturely free choices; and he governs creatures according to the laws of creation, and towards the end or goal he has for his creatures.

In keeping with this view of the scope of divine action in creation, libertarian Calvinism consists of the following claims:

1. God ordains whatsoever comes to pass. (This is a key claim shared with other accounts of meticulous providence.)
2. Free will is inconsistent with determinism. (This is the central claim of incompatibilism, which is espoused by theological libertarians.)

---

[15]David Fergusson, *The Providence of God, A Polyphonic Approach* (Cambridge: Cambridge University Press, 2018), 100–1.

3. God determines the choices of the elect that lead to their salvation. (This is because no fallen human beings can choose salvation without the gift of faith, in keeping with Ephesians 2.)

4. Some human beings are sometimes free and morally responsible. (Not all human are capable of actions that are free in the libertarian sense, and for which they are morally responsible; and not all human actions are ones that are free in the libertarian sense, and for which they are morally responsible.)

These four claims entail several others that are salient for our purposes. For instance, that it is false that a given action can be free in a compatibilist sense, and that determinism is not global – that is, it is not applicable to every single creaturely action. For some, humans are capable of at least some acts that are free and for which they bear moral responsibility.

Libertarian Calvinism and the Sourcehood Problem

How should we understand the scope of free choices according to libertarian Calvinism? Initially, I had thought that libertarian Calvinism should include a version of leeway libertarianism. But I am now not sure that this is a requirement of the view. Instead, and rather like the Anselmian, the libertarian Calvinist might drop the alternate possibilities condition distinctive of leeway libertarianism and settle for a version of source libertarianism instead.[16] As I characterized this earlier, source libertarianism comprises the following: incompatibilism, the denial of determinism, the claim that agents are the source of actions that are free, and the claim that those actions that are free actions are actions for which humans are morally responsible. The libertarian Calvinist can help herself

---

[16]Eleonore Stump has suggested that such a 'modified libertarianism' is Augustinian. If that is right, then surely those Calvinists wishing to align themselves with their Augustinian heritage may find her modified libertarianism attractive, libertarian Calvinists included. See Stump, 'Augustine on Free Will'.

to this sort of libertarianism. Doing so may, in fact, alleviate some concerns about the Reformed *bona fides* of libertarian Calvinism. (Here I have in mind concerns about how a particular view be confessionally Reformed if it allows that free choices include a principle of alternate possibilities.[17])

However, in another respect setting aside the distinctive alternate possibilities condition of leeway libertarianism makes a different kind of worry more pressing. This we might characterize as *the sourcehood problem*. We can put it like this. The libertarian Calvinist affirms that human agents, not God, are in some important sense the source of those human choices that are free. Yet the libertarian Calvinist wants to affirm a doctrine of meticulous providence according to which God ordains all that comes to pass. This poses a problem. For as James Anderson and Paul Manata have recently pointed out, the *Westminster Confession of Faith*, which is the historic subordinate doctrinal standard for Calvinists in the Presbyterian tradition,

> teaches not only that God decrees all things but also that God's decree is not conditioned by or dependent on anything external to him, such as the libertarian free choices of his creatures. Consequently, it's hard to see how one could consistently affirm the theological tradition represented by WCF [Westminster Confession of Faith] yet reject theological determinism. If God ordains all things according to an infallible and immutable decree, and that decree originates entirely in God, how could it fail to be the case that God alone ultimately determines all things?[18]

Meticulous providence presses in the direction of a global theological determinism; libertarian Calvinism resists that claim, allowing for the prospect that some human agents are free in a source libertarian sense on at least some occasions. On the face of it, these two things seem incompatible. Are they *in fact* incompatible?

---

[17]This issue is raised by Anderson and Manata in 'Determined to Come Most Freely: Some Challenges for Libertarian Calvinism'.
[18]Anderson and Manata, 'Determined to Come Most Freely', 48.

Let us explore this a little. The key claim for sourcehood libertarians is that agents are the source of their free actions. But a source in what sense? We can distinguish between *proximate* and *ultimate* sources of a given action. A proximate source is that which gives rise to a particular choice. This is usually an agent, though it may be something else. For instance, it could be an automatic neurochemical switch implanted by a mad scientist in the brain of a human agent that triggers a certain response to particular stimuli, thereby ensuring the agent makes a particular choice in a given situation. As this example indicates, a proximate source is not necessarily an ultimate source. The ultimate source of the neurochemical switch is the mad scientist. It is he who implants it in the agent in order to trigger a particular response to particular circumstances. The agent makes the choice, but the choice is triggered by the neurochemical switch. The switch is the proximate source of the choice, not the agent. But given that the switch is implanted by the mad scientist, he is the ultimate source of the choice.

Relevant to our consideration of proximate and ultimate sources is what is often called *the tracing principle*. This is the idea that a person may be held morally responsible for actions that are not free, provided we can trace the choice that informs that act back to some prior libertarian-free choice.[19] The usual example given is that of a drunk driver. Plausibly, the drunk driver is morally responsible for driving in an intoxicated state even if his action in getting behind the wheel is not entirely free, provided we can trace this decision back to an earlier libertarian-free choice in deciding to become inebriated earlier in the evening. The idea is that an earlier libertarian-free decision may lead to the driver being in a state where he cannot make free choices. But he may nevertheless still be morally responsible while in that drunken state. Now, it might be thought that the drunk driver example shows us that moral responsibility and free choice come apart. For, it might be urged, the example shows that the drunk driver is morally responsible for driving drunk even though his choice to get behind the wheel is not free in a libertarian sense. But that is not quite right, I think. Surely the right lesson to draw here is that an agent can be morally

[19]For discussion, see Anderson and Manata, 'Determined to Come Most Freely', 282–3. See also Stump, 'Augustine on Free Will'.

responsible for a particular choice even when she is not free with respect to that choice *provided* it can be traced back to some earlier choice that was free in the relevant sense. In other words, the drunk driver is the proximate source of the choice to drive drunk, though the choice in question is not a libertarianly free one. But he is held morally responsible for his choice because he (or his earlier self) is also the ultimate source as well, via the tracing principle. For we can trace his choice while drunk back to a previous free choice made while sober, which led to his inebriated state.

This distinction helps us to see that the libertarian Calvinist needs to clarify the different ways in which an agent may be the source of her action. And this, in turn, is salient for the ascription of moral responsibility. Calvinists who are theological determinists deny that fallen human agents are the ultimate sources of their choices, though they are willing to say that they may, in certain circumstances, be the proximate sources. This the libertarian Calvinist cannot allow. Or, at least, the libertarian Calvinist must find a way to avoid the conclusion that ultimate sourcehood lies entirely outside the purview of the human agent.[20]

A biblical example, often cited in the theological discussion of this question, will make this clear. Pharaoh chose to refuse Moses' overtures to let the Hebrews go; but it was God who hardened Pharaoh's heart. God is the ultimate source of Pharaoh's choice, so the theologically determinist Calvinist avers. Nevertheless, Pharaoh is morally responsible for acting as he did because he is the proximate source of his choice. He made the choice, not God,

---

[20]Here I note a possible complication, the pursuit of which would distract from the discussion of sourcehood at issue here though it is relevant in the broader context of Reformed thought. According to the majority report in the Reformed tradition, I am culpable for bearing original sin independent of any actual sins I commit because I also bear original guilt, which is transmitted to all fallen human beings with original sin. But clearly I did not *choose* to bear original sin or original guilt. Hence, for Calvinists who adopt this view of original sin, the ascription of moral responsibility (or perhaps, culpability) does not always depend on creaturely action. Those Calvinists who baulk at the prospect of bearing culpability for original sin may follow John Calvin, Huldrych Zwingli, and several of the early Reformed confessions in rejecting the concept of original guilt and allowing that bearers of original sin are rendered unfit for the presence of God. I have addressed this in more detail in Oliver D. Crisp, 'On Original Sin', *International Journal of Systematic Theology* 17.3 (2015): 252–66.

though God ordained that his heart be hardened towards Moses. Yet, so the objection goes, the libertarian Calvinist cannot say this if she is to avoid compatibilism. She must claim that Pharaoh is both the proximate and ultimate source of his action, if it is truly a free action.

It might be thought that the distinction between proximate and ultimate sourcehood provided by the Pharaoh example shows that the theologically determinist Calvinist has resources that the libertarian Calvinist does not. But perhaps the libertarian Calvinist can avail herself of a similar distinction between proximate and ultimate sourcehood, applying it differently in the context of the metaphysical commitments of libertarian Calvinism. If that is right, then the libertarian Calvinist may well have the tools with which to block the sourcehood problem. It is here that the concurrence theorist may come to the aid of the libertarian Calvinist.

Concurrence and Libertarian Calvinism

Concurrence accounts of meticulous providence are often associated with Thomism, though one need not be a Thomist to find such a view attractive and (as I have already indicated) some historic Reformed theologians seem to be broadly Thomist in their thinking, including their thinking about meticulous providence. The concurrence account holds that meticulous providence, with its claim that God ordains all that comes to pass, is consistent with a notion of libertarian-free choice. In this respect it is very similar to libertarian Calvinism, although the concurrence theorist doesn't necessarily include what I have called the 'mixed' or 'complex' view of libertarian Calvinism that partitions creaturely actions into those that are determined and those that are free in a libertarian sense.

Concurrence theorists maintain that the way in which God's ordination is consistent with creaturely free action has to do with what we might call a *two-source account of creaturely choice*. There is the free choice of the human agent to do a particular thing; and then there is God's concurrence with that choice. But both are sources of the choice that is made. In fact, both are ultimate sources of this choice. In this connection, divine concurrence is a kind of basic action by means of which God ensures that the creaturely choice obtains but without offering violence to that choice and without obliterating creaturely agency. A good example of this can be found in the Old Testament story of Joseph. When Joseph reveals himself to his brothers, who have tried to have him killed, he says to them, 'You intended to harm me, but God intended it for good to accomplish what is now being done, the saving of many lives. So then, don't be afraid. I will provide for you and your children' (Gen. 50.20-21, NRSV). On the face of it, as Joseph reports things, there appear to be two sources of his earlier misfortune: God and his brothers. God intended his brother's choice to harm Joseph for a greater good, whereas his brothers intended their action for his harm. But both God and his brothers concur in bringing about his misfortune.

The Joseph story helpfully illustrates the different ways in which the theological determinist and the concurrence theorist approach the sourcehood problem. A two-source account of creaturely choice could be construed in a way consistent with theological determinism. Then, Joseph's brothers are the proximate source of his misfortune, but God is the ultimate source of it. Nevertheless, God's intention in his ordination of Joseph's misfortune was not to harm Joseph but to bring about his flourishing through the misfortune, whereas the intention of his brothers was simply to bring about his demise. On this way of understanding the story, the brothers are something like the instruments or proxies by means of which God brings about his goal of the 'saving of many lives'. By contrast, the concurrence theorist reads the story rather differently, as an account of two *ultimate* sources. Joseph's brothers freely chose to harm Joseph, intending to do away with him. Because the concurrence theorist maintains that free and morally responsible choice must be ultimately sourced in the agent bringing about that choice, the brothers cannot be mere proxies for divine ordination. They must be ultimate sources of their action if the action in question is to be understood as a genuine exercise of their agency. But God must concur with this, ensuring it comes to pass according to his own good purposes. In this case, he does so in order to ensure the salvation of Joseph and his wider family – including the brothers who would have killed him.

A potentially illuminating way of thinking about the nature of the concurrence account of the Joseph story is suggested by J. L. Mackie's well-known idea of causes as INUS conditions, that is *Insufficient* but *Necessary* parts of an *Unnecessary* but *Sufficient* condition for a particular event or action. The example of an INUS condition usually given in the literature is of several factors that jointly give rise to a house fire: poor wiring, the electrical fault and the spark that catches on some flammable material. Each of these things may be insufficient to cause the house to burn down in and of itself, for each is a necessary but insufficient component needed to bring about this event. Only when all of these different factors are present at a particular time and place in a given building are they jointly sufficient in bringing about the destruction of the house by fire.[21] We might apply Mackie's notion of a cause as an INUS condition to our concurrence interpretation of the story of Joseph, as a way of modelling how a two-source account of creaturely choice might obtain.

Such an INUS model of a two-source account goes like this. God and Joseph's brothers are both ultimate sources for the bringing about of Joseph's misfortune. Both God's concurrence and the libertarian-free choice of the brothers are individually insufficient but jointly necessary for bringing about the unnecessary but sufficient event of Joseph's misfortune. God's ordination and concurrence are insufficient but necessary for this outcome in the sense that it must also be the free (ultimately sourced) choice of the brothers. But the brothers are also insufficient but necessary for this outcome in the sense that their choice must be concurred with by divine (ultimately sourced) fiat in order for it to obtain. Taken together both God and the brothers are ultimate sources of the action. The outcome itself is unnecessary in the sense that it is dependent on the free choice of the brothers, and upon the free choice of God who ordains the circumstances of Joseph's misfortune and the free choice of the brothers meticulously. (Of course, in another sense the action is necessary in that God has ordained it, but it is only hypothetically necessary, that is, necessary given God's choice to bring about this particular state of affairs including the free choices of Joseph's brothers, rather than some other state of affairs.) But taken together, the two ultimate sources of divine ordination and concurrence and the free creaturely choices of the brothers were sufficient to bring about Joseph's misfortune.

---

[21]See J. L. Mackie, 'Clauses and Conditions', *American Philosophical Quarterly* 2 (1965): 245–64. He writes, 'A is an INUS condition of a result P if and only if, for some X and for some Y, (AX or Y) is a necessary and sufficient condition of P, but A is not a sufficient condition of P and X is not a sufficient condition of P.'

Now, as I indicated earlier, this is offered as a model of how we might think about a two-source account of creaturely choice that is consistent with a concurrence view of meticulous providence. As it stands, it has an important shortcoming. This is that the INUS condition account presumes several physical conditions that give rise to a particular event, whereas in the case of concurrence God is an ultimate source of creaturely free choice, and the human agent is also an ultimate source of her choice. They are not both partially ultimate, or only jointly ultimate. Both are ultimate sources. The INUS model would need to be adjusted in order to account for this important qualification. That said, even if the model does not give a complete explanation of how a two-source account might go, it does provide a way of thinking about these things that we can get some conceptual grip on. But there may be additional theological reasons for motivating a two-source account as well.

To see this, we will need to turn to briefly consider aspects of a classical theistic way of thinking about God's relation to creation that is common to both traditional concurrence theorists (like Thomists) and confessionally Reformed libertarian Calvinists. Such theologians affirm the aseity of God, and, as part of that doctrine, the claim that God does not have a real relation to creation. But if he doesn't have a real relation to creation, then it is difficult to see how he can be the cause of any creaturely action. In a recent paper on the subject, W. Matthews Grant has proposed that God has reasons for concurring with the volitions of creaturely agents, but that strictly speaking there is nothing in virtue of which God brings about the effect of the creaturely volition because God has no real relation to creation – that is, no relation God bears to the creation that is intrinsic to the divine life. In this connection, Grant writes, 'God's willing, choosing, or intending E [the creaturely volition] is not an act distinct from God's causing E.' For there is nothing intrinsic to God in virtue of which God brings about the volitional effect in the creaturely agent. 'Rather', Grant remarks, 'God's causal act consists entirely in items extrinsic to God, that is, in E [the creaturely volition] plus the causal relation between God and E.'[22] So God's act in ordaining particular creaturely choices

---

[22]Grant, 'Divine Causality and Libertarian Freedom', in Kevin Time and Daniel Speak, eds, *Free Will and Theism: Connections, Contingencies, and Concerns*

does not entail those choices because, for any given creaturely choice one alights upon, it is possible to conceive of God existing without the particular choice obtaining. Creaturely choices on this way of thinking bear a relation to God rather like mere Cambridge relations. They do not bring about any intrinsic change in the divine nature any more than a son outgrowing his father brings about any intrinsic change in the father.

Put in a more dogmatic register, if God is an absolute sovereign over all he has created, and is metaphysically and psychologically independent of his creation (existing *a se*, or from himself), then his concurrence with creaturely action cannot affect or change his being. And if God is metaphysically simple, there can be no act of concurring with particular creaturely volitions 'in' God, so to speak. For that would imply the very notion of metaphysical complexity in God that many traditional defenders of concurrence want to deny. Instead, according to Grant's way of construing matters, there is God, God's reason for concurring with the creaturely volition, and the relation that obtains between God and the creaturely volition – though this cannot be a 'real' relation, that is, one that actually presumes some sort of real or intrinsic change in God.

What is more, God is not in time according to both traditional concurrence theorists and confessional Calvinism. So although God's concurrence with creaturely free choices is in one sense conceptually or logically prior to that choice, it cannot be that God is a *temporally* prior cause of creaturely free choice because (on this way of thinking) his action is eternal. His ordination of a particular creaturely choice is neither diachronically nor synchronically prior to the creaturely choice, though it is a necessary condition of such choice – a kind of hypothetically necessary condition, dependent on the content of divine will and intellect.

These two theological considerations, about God's relation to the world and about God's priority in creation, are grist to the mill of the confessionally Reformed libertarian Calvinist, just as they are grist to the mill for the concurrence theorist. To the extent that the libertarian Calvinist can avail herself of the resources of a two-source account of creaturely freedom such as that offered by the concurrence theorist, they may also provide reasons for thinking that libertarian Calvinism is more deeply embedded in a kind of classical theological way of thinking about God's relation to creation and his action in meticulous providence, than some objectors might imagine.

The Theological Upshot

What is the upshot of all this? First, that meticulous providence is a doctrine that is consistent with a number of different metaphysical pictures of God's action in the world, not all of which are theologically compatibilist or determinist in nature. One such version of meticulous providence (though by no means the only one) is the libertarian Calvinist view. It is not much discussed in the history of Reformed thought,[23] but it seems to me to be a viable account of meticulous providence that is recognizably Reformed, and clearly not determinist – at least not in the sense that it requires all of God's actions in the world to be determinist in form. Second, that the sourcehood problem is not just a concern for libertarian Calvinism, but is, in fact, a problem common to concurrence accounts as well. Third, if the parallels I have drawn between concurrence doctrines and libertarian Calvinism hold, then potential solutions to the sourcehood problem proffered by aficionados of concurrence accounts of meticulous providence can be taken up and adapted by libertarian Calvinists as well. Finally, I outlined one way in

---

[23]Although, as I point out in *Deviant Calvinism* and *Jonathan Edwards Among the Theologians* (Grand Rapids: Eerdmans, 2015), it is a minority report that can be found hinted at here and there. Recent historical-theological work on early Reformed theology has suggested that Reformed theologians were in some cases Thomists, holding to a doctrine of concurrence, and that many thought in terms other than the contemporary determinist-libertarian debate, preferring to think in terms of the bondage and liberation of the will, and of divine necessity of various sorts. But, as Anderson and Manata point out, this doesn't really address the issue but rather elides it. See in particular, Muller, *Divine Will and Human Choice*, and Asselt, Bac and te Velds, eds, *Reformed Thought on Freedom: The Concept of Free Choice in Early Modern Reformed Theology*. Texts and Studies in Reformation and Post-Reformation Thought (Grand Rapids: Baker Academic, 2010).

which we might model the concurrentist two-source account of free creaturely action, adapting Mackie's notion of an INUS condition to do so, supplemented by some theological suggestions culled from recent work by W. Matthews Grant. This does not *resolve* the problem of meticulous providence and human free choice, but it does indicate that there are resources in the tradition that the libertarian Calvinist can avail herself of in attempting to address this issue, which may prove fruitful, and which indicate a significant conceptual convergence between two historic theological streams of thought concerning meticulous providence and human free choice within the Christian tradition.

2

Sin in Reformed Theology

According to the *Westminster Shorter Catechism*, sin is 'any want of conformity unto, or transgression of, the law of God' (Answer to Question 14). That seems like a useful working definition with which to begin. We might distinguish further between sin in general or sin *simpliciter*, and original sin, that morally vitiated state into which all human beings barring Christ are born as a consequence of the actions of our first parents. Clearly, one need not hold to the doctrine of original sin in order to have an account of sin *simpliciter*, and there have been thinkers who embraced the latter while rejecting the former. Immanuel Kant may be the best-known philosophical exemplar of this sort of view; Pelagius is surely the most notorious theological representative. While it is tempting to restrict the scope of this chapter to sin *simpliciter*, that is not really feasible in a theological account of the notion. For, as I understand it, the traditional theological position is that human sin obtains because of the presence of original sin in creation; and without original sin there would not be individual acts of human sin because there would be no human sin per se. Original sin obtains because of the sin of an individual – at least, on traditional versions of the doctrine, as we shall see presently. But this primal or first act of sin gives rise to the condition of original sin with which we are all generated. Thus, sin exists in the world because of the fault of an individual – an act of sin – but it is this fault that is transmitted in the condition of original sin from which all human beings now suffer, and which gives rise to all subsequent individual acts of sin.[1]

---

[1] Possibly, there would still be sin in the creation if there is an angelic fall prior to the human one. But that is a matter we shall not delve into here.

Hence, a theological account of human sin must place it in the wider context of a doctrine of original sin, in which it is properly situated, dogmatically speaking.

In what follows we shall address ourselves to what I take to be the central dogmatic constituents of the doctrine of original sin with primary reference to theology in the Reformed tradition. In the course of this discussion, I shall offer a defence of one neglected strand of this tradition that is quite distinct from the majority report – the doctrine offered by the Swiss Magisterial Reformer, Huldrych Zwingli (1484–1531). Or, more precisely, I shall outline a constructive account of original in the course of presenting the dogmatic lay of the land from a Reformed perspective, which draws on a broadly Zwinglian version of the doctrine as one viable way forward for contemporary Reformed theology.[2] A defence is not an endorsement, of course (ask any attorney). But a Zwinglian account of original sin certainly merits more attention that it typically receives in textbooks of dogmatics like this one.

We begin with some remarks on method. Following this, there is a second section on the nature of original sin. The third section considers the transmission of original sin, comprising the union between Adam and his progeny envisaged in such transmission, and the manner of transmission. The conclusion offers reflections on the success of the doctrine, with particular reference to the Zwinglian account.

Methodological Preamble

There are broadly two sorts of theological approaches to original sin. The first attempts to shore up the traditional doctrine. The second revises it. There are different versions of the doctrine in the Christian tradition, and today there are significant doctrinal differences between, say, Protestant theologians, Orthodox

---

[2]'Zwinglian' because this is not an exposition of Zwingli's account, but the use of some ideas that are central to it. For instance, no account will be given here of the relationship between sacramental theology and original sin, or predestination and the ordering of the divine decrees and original sin, though these are both matters that would be important if we were giving an exposition of Zwingli's doctrine.

theologians and Roman Catholic theologians on this topic – not to mention differences between theologians in a given branch of the tradition, especially among Protestants.[3] Consequently, it might be thought that to refer to *the* traditional doctrine is question-begging: Which doctrine is the traditional one? Aren't there many traditional versions of the doctrine? Part of the reason for this is that there is no canonical definition of the doctrine as there is for some other Christian tenets such as the two-natures doctrine of the incarnation. (Some Roman Catholics might dispute this, given that the Council of Trent pronounced on the doctrine. However, with deepest respect to those who might take such a view, the deliverances of one branch of the Christian church cannot constitute an ecumenical consensus on the matter, and therefore cannot be binding upon all Christians in the way that members of the different communions of the church are bound to accept some other dogma upon which there is such universal agreement, such as the Nicene view of the Trinity.[4])

---

[3]On the debate about the development of the Augustinian view, see N. P. Williams, *The Ideas of the Fall and of Original Sin* (London: Longmans, Green, and Co., 1927), and Pier Franco Beatrice, *The Transmission of Sin: Augustine and the Pre-Augustinian Sources* (New York: Oxford University Press, 2013). For a recent sophisticated restatement of the Augustinian position, see Jesse Couenhoven, *Stricken by Sin, Cured by Christ: Agency, Necessity, and Culpability in Augustinian Theology* (New York: Oxford University Press, 2013). For a readable modern Orthodox view, see John S. Romanides, *The Ancestral Sin* (Ridgewood, NJ: Zephyr Publishing, 1998). In addition to the *Catechism of the Catholic Church* (New York: Doubleday, 1995), Ludwig Ott's *Fundamentals of Catholic Dogma* (Rockford, IL: Tan Books, 1955) is a useful field guide to Roman Catholic teaching on the subject. An example of a moderate contemporary Reformed restatement of the doctrine can be found in Marguerite Shuster, *The Fall and Sin: What We Have Become as Sinners* (Grand Rapids: Eerdmans, 2004). A much more revisionist recent Protestant account is given in Patricia A. Williams, *Doing Without Adam and Eve: Sociobiology and Original Sin* (Minneapolis: Augsburg Fortress, 2001). Perhaps the most comprehensive treatment in print is Thomas H. McCall, *Against God and Nature: The Doctrine of Sin. Foundations of Evangelical Theology* (Wheaton: Crossway, 2019). A good one-stop shop overview of a range of contemporary views on original sin is J. B. Stump and Chad Meister, eds, *Original Sin and the Fall: Five Views* (Downers Grove, IL: IVP Academic, 2020).

[4]Here I presume a distinction between a doctrine or teaching of Christian theology, such as the atonement, and a dogma, which is a doctrine that has some canonical definition, as the doctrine of the Trinity does in the ecumenical creeds shared between all Christian communions. I take it that the conciliar decisions of Roman Catholic councils and synods has a dogmatic status in some ways analogous to that of the

Nevertheless, although there are not insignificant differences of opinion on the matter of the nature of original sin and its transmission (and what it is that is transmitted from some putative first humans to their progeny), there is broadly historic ecumenical agreement on the following matters: *first*, that there was an original pair from whom we are all descended; *second*, that this pair introduced the morally vitiated condition from which all subsequent human beings suffer; and *third*, that all human beings after the fall of the original pair possess the condition of original sin and are in need of salvation, without which they will perish. Some theologians (particularly in the Augustinian tradition) want to add to this the claim that all human beings after the fall (barring Christ) bear the guilt of Adam's sin, so that in addition to possessing the condition of original depravity they also bear original guilt. However, this is not a doctrine universally affirmed and has generated a number of significant problems, as we shall see.[5]

For present purposes when I refer to *the traditional doctrine of original sin* in what follows, I mean by this the concatenation of these three doctrinal tenets without any commitment to the doctrine of original guilt. These three tenets are fairly broad, and dogmatically unspecific enough to encompass most of the different communions of historic Christianity. Although my usage is a term of art that will not satisfy everyone, it will be easier to use this shorthand rather than give a potted version of the long and

---

confessions and synodical decisions of Protestant churches. Analogous, but not the same, for Protestants still hold that confessions, though good and useful summaries of the faith, are subject to Scripture and may err, whereas Roman Catholics ought to believe what the church promulgates in her canonical decisions, including decisions by councils like Lateran IV or Trent.

[5]In his recent study, Ian McFarland carves up the doctrine in a similar fashion. He divides it according to (1) the degree to which the story of the Fall in Genesis 1–3 should be interpreted literally; (2) whether the story told there implicates the rest of the human race and (3) whether or to what extend the sin of our first parents affects the freedom of subsequent human beings (Ian A. McFarland, *In Adam's Fall: A Meditation on the Christian Doctrine of Original Sin* (Oxford: Wiley-Blackwell, 2010), 32). By contrast, Richard Swinburne writes of the proneness to sin in all human beings; the question of its cause (and whether that has to be an original human pair); and whether guilt for this original sin distributes to all other human beings. (Swinburne, *Responsibility and Atonement* (Oxford: Oxford University Press, 1989), ch. 9.)

convoluted historical narrative that gave rise to these three tenets of the traditional doctrine.[6]

The Nature of Original Sin

Having dealt with these methodological concerns, we may turn to exposition. The doctrine of original sin has several parts. Some theologians argue that original sin is a moral corruption that affects human beings in such a way that they are prone to sin. However, the sort of doctrine I am interested in stipulates that the moral corruption affecting human beings means that they will *inevitably* fall into actual sin on at least one occasion. This needs to be parsed a little more finely, however. What is this corruption, and what does it mean to 'fall into sin' if one already possesses such a moral corruption?

As to the first matter, I take it that original sin is a condition that affects all human beings (barring Christ[7]). Zwingli characterized original sin as analogous to an inherited disease or defect that inevitably gives rise to actual sin, for which humans are culpable. Possession of original sin was not itself culpable, said Zwingli, any more than being born a slave is a circumstance for which one is culpable. Yet it implies a separation from God that leads to damnation and (inevitably) to actual sin for which the individual is culpable in the sight of God. What is more, those born with original sin will perish and be separated from God without the interposition of divine grace in Christ.[8] He sums up his view like this, 'original

---

[6]For the historical development of the doctrine, N. P. Williams, *The Ideas of the Fall and of Original Sin*, is still the benchmark. A more recent account can be found in Tatha Wiley, *Original Sin: Origins, Development, Contemporary Meanings* (Mahwah, NJ: Paulist Press, 2002). Alan Jacobs's *Original Sin: A Cultural History* (San Francisco: HarperOne, 2008) also bears scrutiny. An interesting constructive account of the doctrine that takes account of evolutionary biology is Robin Collins, 'Evolution and Original Sin', in Keith B. Miller, ed., *Perspectives on an Evolving Creation* (Grand Rapids: Eerdmans, 2003), 469–501.

[7]Roman Catholics will want to include Mary *Theotokos* as another sinless post-fall human, and, perhaps, her mother, Anne. Such Christians are invited to make the relevant adjustment in what follows.

[8]Zwingli touches on original sin in several places in his works. The most developed account is in his *Declaration of Huldreich Zwingli Regarding Original Sin, Addressed*

sin, as it is in the children of Adam, is not properly sin . . . for it is not a misdeed contrary to law. It is, therefore, properly a disease and condition – a disease, because just as he fell through self-love, so do we also; a condition, because just as he became a slave and liable to death, so also are we both slaves and children of wrath . . . and liable to death.'[9]

Later, Reformed theology spoke of original sin in rather different terms as a deformity of the soul or *macula*[10] possession of which is itself grounds for culpability (see, for example, *Westminster Confession of Faith* 6.5). It is tempting to try and locate this condition, much as one might want to locate specific recessive genes that may affect a person adversely. However, although original sin does have perceptible consequences, for example, in the manifestation of moral corruption evident in the lives of sinners, it has no location because it is not a physical thing. Rather, it is a property that, when instantiated, gives rise to a particular moral condition in a person. Much as a human being may be born with the property of being capable of conscious thought, so, on this way of thinking, fallen human beings are bearers of a property that means they are morally disordered in some fundamental respect, such that they will inevitably sin on at least one occasion. The condition of sin with which we are generated gives rise to acts of sin. Usually, such acts of sin are distinguished from the moral condition of original sin, as actual sins that are performed because a person is in a state of sin, that is, that proceed from the moral condition of original sin.

Does this mean that fallen human beings are only guilty for the actual sins they (inevitably) commit because they are born with the moral condition of original sin? There is not one answer to this question. Much of the Western (Catholic) tradition replies in the affirmative, for example, St Anselm of Canterbury in his work, *On*

---

to *Urbanus Rhegius, August 15 1526.* He summarizes this view in *An Account of The Faith of Huldreich Zwingli, Submitted to The German Emperor Charles V, at The Diet of Augsburg. July 3, 1530.* Both works are translated in *On Providence and Other Essays,* ed. Samuel Macauley Jackson (Durham, NC: Labyrinth Press, 1983 [1922]). A useful digest of Zwingli's views can be found in W. P. Stephens, *Zwingli, An Introduction to His Thought* (Oxford: Oxford University Press, 1992), ch. 7.
[9]Zwingli, *Account of the Faith to Charles V* in *On Providence and Other Essays,* 40.
[10]See Heinrich Heppe, *Reformed Dogmatics,* trans. G. T. Thomson (London: Collins, 1950), 325.

the Virginal Conception and Original Sin. And, as we have already noted, there are Protestant defenders of much the same view – Zwingli being the best known among the orthodox. However, at least since St Augustine, there has been a presumption in much theology that has followed his lead that possession of the condition of original sin is itself sufficient for culpability independent of any actual sin committed. In fact, the performance of actual sins is a reason for additional culpability.

We shall consider the objections to this sort of view in a moment, when considering the transmission of original sin. For now it is important to note that there is a significant difference of opinion on the nature of original sin that turns on whether fallen human beings are culpable for being in a state of original sin. This question of innate culpability implies that fallen human beings bear Adam's sin *and guilt*. Often, textbook accounts from a more Augustinian or Reformed perspective suggest that original guilt is a constituent of the doctrine (or ought to be), and that alternative accounts that have no doctrine of original guilt are defective. However, Zwingli and St Anselm (to name but two theologians that defend a doctrine without original guilt) are hardly liminal or unorthodox figures in Western theology. Nor are they non-Augustinian in the general thrust of their thinking. Yet both presume that fallen human beings do not possess original guilt, though (in the case of Zwingli at least) they are in a serious condition that will yield spiritual death without saving grace in Christ.[11] Although the Reformed confessions by and large do not support Zwingli's position, and, as they developed, moved away from Zwingli's view to include original guilt, this is not true of *all* Reformed symbols. For instance, Article 9 of the Thirty Nine Articles of Religion states,

Original sin . . . is the fault and corruption of the Nature of every man, that naturally is engendered of the offspring of Adam;

---

[11]To be fair, the language of infection that Zwingli utilizes can also be found in Augustine. See, for example, 'Made an exile from thence after his sin, he [Adam] bound also his offspring, whom by sinning he had marred in himself as root in the penalty and death of damnation: with the result that all the children born of him . . . were infected with original sin." Augustine, *Enchiridion* trans. Ernest Evans (London: SPCK, 1953), ch. 26, 24.

whereby man is very far gone from original righteousness, and is of his own nature inclined to evil, so that the flesh lusteth always contrary to the Spirit; and therefore in every person born into this world, it deserveth God's wrath and damnation. And this infection of nature doth remain, yea in them that are regenerated; whereby the lust of the flesh, called in Greek, *phronema sarkos* . . . is not subject to the Law of God. And although there is no condemnation for them that believe and are baptized; yet the Apostle doth confess, that concupiscence and lust hath of itself the nature of sin.[12]

This is very like Zwingli's view in what it affirms about the nature of original sin as corruption as well as what it omits, for example, original guilt. It is my view that such a Zwinglian account is underappreciated in Reformed thought. What is more, given the problems associated with defending a doctrine according to which I am guilty for the sin of an ancestor many generations removed from me, whose action I did not concur with or approve, there does appear to be a significant moral objection to those Augustinian and Reformed views that include original guilt. If a strong doctrine of original sin can be had that does not include this element, it might be preferable to the stronger alternative including original guilt, at least in part because it does not have to circumvent this significant moral objection. (It may incur other objections, of course, but these are, I think, less serious in part because the doctrine is weaker in what it asserts about the moral consequences of original sin for fallen human beings.) There are a number of places where the traditional doctrine of original sin *plus* original guilt is defended.[13]

---

[12]Compare Article 15 of the *Belgic Confession*, which, like the 39 Articles, has no clear doctrine of original guilt. It states that original sin 'is a corruption of the whole human nature – an inherited depravity which even infects small infants in their mother's womb, and the root which produces in humanity every sort of sin. It is therefore so vile and enormous in God's sight that it is enough to condemn the human race, and it is not abolished or wholly uprooted even by baptism, seeing that sin constantly boils forth as though from a contaminated spring.' It goes on, 'Nevertheless, it is not imputed to God's children for their condemnation but is forgiven by his grace and mercy.'

[13]John Murray's little study, *The Imputation of Adam's Sin* (Grand Rapids: Eerdmans, 1959), is perhaps the best place to begin.

In the next section, dealing with the transmission of original sin, I shall outline the major views from a broadly Reformed perspective, and end up offering a defence of the Zwinglian view as a viable alternative that the Reformed (and other interested theologians) might want to reconsider.

The Transmission of Original Sin

There are two related but distinct dogmatic questions pertaining to the transmission of original sin. The first of these has to do with the nature of the union between Adam and his progeny on the basis of which original sin is transmitted. The second of these has to do with the imputation of original guilt. Some theologians argue that original guilt is applied *immediately* so that the condition of original sin is (somehow) communicated to all of Adam's progeny upon commission of the primal sin. Others claim that it obtains *mediately*, as we shall see.

(a) Concerning the Union between Adam and His Progeny

We turn to the matter of the union between Adam and his progeny first. In Reformed theology, there have been two important strands of thought on the question of the mode of transmission of original sin. The first of these is often called federalism, since it depends on a story about different covenants between God and human beings (the Latin term for such a covenant being *foedus*), beginning with a 'covenant of works'. This had as its condition that Adam and Eve refrain from eating of the tree of the knowledge of good and evil that stood in the midst of the Garden of Eden (Gen. 2.17).[14] This view is also sometimes called representationalism, for the central theological claim here is that Adam represents the rest of the human race in committing the primal sin; he acts on our behalf; and God

---

[14]Federalism is 'first' in that it is the more widespread view in Reformed thought even though, as a matter of fact, it postdates realism in theological discussions of the matter.

imputes his sin to us as a consequence. The other main view in Reformed theology is Augustinian realism, so called because it was thought to originate with St Augustine of Hippo.[15] On this way of thinking, Adam's progeny are somehow really present with Adam when he commits his first sin so that the culpability for that sin is transmitted from Adam to his progeny who are united with him at that moment, either seminally (in his loins, so to speak), or in some other mysterious manner, often thought to be beyond our ken.

We have already mentioned in passing the two main concerns that the transmission of sin raises, namely the apparent immorality and injustice involved in ascribing the sin and guilt of one person to another. How can I be guilty of Adam's sin if he lived many hundreds of years ago, and I had no say in his wickedness? How is it moral for me to suffer for the sin of a long-dead ancestor?[16] The thought here is this: guilt cannot be ascribed to a person that has not authorized or otherwise participated in the sin of another individual. Yet this is just what is said to obtain in the case of the imputation of Adam's guilt to his offspring in the doctrine of original guilt.

There are two related lines of argument developed by federalists that attempt to rebut these worries. The first of these depends on the claim that Adam acts as the head of the human race in sinning as he does. There is a natural union between him and us because he is the first human being, and we are his offspring. So, the tragic events in Eden that led to the primal sin have consequences for

---

[15]For instance, 'In fact, because of the magnitude of that offence, the condemnation changed human nature for the worse; so that what first happened as a matter of punishment in the case of the first human beings, continued in their posterity as something natural and congenital. . . . Therefore the whole human race was in the first man, and it was to pass from him through the woman into his progeny, when the married pair had received the divine sentence of condemnation. And it was not man as first made, but what man became after his sin and punishment, that was thus begotten, as far as concerns the origin of sin and death.' Augustine, *City of God* Bk. XIII: III, trans. Henry Bettenson (Harmondsworth: Penguin, 1984), 512.

[16]The nineteenth-century Southern Presbyterian Robert Dabney puts it like this, 'the grand objection of all Pelagians and skeptics, is still repeated: How can it be justice, for me, who gave no consent to the federal arrangement, for me, who was not present when Adam sinned, and took no share in it, save in a sense purely fictitious and imaginary, to be so terribly punished for another man's deeds.' *Lectures in Theology* (aka *Systematic Theology*) (Edinburgh: Banner of Truth, 1985 [1871]), 338.

all subsequent human beings because he was the natural head of the race. Had he been born several centuries after the first human beings, then he would not have been the natural head of the race, and his primal sin would not have been distributed to all humanity, for some human beings would have lived and died before him, and not all humanity would have proceeded from him.

The second line of reasoning depends on the claim that there is a legal bond between Adam and his progeny. God justly imputes Adam's sin to us because Adam is our legal representative, acting on our behalf. When he sins, this act has the legal ramifications of committing those with whom he has this legal bond to the consequences attending his primal sin, namely condemnation and the inheritance of the condition of original sin. In a similar manner, if Jones engages Smith to act as his legal representative in certain matters, then Smith's actions in that capacity are binding upon Jones. He is legally warranted to act on behalf of Jones in these matters. Something similar obtains with Adam and his progeny on this view. His action in primal sin is binding upon his progeny because he is warranted by divine fiat to be our legal representative.

So, according to the federalist, it is just that Adam acts on our behalf in his primal sin because God has authorized him to act in this manner, both as the natural head of the race so that the moral effects of his action may distribute to all subsequent human beings and as our public representative, whose fall has legally binding consequences for the rest of the human race that proceeds from him. Clearly, these two lines of argument are related, though distinct.

However, there are several significant drawbacks to the federalist view. Perhaps the most serious problem is that the appointment of Adam as our legal representative is dependent on the divine will alone. This means that the grounds for Adam being our natural and legal head is divine convention, nothing more. God makes truth in this matter. Not merely in the sense that he creates a world in which a certain person, Adam, is the first human being (according to traditional theology, at least). But, additionally, he makes it the case that Adam acts as a legal representative of the human race when he commits the primal sin. In other words, it is God alone who is responsible for the state of affairs in which Adam's commits the primal sin, which is communicated to his offspring. And God alone is responsible for ordaining that original sin is communicated from Adam to his progeny, as well as the mechanism by means of which original sin is transmitted from Adam to his progeny. So God alone is responsible for bringing about what appears to be a deeply immoral and unjust arrangement whereby all those who come after Adam are culpable and punishable for his primal sin, a sin which they did not commit, and which they did not authorize a representative to commit either. But God cannot bring about a state of affairs for which he is solely responsible that is both unjust and immoral (Deut. 32.4; Hab 1.13; 1 Jn 1.15). Hence, there must be something amiss with the federalist account of the transmission of sin. Call this *the arbitrary divine will objection.*

A second problem is closely related to the first, though it may be distinguished from it. Call it, *the authorization objection.* It goes like this: I have not authorized Adam to act on my behalf as Jones authorizes Smith. Whether I would have done the same had I been in Adam's place is irrelevant for the purposes of establishing a proper legal warrant. Normally we would expect that someone who acts on behalf of another individual or on behalf of another group does so because he is authorized to do so by some appropriate authority. Although it might be claimed that God is the relevant authority here, it is not clear that anyone has the authority to make Adam the legal representative of a whole race that has no say in the matter – which yields the divine arbitrary will objection once more. It is not clear that God has the authority to impute the consequences of Adam's primal sin to the rest of humanity given that they have not authorized him to act on their behalf, and have not colluded with him, or otherwise been a party to his sinful action. The fact that Adam is said to be the natural head of the race does not work in resolving this legal problem, of course, since this aspect of the federalist argument does not depend on any established legal arrangement independent of the divine will. What is more, the imputation of the moral consequences of the primal sin of the first human to the rest of humanity is itself a seemingly arbitrary arrangement. (Why the first sin only? Why the first sin of the first human being only? And so on. The first virtuous act of Adam isn't imputed to all his offspring in a similar manner. So this seems arbitrary.) On the face of it, defenders of the federalist argument appear to be saddled with a rather difficult version of the injustice problem for the transmission of original sin.

Might the federalist notion that original sin is imputed from Adam to his progeny help alleviate the moral problem of the transmission of original sin? Not obviously. For clearly we would normally think it is immoral to impute sin and guilt from one party who is culpable to another that is innocent. Adam is the agent that commits the primal sin, the rest of humanity do not; they are innocent of committing the primal sin for which they are said to be culpable and punishable. Consequently, it appears that the federalist is in a bind regarding both the legal and moral objections to the transmission of original sin because Adam's progeny have not authorized or otherwise approved his action on their behalf.

Finally, it seems that the federalist scheme rests upon what we might call a legal and moral fiction, generating *the fiction objection*: God imputes Adam's sin to his progeny; he holds them responsible for Adams sin – or at least, he holds them jointly culpable with Adam, because they are punishable for his sin in virtue of possessing original sin quite apart from any actual sin they may perform. But clearly Adam's progeny are not the ones guilty of performing the act of primal sin; Adam is. So imputing it to them involves a fiction, one that has both a legal and a moral dimension given the federalist argument. However, the fact that God is said to impute original sin to Adam's progeny on the basis of a natural and legal union with Adam does not make this act any more appropriate. Often defenders of the federalist view argue that because God is an absolute sovereign, he may distribute matters as he sees fit, and we are not to question him in this regard (relying in part on St Paul's comments in Romans 9). Furthermore, the fact that an entity is an absolute sovereign in and of itself conveys no moral *imprimatur* to that entity's actions.[17] Such an entity could be a tyrant, after all, with

---

[17]Question: suppose Adam didn't sin. Would it have been unjust for God to have granted eternal life to all of Adam's progeny on the basis of his obedience? Maybe not. However, I am attracted to the view that without union with Christ eternal life is impossible even for those who are sinless. If that is right, then the incarnation would have happened irrespective of Adam's primal sin. For recent discussion of this matter, see Marilyn McCord Adams, *Christ and Horrors: The Coherence of Christology* (Cambridge: Cambridge University Press, 2006), ch. 7; Edwin Christian van Driel, *Incarnation Anyway: Arguments for Supralapsarian Christology* (New York: Oxford University Press, 2008), and Justus H. Hunter, *If Adam Had Not Sinned: The Reason for the Incarnation from Anselm to Scotus* (Washington, DC: Catholic University of America Press, 2020). For my own view, see Oliver D. Crisp, *Analyzing Doctrine: Toward a Systematic Theology* (Waco: Baylor University Press, 2019), ch. 6.

his acts evidence of megrim. The fact is, the federalist account hangs upon the divine will, and what God decides to bring about according to his goodwill and pleasure. Yet this alone is an insufficient ground for an argument for the conclusion that the transmission of original sin is just and moral, unless one is willing to embrace the view that God *makes* certain things just and moral. Even if one factors in the divine character so that the argument is not purely voluntarist (i.e. stemming from the divine will alone) but intellectualist (i.e. involving God acting as he does because of the character he has), it is still not clear how this in and of itself provides any moral or legal justification for the act of transmitting original sin. Something more needs to be said. If, in the final analysis, the federalist appeals beyond the divine will to mystery or antinomy, it is not clear how this will help. For in the case of the imputation of a thing from one party to another, we have deep-seated moral intuitions about what is morally and legally appropriate, such that it would be clear in a more mundane context that such an arrangement as that given by the federalist for the transmission of original sin, would be unjust and immoral.[18]

---

[18]The federalist may reply that this objection proves too much. In undercutting reasons for the imputation of Adam's sin, we also undercut reasons for thinking that Christ's righteousness may be imputed also; but we don't want to set aside the imputation of Christ's righteousness in redemption; so we have a christological reason for thinking that imputation obtains in the case of Christ's work, and that a similar sort of reasoning obtains, *mutatis mutandis*, with respect to the imputation of Adam's sin. Here the federalist can appeal to Rom 5: 12-19, which turns on the parallel between the work of both Adam and Christ.

One line of response here is to point out that there are significant dissimilarities between the work of Adam and Christ that bear upon the question of imputation. Adam's headship is natural and legal (according to federalism); Christ's is neither. Perhaps the imputation of sin on the basis of a natural and legal headship is problematic (for the reasons given above), whereas the supernatural basis for the imputation of Christ's righteousness is not. This is the realist way of distinguishing between the two 'Adams'. (See, for example, William Shedd's *A Critical and Doctrinal Commentary on the Epistle of St. Paul to the Romans* (Eugene, OR: Wipf and Stock, 2001 [1879]).) Another answer involves acceding to the federalist objection and appealing to a doctrine of atonement that does not include the notion that Christ's righteousness is imputed to the saints. One historic example of this is Anselm's doctrine of atonement in *Cur deus homo*. Given his influence in historic Reformed theology, this seems to be an alternative to penal substitution worth exploring. I have attempted a different (more modern) version of a consistent realist response

For these reasons, I judge that the federalist argument, taken on its own merits and without augmentation by appeal to other accounts of the transmission of sin, fails to overcome the moral and legal problems with which we began our assessment.[19]

What of the realist alternative? According to at least one recent treatment of the Reformed doctrine of original sin, this is very much a minority report in the tradition associated with one nineteenth-century American Presbyterian theologian in particular, namely William Shedd.[20] But as Shedd himself argues in his *Dogmatic Theology*, the realist position is found in much earlier Reformed theology, at least implicitly, and is present in the work of several other eighteenth- and nineteenth-century theologians, including Samuel Baird, James Thornwell and the Reformed Baptist Augustus Strong. There are strong overtones of this view in the work of others too, for instance Robert Dabney and Robert Landis, as well as Jonathan Edwards.[21]

---

in 'Original Sin and Atonement', in Thomas P. Flint and Michael C. Rea, eds, *The Oxford Handbook of Philosophical Theology* (Oxford: Oxford University Press, 2009), ch. 19.

[19]One could augment the federalist account with a realist account, as some Reformed theologians seem to have done, for example, Jonathan Edwards. In such cases the federalist account is no longer doing all the metaphysical heavy-lifting. It may be that such hybrid doctrines are able to avoid the problems set forth here. For further discussion, see Oliver D. Crisp, 'Jonathan Edwards on the Imputation of Sin', in *Retrieving Doctrine: Essays in Reformed Theology* (Downers Grove, IL: IVP Academic, 2011), ch. 3. Some early Reformed accounts of the imputation of sin are not clearly federalist or realist having aspects of both later accounts, for example, John Calvin, *Institutes of the Christian Religion*, ed. John T. McNeill, trans. Ford Lewis Battles (Philadelphia: Westminster Press, 1960 [1559]), 1.2.7. Some federalists maintain that their position doesn't fall foul of the arbitrariness objection because imputation is grounded in an existing natural union between Adam and his offspring. Suppose that is right. The fiction objection still obtains because God has to ascribe to Adam's offspring a property they do not naturally possess. If the federalist wants to argue that God does transmit Adam's sin to his offspring as parts of a natural or organic whole, then this begins to look much more like a realist view.

[20]See Donald Macleod, 'Original Sin in Reformed Theology', in Hans Madueme and Michael Reeves, eds, *Adam, the Fall, and Original Sin: Theological, Biblical, and Scientific Perspectives* (Grand Rapids: Baker Academic, 2014), 129–46.

[21]For discussion of this, see George P. Hutchinson, *The Problem of Original sin in American Presbyterian Theology*. Biblical and Theological Studies Series (N.P.: Presbyterian and Reformed Co., 1972). Augustus Strong's views are set forth in his *Systematic Theology* [3 Vols. in 1] (Valley Forge, PA: Judson Press, 1907). Jonathan

According to the realist view, the way to avoid the moral and legal problems that beset the transmission of original sin is to opt for a real union between Adam and his progeny rather than a union that is a moral and legal construct. Making good on this claim is a tall order, however. There are several historic realist arguments for this conclusion. The first of these we may call *the seminal argument*, since the idea is that somehow all of Adam's descendants were seminally presents with him in his act of primal sin. Appeal is often made to Heb. 7.9-10, where Levi is said to have been in the loins of Abraham when he was blessed by Melchizedek, so that he may be said to have paid out a tithe with Abraham, figuratively speaking. Just as Levi was in the loins if Abraham, so we were in the loins of Adam. And just as Levi paid out a tithe via his ancestor to Melchizedek, so we sinned in Adam.

The problems with such a view are obvious. First of all the passage in Hebrews does not require that Levi was actually seminally present in Abraham's loins, so it is a frail reed upon which to rest and argument for the conclusion that all humanity was really present in Adam's loins. Moreover, given what we now know of human biology and procreation, the seminal argument is a non-starter. Furthermore, even if some sense could be made of it, it doesn't solve the moral problem for the transmission of original sin because a seminally present entity is not an entity that can authorize the sin of Adam or participate in his sin.

Another realist argument is that Adam's human nature is a sort of mass from which all subsequent human natures are drawn. His nature is either fissiparous or parturient, so that subsequent human natures are individualized from his greater nature as a piece of clay is taken from a lump, and fashioned into a particular artefact. On this view, then, we are literally chips off the old Adamic block! Parts of Adam's human nature are passed on from him to his children, and they in turn pass on a part of their human nature to their children and so on, down through the generations, so that each subsequent instance of human nature is individualized as it is generated from the substance of the parent human nature, just as

---

Edwards' views are not straightforwardly realist, but could be characterized as a sort of rogue realism. See his *Original Sin, The Works of Jonathan Edwards*, vol. 3, ed. Clyde A. Holbrook (New Haven: Yale University Press, 1970), IV. III.

one might take a piece of clay from the lump, and then another piece from the smaller lump, and another piece and so on, fashioning each individual lump into a particular artefact. Let us call this *the unindividualized nature argument*. This version of realism appears to require the doctrine of traducianism according to which human souls are passed down the generations in a manner analogous to the passing on of genetic material from parents to children. On this realist account, human nature (whatever that is, exactly) is passed down through natural generation.

The benefit of this unindividualized nature realist argument is that it can provide an argument that ameliorates the moral problem of the transmission of original sin. We really were 'in' Adam because we were literally parts of his human nature, which is the Ur-nature for all humanity that is passed down the generations and individualized in each of us in part. However, for most contemporary theologians, the cost of this solution will be too high. Few modern theologians want to embrace traducianism in any form, and the notion that Adam has some sort of Ur-nature or Ur-soul from which all subsequent humans are derived is, to say the least, fanciful – provided some sense can be made of the notion of a fissiparous Ur-nature.

A recent peroration on this Ur-nature realist argument that draws on the work of Jonathan Edwards claims that we literally sin 'in' Adam because we all share a temporal part or stage with Adam – the part or stage that commits primal sin. The idea is something like this. Suppose that we are all four-dimensional beings that persist through time in virtue of having temporal parts or, perhaps, stages that are segued together, on analogy with the physical parts that make a human person.[22] Just as I have a hand and foot as distinct physical parts, so perhaps I have distinct temporal parts: the part of me that existed yesterday, the part that existed thirty

---

[22] I am skating over an important difference between stage theory and temporal parts theory, two ways of carving up four-dimensional wholes that are distinct. I have had to do this in the interests of space. But the reader should be aware that this difference entails two distinct four-dimensionalist accounts of persisting objects that utilize the same background ontology, carved differently. The distinction is clearly set forth in Sally Haslanger, 'Persistence Through Time', in Michael J. Loux and Dean W. Zimmerman, eds, *The Oxford Handbook of Metaphysics* (Oxford: Oxford University Press, 2003), ch. 11.

years ago today and so forth. Now, assume that this is true of all human beings, Adam included. Then he has a temporal part or stage that committed primal sin. Imagine that at the moment of primal sin that stage fissions into innumerable stages that are qualitatively identical to one another, though numerically distinct. These innumerable stages or parts become the first part or stage of the lives of subsequent human beings so that each and every human being (barring Christ, perhaps) shares a fissioned stage with Adam. Then, the first moment of our lives, so to speak, is a stage that obtains thousands of years ago when Adam sinned. Like other realist arguments, this one involves the claim that somehow I have a pre-existence before my conception in the womb. Unlike the Ursoul argument, however, on this view that which pre-exists my first moment in the womb is a fissioned stage or a temporal part that is shared with Adam.

This updating of a sort of realist view uses contemporary metaphysical discussion of persistence through time to make a case for a real union between Adam and his progeny. But it has a considerable cost, and many will think the notion that I have a fissioned part that I derive from Adam, though possible, is not terribly plausible, and begs other important questions about my pre-existence 'in' Adam, and about the so-called 'gappy' existence (for then I would have a temporal part or stage shared with Adam, and a huge temporal gap between it and my next temporal part or stage that obtains when I begin to exist in my mother's womb). If one has independent reasons for thinking an entity cannot have two beginnings of existence, or cannot have a gappy existence like this, then one will find little attractive about this modern relative of a realist solution – what we might call *the fission argument*.[23]

Yet another peroration on a realist theme (and one that also draws on the work of Jonathan Edwards) is what we might call

---

[23]The argument is found in Michael C. Rea's essay, 'The Metaphysics of Original Sin', in Peter van Inwagen and Dean Zimmerman, eds, *Persons: Human and Divine* (Oxford: Oxford University Press, 2007), ch. 14. It is discussed by Hud Hudson in *The Fall and Hypertime* (Oxford: Oxford University Press, 2014), who finds problems with it, though he thinks it a remarkable piece of metaphysics. As will be clear from a perusal of Rea's paper, his argument is inspired by Edwards' discussion in *Original Sin* IV. III.

the participation argument.[24] On this view, sin is 'transmitted' from some first human community to all subsequent humans (barring Christ) because God constitutes the part of this human community that sins and all subsequent human beings (barring Christ) as one metaphysical whole, with myriad different parts scattered across space-time. You and I are both 'parts' of this one whole entity, so that we share together certain properties in common, much as a composite whole has parts that shares properties in common, though not all properties and not all parts. For instance, consider my cat Tigger. He is a ginger cat. He is a composite whole made up of many parts. Some of those parts share in common the property 'being ginger', which is why we think of him as a ginger cat. However, not all his parts have the property 'being ginger' for not all his parts are ginger. His whiskers are not ginger, nor are his claws, his bones, his intestines and so on. Yet he is a ginger cat. In a similar way, perhaps humanity is a whole entity that is scattered across space-time. Some of its constituent members share the property of original sin just as some of Tigger's parts share the property 'being ginger'. Not all the parts of this four-dimensional whole that we might call Composite Humanity are fallen (e.g. Adam and Eve prior to their primal sin, or Christ). Yet many members have this property. Together they comprise a scattered entity, which shares certain parts and properties in common.

Like other versions of realism, the participation argument presumes that there must be some real unity between Adam and his progeny on the basis of which God is able to 'transmit' original sin from one part of the composite whole of humanity to the others. This real unity is ordained by God, of course. But he has set the world up so that, in addition to conventional artefacts like tables and chairs, there are unconventional or exotic entities like Composite Humanity. Like the federalist arguments, there is a reason why this involves the 'transmission' of the moral condition generated by the primal sin of the first human, Adam, rather than some later sin of a later human being. Only the primal sin can infect all the later stages of Composite Humanity, just as only an infected acorn can be the cause of the chronic disease afflicting the oak tree at each and every stage of its later development. To change the

---

[24]For elaboration of this argument, see Oliver D. Crisp, 'Original Sin and Atonement'.

metaphor, if one introduces a flaw into the blueprints for a new vehicle, then that flaw will be present in every production line model of the motorcar. The same would not be true if the flaw occurred on the production line of one of the factories manufacturing the vehicle as a consequence of equipment failure. For in that case there are other factories making the same model that remain unaffected by the mechanical failure at the first factory, and examples of the model being driven around that would not have the flaw. *Mutatis mutandis*, Adam's primal sin must be the sin that is communicated to the other parts of Composite Humanity, if it is to be 'transmitted' via natural generation.

But we must ask: Does the participation argument offer a moral or a just arrangement (more moral and more just than the realist alternatives)? And does it overcome the problems of the transmission of original sin? Edwards thinks it is just for God to do as he pleases, because God 'makes truth in affairs of this nature'. This seems too strong, and has the unintended outcome of collapsing Edwards's four-dimensionalist argument for the transmission of original sin into a matter of divine fiat. Nevertheless, God may arrange matters so that Adam and his progeny constitute one scattered composite whole much as, in a soteriological context, Christ and his elect constitute another scattered whole, the whole comprising the Saviour and those united to him by the secret working of the Holy Spirit. The union is different, of course. In the case of Adam and his progeny, it is a natural union between the first human and his sin, and later humans. In the case of Christ and the elect, the union is not a natural one but a supernatural one that has a proleptic component: Christ is the firstborn from the dead, the first fruits of resurrection, the New Adam, and the head of a new race of those who, through union with him, are redeemed (as the Pauline language of the New Testament makes clear), including those saints that lived prior to Christ.

Recall that a worry raised with seminal and unindividualized nature versions of realism were that they did not address the matter of the culpability of Adam's progeny in his sin, since seminal or unindividualized presence with Adam is hardly the same as being complicit in the sin of Adam, and cannot include the notion of agreeing with Adam in his sin (for seminal and unindividualized presence does not include agency on the part of those seminally present or present in an unindividualized state).

Does the participation argument fare any better on this score? It certainly involves Adam's progeny as agents capable of acceding to Adam's sin. But they do not actually accede to his sin on this version of realism. So it might appear that the argument fails to overcome the moral problem for transmission of original sin. But such a judgement would be overhasty. The participation argument presumes that Adam and his progeny form one organic whole, Composite Humanity.[25] What the first part does in the act of primal sin has implications for later parts of the same entity scattered across space-time because Composite Humanity is an aggregated object. God treats as one what is, in fact, one aggregated object for the purposes of the transmission of original sin. There are parallels to such arrangements in corporate law where the different assets of a particular company can be treated as parts of one legal entity for certain legal purposes. The difference in the case of the participation argument is that Adam and his progeny are not merely a legal entity (as with federalism) but a real four-dimensional metaphysical whole. Nevertheless, like the legal corporate entity, the metaphysical four-dimensional entity that is Composite Humanity can have ascribed to some of its parts the moral properties of other parts because they are parts of one entity.

We have been using the language of the traditional account of original sin here deliberately, and in the interests of economy of style. However, if one thought of 'Adam' as a placeholder for some early human community, the argument could still be run with only minor changes being made. Nor does it matter that 'Adam' is not the first hominid. What matters for the purposes of the participation argument is that 'Adam' is the first member or the first community of the whole that comprises Composite Humanity. God certainly 'makes truth' in that respect: he decides which hominid community

---

[25]Question: Aren't Adam and his progeny one composite whole according to federalism as well? He is the natural and legal head of the race and his sin is imputed to them. But this is a different arrangement than the realist one. Adam and his offspring are not one organism or one organic whole; the union envisaged in federalism is more like that of an artefact than an organism, that is, it is more like a collection of distinct parts organized into a whole than it is a whole that has certain parts – the difference between, say, a chair made of wooden parts fashioned into a serviceable object, and a tree, which is an organism made of wood.

will be the community upon which he bestows his image, and with which he enters into covenant relationship.[26]

(b) Concerning the Guilt Transmitted

A final matter remains to be explored. This is the question of the manner of the transmission of original sin. Does God transmit it immediately upon the commission of the primal sin so that once Adam sins God transmits original sin to all subsequent humans, as it were, automatically and prior to the existence of subsequent human natures? This is a common view in Reformed theology.[27] But it has some significant drawbacks. On this view, the immediate imputation of original guilt logically precedes, and is the cause of inherent corruption. But this means that I am born in a state of sin, possessing original sin, because God imputes the guilt of another individual to me logically prior to me becoming a moral agent. For reasons already touched upon, this seems intolerable, the sort of arrangement that would never be thought just or moral in more mundane circumstances.

The alternative view developed by the theologians of the post-Reformation French Saumur Academy, and Josue Placeus in particular, is mediate imputation. In this view the inheritance of a corrupt nature gives rise to the guilt of Adam's sin. That is, guilt for Adam's sin is consequent upon possessing the corrupt nature inherited from Adam. Placeus's view was censured at the Synod of Chareton, though in clarifying his view after the censure, Placeaus made it clear that his position was not identical to the one the Synod had condemned. Nevertheless, though it is intriguing, mediate

---

[26]Does this not fall foul of the arbitrary divine will objection? Perhaps it does. But perhaps not in quite the same ways as federalism. The worry with federalism is that it attributes an arbitrariness to God that raises moral objections. The same objections cannot be raised here because (we presume) no hominid group deserves special treatment by God, and God may elect according to his good pleasure and will (Eph. 1.9; Rom. 8.28-30; 9:).

[27]See *Westminster Confession of Faith* 6.3; The *Formula Consensus Helvetica* of 1675 also takes a firm stand against the mediate view of the Saumur theologians in favour of immediate imputation.

imputation has remained relatively undeveloped in subsequent Reformed theology.[28]

(c) The Zwinglian Alternative

Zwingli's view, to which we have already made reference, is that human beings inherit a disease or defect, a moral condition from fallen Adam that includes no guilt at all. We are not culpable for the corruption that we are generated with, and which we bring with us into the world. Thus, on the Zwinglian view neither immediate or mediate imputation applies, for two reasons. First, Adam's guilt is not transmitted to his progeny; second, the condition of original sin is inherited, passed down the generations like genes. It is not imputed; it is a disease consequent upon Adam's primal sin, akin to contracting a chronic and debilitating malady which is then passed on to one's offspring through natural generation. Being born in sin, on this Zwinglian view, involves having moral corruption – that much is held in common with other Reformed thinkers. But without a doctrine of imputed original guilt, there is no need for elaborate metaphysical distinctions between immediate or mediate imputation, or between the punishable aspect of original guilt and the inherent aspect, or even explicit commitment to four-dimensional parts and wholes. So his view, or a variant of it, has a certain theological parsimony in making sense of the transmission of original sin that is attractive, and, perhaps, preferable to the alternatives.

Does it overcome the moral problem and the injustice problem for the transmission of original sin? Does it fare any better than federalism or realism in this regard? In answer to the immorality objection to the transmission of original sin, the Zwinglian can say that it is not immoral for God to allow Adam to freely choose to commit the primal sin. Nor is it immoral that the consequences of this act are transferred to all his progeny as a spiritual disease, moral defect and inherited condition on analogy with the inheritance of

---

[28]See Philip Schaff, *Creeds of Christendom with a History and Critical Notes. Vol. 1. The History of the Creeds* (New York: Harper and Brothers, 1877), 484–5; Anthony A. Hoekema, *Created in God's Image* (Grand Rapids: Eerdmans, 1986), 156–7; G. C. Berkouwer, *Sin* (Grand Rapids: Eerdmans, 1971), 454–8.

serious medical conditions that are recessive in nature. This is just the natural outworking of Adam's primal sin, just as, in a different context, the selling of oneself into slavery is the reason why one's offspring and their offspring and so on, are all born into slavery. For, in a sense, and metaphorically speaking, that is just what Adam has done: he has sold his offspring into a condition of bondage to sin. This means that each of his offspring (barring Christ) is generated with original sin, a condition that will lead to spiritual death if left unaddressed.[29]

What about the injustice objection to the transmission of original sin? Here too, Zwingli's position has distinct advantages. Zwingli can say something different from federalism and realism. God justly transmits Adam's sinful condition to me through natural inheritance. (Perhaps, we might think, God does this via some sort of spiritually recessive 'gene' that both parents of any fallen person possess – though this goes beyond what Zwingli actually says.) He does not transmit Adam's guilt to me, so the condition in which I find myself (i.e. being born with the condition of original sin) is not one for which I am culpable, though it will lead to my death without the interposition of divine grace, just as some inherited conditions lead to death without medical intervention.

Note that Zwingli clearly does endorse original sin. He is not a Pelagian (*pace* Luther), for Pelagians deny the doctrine of inherited sin, opting instead for the view that sin obtains by imitation, not imputation (nor inheritance).[30] Clearly, Zwingli does think sin obtains through inheritance, the inheritance of a vitiated moral condition that leads inevitably to acts of sin. Is he semi-Pelagian? Semi-Pelagians hold to a doctrine of synergism in the matter of salvation. That is, they teach that humans beings are able to exercise their free will independent of divine grace in order to

---

[29]Granted, the federalist and realist can use similar language about Adam selling his descendants into slavery, but the theological account of the transmission of sin underpinning this trope is quite different.

[30]For Pelagius's writings see B. R. Rees (trans.), *The Letters of Pelagius and His Followers* (Woodbridge: Boydell Press, 1991), and *Pelagius's Commentary on St Paul's Epistle to the Romans*. Oxford Early Christian Studies Series, trans. Theodore de Bruyn (Oxford: Oxford University Press, 1993). For a brief introduction to Pelagius, see John Ferguson, *Pelagius, A Historical and Theological Study* (Cambridge: W. Heffer and Sons, 1956).

cooperate with divine grace in bringing about their own salvation. But Zwingli emphatically denies this, and the Zwinglian can do the same: salvation is entirely a matter of divine grace for which fallen human beings can do nothing to prepare themselves. This Zwinglian view is clearly monergistic, and therefore not semi-Pelagian.[31]

There are other things about the Zwinglian view that seem appealing as well. Although Zwingli thought of original sin as originating with a historic human pair, it might be that a broadly Zwinglian account of original sin could be had that makes room for a more expansive understanding of the acquisition of original sin. Perhaps the disease is introduced by the actions of more than one pair, or by the action of a community (i.e. by 'Adam'). It comes to afflict all the members of the community, and, as a consequence, is passed on to all their offspring and so on, down through the generations.

Such a variation on the Zwinglian position would not require that the humans from which all have descended were specially created, or were the only hominids at the time the primal sin is committed. And it could provide a plausible account of the transmission of original sin down through the years via (or accompanying) natural generation.[32] It would offer a strong doctrine of human moral disorder, but one that does not have the problems that the more metaphysically elaborate notions of federalism or realism require. Without imputation and original guilt, such a Zwinglian doctrine is also freed from the need to defend implausible or objectionable notions such as moral and legal fictionalism, or the culpability of the innocent. It is not without cost, of course. But it may be that a Zwinglian doctrine taken along these lines has more to be said for it in a post-Darwinian world than does the sort of doctrine beloved of

---

[31]There are aspects of Zwingli's position that are less attractive. In *On the Providence of God*, he argues that hard determinism obtains; that human free will and agency is an illusion; and that God is the only real cause of all that takes place in the world. He also advocates a strong version of supralapsarianism that will not appeal to everyone. However, one can extract his doctrine of original sin from these wider, though related, theological commitments in which it is embedded without damaging the substantive claims he makes about original sin and its transmission. That is what I am proposing here.

[32]Here I have in mind the notion of a hominid community chosen by God, from which all subsequent humans are descended.

many Reformed divines after Zwingli, whose views are encumbered by various elements that make them much less attractive or straightforward, much of which stems from their inclusion of a doctrine of original guilt.

Conclusions

Can a traditional account of original sin be defended? Recall that we characterized the three constituents of the traditional view as follows: *first*, that there was an original pair from whom we are all descended; *second*, that this pair introduced the morally vitiated condition from which all subsequent human beings suffer; and *third*, that all human beings after the fall of the original pair possess the condition of original sin and are in need of salvation, without which they will perish. Clearly some Reformed account can be given of the doctrine that does satisfy these three criteria, though I have indicated that a more expansive understanding of the first constituent is required given what we now know about human evolution. I have also commended the Zwinglian view as one that has certain obvious advantages over extant alternatives in the Reformed tradition, chief among which is that it does not require a doctrine of original guilt. Not only is original guilt not a constituent of the traditional view as set forth here, it also generates significant dogmatic problems for the federalist and realist doctrines that presume it. Does something like the Zwinglian alternative seem plausible – perhaps *more plausible* than the alternatives that presume original guilt? I have answered in the affirmative. What is more, a version of this Zwinglian story of original sin can be had that is consistent with much of the story of human development told by contemporary biology and allied sciences. If that is right, then this neglected strand of Reformed anthropology may well be both dogmatically and scientifically plausible – or at least, dogmatically plausible and not scientifically *im*plausible, and at least as plausible as the alternatives, perhaps more plausible on balance. That may be the best one can ask for when considering such a difficult and perplexing theological topic.

PART TWO

Person of Christ

3

Andrew Loke's
Preconscious Christ

How should we think about the hypostatic union? In a series of articles and essays and a recent monograph, Andrew Loke has argued that existing models fail to give an adequate account of this central theological mystery.[1] In place of these different views, he offers his own model of the hypostatic union as one possible way in which to meet worries about the coherence of the incarnation. In this chapter I will outline his model and offer two sorts of pushback against some of its key claims. The first sort has to do with the coherence of the model proposed by Loke, which has recently been articulated by James Arcadi. I try to strengthen and extend Arcadi's line of criticism against Loke. Following on from this, the second sort of pushback has to do with whether Loke's view is a more plausible account of the incarnation than that favoured by many contemporary analytic theologians, namely the two-minds model.

The Divine Preconscious Model (DPM)

Let me begin by outlining Loke's understanding of the incarnation. In the twentieth century several theologians attempted to provide an account of the hypostatic union that drew on modern psychology. Perhaps the best known of these models was that of the

---

[1]In what follows, I shall refer to Loke, *A Kryptic Model of the Incarnation*. All references to this work are given parenthetically in the body of the text, as 'Loke', followed by the page reference.

Anglican Oxford theologian, William Sanday. He put forward the *Divine Subconscious Model* (DSM) of the incarnation, according to which the divine nature of Christ becomes something like the subconscious or 'subliminal self' of Christ from the first moment of incarnation onwards. This is a kind of functional kenotic model of the incarnation, where the Word restricts the exercise of his divine attributes by relegating his divine nature to the subconscious of the incarnate Christ. As Sanday puts it,

> On the one hand we think of the human consciousness of the Lord as entirely human; we make no attempt to fence off one part of it as human and another part as divine. Whatever there was of divine in Him, on its way to outward expression whether in speech or act, passed through, and could not but pass through, the restricting and restraining medium of human consciousness. This consciousness was, as it were, the narrow neck through which alone the divine could come to expression.[2]

Loke's contribution to the literature on the incarnation stands in this tradition of what we might call psychological models of the incarnation. In many ways it is an updated and amended version of the sort of approach to the incarnation Sanday commended to theological readers over a century ago. Loke calls his own contribution, *the Divine Preconscious Model of the incarnation*, or DPM. We can summarize it thus. Following the two natures doctrine of Chalcedonian Christology, Loke claims that Christ is one divine person with two natures: one divine nature (which he has in virtue of being a divine person) and one human nature (which he acquires at the first moment of incarnation). However, unlike those who in the recent analytic-theological literature have adopted a two-minds model of the incarnation as a way of construing the metaphysics of the two natures doctrine, Loke believes that Christ has only *one* consciousness, though he has two minds. This, he maintains, is vital in order to avoid worries about Nestorianism, which (so he thinks) the defenders of two-minds Christology find it difficult to avoid.

Well then, how does Loke think Christ can have *one* consciousness and yet *two* minds? To begin with, he adopts a three-part concrete

---

[2]Sanday, *Christology and Personality*, 167. Compare Andrew Ter Ern Loke, 'Sanday's Christology Revisited', *Journal of Theological Studies* 63.1 (2012): 187–97.

nature view of the incarnation as his metaphysical framework. According to the concrete nature view of the incarnation, Christ's human nature is fundamentally a concrete particular. Loke presumes some species of substance dualism is true for the purposes of his model, such that a given human nature is normally composed of a human body and a human soul rightly related or configured. Add to this the assumption of such a human nature by the Word of God, and the result is a three-part Christology comprising the Word, and the human nature he assumes in the act of incarnation, that is, a human body and human soul rightly configured.

Prior to the incarnation the Word had a divine mind but no body. At the first moment incarnation, says Loke, the divine mind 'came to include a [human] consciousness and a [human] preconscious' (Loke, 69). Following contemporary textbook psychology,[3] Loke maintains that the human *conscious* is that which, 'when it is active, exhibits a mental condition characterised by the experience of perception, thoughts, feelings, awareness of the external world, and, often in humans, self awareness' (Loke, 65). A *preconscious* is defined as 'mental contents that are not currently in consciousness but are accessible to consciousness by directing attention to them' (Loke, 66). For instance, one might have memorized in one's preconscious Pi to three decimal places (i.e. 3.142). Although in one sense it is true to say that I know Pi to three decimal places, this knowledge is not occurrent, but dispositional. One has to access it by directing attention to it, 'retrieving' it from the preconscious, so to speak, in order to make use of it in one's mathematics homework.[4] In the case of Christ, this preconscious has two 'parts': Part A that has certain properties of divinity, which the Word relegates to his preconscious at the first moment of incarnation, and Part B that has the properties of a human preconscious generated with the human nature in the first moment of incarnation.[5]

---

[3]Andrew M. Coleman, *A Dictionary of Psychology* (Oxford: Oxford University Press, 2001).

[4]Loke uses the example of calculus instead of Pi, but the point is the same. See *A Kryptic Model of the Incarnation*, 114.

[5]Summarizing his view, Loke writes 'at the Incarnation the Logos had a consciousness (which included access to the divine preconscious), a preconscious that had two parts (Part A having the properties of divine and Part B having the properties of a human preconscious), and a human body'. *A Kryptic Model of the Incarnation*, 69.

However, matters are complicated by the fact that on Loke's way of thinking the 'human soul'[6] of Christ is the immaterial part of his person distinct but not separate from his divine nature, which includes 'the aspect of his consciousness which had human properties, and the human preconscious' (Loke, 70). This 'human soul' of Jesus has a human and a divine aspect, the former being the 'human soul', that is, his human consciousness and preconsciousness, the latter being the divine nature, including the divine preconsciousness that begins to exist at the first moment of incarnation. This 'one soul' of Christ is, he says, 'truly human and truly divine' (Loke, 71) from the first moment of incarnation onwards.

Yet Christ has two minds. He has a divine mind, which comprises 'the aspect of his consciousness having access to the divine preconscious, and the divine preconscious' (Loke, 75) and a human mind, 'the aspect of his consciousness having human properties, and a human preconscious' (Loke, 75), yet only one consciousness and one self-consciousness 'because the two minds shared [sic] one consciousness which had distinct divine and human aspects' (Loke, 75).

The upshot is this. At the incarnation, the Word assumes a human nature. This involves the acquisition of a concrete particular (a human body and human soul, rightly configured). It also involves significant change to the conscious life of the Word. For from the incarnation onwards he comes to have a human consciousness as an aspect of his (divine) conscious life, as well as a human preconsciousness. In addition to this, he relegates divine powers like omniscience and omnipotence to a divine preconsciousness, to which he has access in addition to his access to the human preconsciousness acquired in the act of incarnation. So Christ retains the one conscious life of the Word, augmented in significant respects with the properties of a human consciousness, and a human preconsciousness. And he partitions his divine consciousness at the first moment of incarnation so that those powers that would potentially interfere with a truly and merely human conscious life are relegated to a *divine* preconsciousness. There is, then, an important sense in which Loke preserves the functional kenoticism of Sanday's DSM (the 'narrow neck through which alone the divine could come to

---

[6]Loke places the term 'human soul' in parentheses, in order to indicate that his way of construing the human soul of Christ is idiosyncratic.

expression' in the human Christ, as Sanday puts it), while offering a different way of understanding the conscious life of Christ. It is also important to note in this connection that although Loke affirms that Christ has a human and divine preconsciousness as aspects of his *subconscious* mental life (where subconscious mental life is just mental content existing outside the conscious), he denies that Christ has a human or divine *unconscious*. Christ cannot have either a human or a divine unconscious because this would jeopardize the retention of divine attributes like omnipotence and omniscience. For the unconscious contains repressed instincts, wishes, ideas and images not accessible to direct examination. Thus, possession of a human or a divine unconscious would mean that Christ did not have direct access in his conscious life to the mental content of his unconscious. In which case, Christ would not be omniscient from the first moment of incarnation onwards, for he would not know or have access to the content of his unconscious from the first moment of incarnation onwards. But the kind of historic orthodox theology with which Loke aligns himself requires that Christ does remain omniscient from the first moment of incarnation onwards. So, he cannot have a human or a divine unconscious (Loke, 66).

Objections

This completes our exposition of Loke's model. In one respect, the DPM is an intriguing variation on earlier psychological models of the incarnation. Nevertheless, it is liable to several kinds of objection. The first of these has to do with the coherence of the model, and specifically, whether it is internally disordered in some respect. In light of these worries, a second sort of objection has to do with whether the DPM is a more adequate model of the incarnation than more traditional two-minds Christologies, as Loke maintains. We shall consider each of these objections in turn.

(a) The Incoherence Objection In the recent literature James Arcadi has argued that Loke's DPM has difficulty in explaining how Christ's conscious life is truly human. He writes:

On Loke's version of the DPM, the one consciousness of Christ is possessed by Christ in virtue of his divine nature, he is not conscious in virtue of his human nature, he is only conscious in virtue of his divine nature. But then given the concrete-nature picture of natures, and a human consciousness being a necessary feature of human nature, Christ did not take on a complete human nature in the incarnation. Christ was conscious, he was divinely conscious, but he was not humanly conscious, and was thus not fully human.[7]

Arcadi concludes that 'If Christ does not have a human conscious, as on Loke's view, then he cannot humanly be aware of himself or anything else, and thus he fails to be like all other humans in an essential respect'.[8] Arcadi's worry seems to be this. The consciousness that Christ has is the consciousness of the Word. At the first moment of incarnation, the Word acquires a human consciousness in addition to a divine consciousness, which comprises the properties necessary and sufficient to exemplify a human consciousness. Since a human consciousness normally goes hand in hand with a human preconsciousness, he also has a human preconsciousness. (Though, note, Christ does not have a human unconscious as previously mentioned. We shall return to this point in a moment.) In addition to augmenting his divine mental life with these properties of human mental life, the Word also brings about a divine preconsciousness in his own mind, so that he is not immediately aware of being omniscient and omnipotent. The 'human soul' or mental aspect of Christ comprises his divine consciousness, the divine preconsciousness brought about by fiat, the acquired human consciousness and the acquired human preconsciousness.

Now, recall that Loke adopts a concrete nature, three-part Christology. If human nature is a concrete particular comprising a human body and human soul rightly configured, then what does Loke mean by claiming that the human consciousness and preconsciousness of Christ are aspects of the divine consciousness assumed at the incarnation? By Arcadi's estimate, this seems tantamount to an abstract view of the human soul of Christ, not a concrete nature view. Or, if not that, it seems to be a case of smuggling

---

[7]James M. Arcadi, 'Kryptic or Cryptic? The Divine Preconscious Model of the Incarnation as a Concrete-Nature Christology', *Neue Zeitschrift für Systematische Theologie und Religionsphilosophie* 58.2 (2016), 229–43; 238.
[8]Ibid., 240.

in an abstract nature view into Loke's account of the mental life of Christ. In which case, Loke's model is in trouble for two reasons. First, because it is not internally consistent; and, second, because it yields an account of Christ's human nature that implies Christ's human nature is significantly unlike other mere human natures like that possessed by you or me, contrary to Heb. 4.15 and the classical Chalcedonian Christology he takes himself to be defending. For if Arcadi is right, it looks like Loke is committed to a three-part concrete nature model of incarnation that includes a 'human soul', the human mental aspects of which are fundamentally properties rather than a concrete particular as would be the case with a normal mere human soul like yours or mine. (Recall, Loke concedes that the conscious life of Christ is the conscious of the Word, not a human consciousness. What is added to the consciousness of the Word at the incarnation are the properties necessary and sufficient for the Word to exemplify human nature in addition to the consciousness of the Word. The Word does not *become a human soul* on Loke's account. Nor does he *take the place of a human soul* as with Apollinarianism. Instead, he acquires the properties necessary and sufficient for exhibiting the requisite mental life in order for his incarnate consciousness to be considered a 'human soul' in addition to remaining the consciousness of the Word.)

Alternatively, it could be that Loke thinks the additional (and presumably concrete) aspects of the human soul of Christ added at the incarnation – that is, the human consciousness and preconsciousness of Christ – comprise a concrete particular, or concrete particular-like thing that somehow becomes united with the divine consciousness from the first moment of incarnation onwards. But then, how does Loke maintain that Christ has unity of consciousness if his conscious life post-incarnation includes the concrete particular of the divine nature and the concrete particular of the human mental life of Christ – where the 'concrete particular' of the human mental life of Christ is a human soul? The worry according to this line of objection is that Loke has not provided an adequate explanation of how on his three-part Christology the human mental life of Christ is distinct from the divine mental life of Christ yet without these two 'parts' of Christ's mental life being different entities. And, as we have already noted, Loke is clear that he wants to avoid two mental lives in Christ because he worries that would imply Nestorianism.

However, if he wants to say that the 'human soul' of Christ comprises two concrete parts, a divine part and an acquired human part (i.e. a human soul), it is not clear how he can avoid Nestorianism. At the very least this way of understanding his position appears to ascribe too many mental lives to Christ – which is the main reason Loke rejected the two-minds Christology in the first place.

Now, Loke could claim that the addition of a concrete human mental life to the concrete divine mental life from the first moment of incarnation onwards does not have this problematic implication. He could claim that the concrete human mental life assumed by the Word is the natural endowment of a human person but not a human person per se. The natural endowment of a human person is not a human person per se because it is not a fundamental substance or *supposit*, for it never exists independently of the Word in order to form an independent substance. But if he takes this route, it is difficult to see what motivates him to reject the two-minds model of the incarnation. In fact, it is difficult to see what separates this way of construing his position from (at least one version of) a two-minds Christology.

Loke has responded to Arcadi. However, it is not clear to me that he has met Arcadi's objection. (Or at least, the refinement of it given here.) In reply to what I am calling the incoherence objection Loke writes, 'On my view, Christ's human consciousness did not come about by adopting a complete human being, rather it came about by the consciousness of the pre-existing Second Person of the Trinity acquiring certain human properties at the Incarnation.'[9] Loke worries that if the concrete human nature of Christ is a complete human nature at the first moment of incarnation, then it looks like adoptionism follows. (This is the view that the Word assumes – that is, 'adopts' – an existing human person, the person of Jesus of Nazareth.) But adoptionism is unorthodox. So, in order to safeguard against this worry while endorsing the Chalcedonian claim that Christ possesses a complete human nature, Loke opts for the idea that at the first moment of incarnation the consciousness of the Word begins to exemplify the properties necessary and sufficient for human consciousness in addition to his divine consciousness.

---

[9]Andrew Ter Ern Loke, 'On the Divine Preconscious Model of the Incarnation and Concrete-Nature Christology: A Reply to James Arcadi', *Neue Zeitschrift für Systematische Theologie und Religionsphilosophie* 59.1 (2017): 26–33; 31.

Later on in his reply to Arcadi, Loke adds, 'On my view, Christ's human soul is distinct but not independent and separate from the Word. It is distinct in being a distinct concrete aspect of the one soul of Christ, and it is not independent and separate because it is a component of the one soul of Christ.'[10] He seems to think that provided Christ has the capacity to experience human states and sensations via his physical organs, he has a human consciousness.[11]

But this does not turn back the incoherence objection raised by Arcadi for the following reasons. First, if the human mental life of Christ (what would normally be thought of as the human soul of Christ) is fundamentally a property of the Word incarnate, not a concrete particular as is the case with other mere human beings like you and me, then Christ's human mental life is significantly different from that of other human beings in a way that seems theologically problematic. Arcadi suggests that one way out for Loke is to reject a three-part concrete nature view of the incarnation in favour of an abstract nature understanding of the incarnation. Then it would make sense to say that the assumption of human nature by the Word involved the acquisition of those properties necessary and sufficient to exemplify a human mental life. Yet even if Loke were to go down this route, he would still have to explain how Christ can be 'like us in every way, sin excepted' (Heb. 4.15) when he lacks a human unconscious, which he seems to think all other mere human beings apart from Christ possess. In this connection he claims that a human unconscious is not a requirement of human psychology. His argument for this conclusion is that it is theoretically possible that future psychological techniques may become so sophisticated that the repression of the unconscious is overcome such that no region of the human mind is beyond human access (Loke, 69). But even if that is right (a matter that I am not competent to judge), it is not clear to me how this is salient. For if Christ comes to reconcile

---

[10]Ibid., 32.

[11]This is how I construe these rather gnomic sentences at the end of his essay: 'On my view, Christ is not only able to constrain his consciousness to only execute those things a human consciousness could do, as Arcadi noted. Rather, its consciousness has human aspect and properties such as the capacity to experience physical pain, to have sensations through physical organs and to have the desires for food, for sleep, etc. Given this, Christ evidently has a human consciousness.' Loke, 'On the Divine Preconscious Model', 33.

the whole human person, and all mere human beings to the present have an unconscious, then it looks like Christ lacks a mental trait all other mere humans to the present possess. And on the basis of the venerable catholic claim that 'that which Christ has not assumed is not healed',[12] one might infer that if Christ does not have a human unconscious, he has not healed the human unconscious.

But, in any case, Loke rejects Arcadi's suggestion that he adopt an abstract nature account of the incarnation. Well then, what about the concrete particular alternative I have offered here? That is, if Loke is serious about his adherence to a three-part, concrete nature account of the incarnation, then why not say that the human mental life of Christ is a concrete particular as is the case in all other mere human beings? In other words, what distinguishes a mere human soul from the 'human soul' of Christ on Loke's view?

Recall that, in response to Arcadi's objection, Loke replies by saying, 'On my view, Christ's human soul is distinct but not independent and separate from the Word. It is distinct in being a distinct concrete aspect of the one soul of Christ, and it is not independent and separate because it is a component of the one soul of Christ.' But that sounds very much like the sort of view I outlined above, according to which the Word assumes a concrete particular, the human soul of Christ; at the moment it is generated making it his own human soul so that it never exists independently of the Word as a fundamental substance, forming a person distinct from the Word. This would appear to be sufficient to block his worry about Nestorianism. But it does have the consequence that Christ has at least two ranges of consciousness – the consciousness of the Word, and the consciousness of his acquired human soul. This is a 'cost' to Loke's model because he explicitly denies that Christ has two ranges of consciousness. But it is one way of construing his model that makes it a consistent three-part concrete nature view. So perhaps the cost is worth bearing.

(b) More Adequate than the Two-Minds Alternative? Earlier I wondered whether Loke's position is really an improvement on the two-minds model that he rejects. I have now given reasons to doubt

---

[12]Gregory of Nazianzus, 'For That Which He Has Not Assumed He Has Not Healed; but That Which Is United to His Godhead Is also Saved', *Letter to Cledonius the Priest Against Apollinarius* in *On God and Christ: The Five Theological Orations and Two Letters to Cledonius*, trans. Frederick Williams and Lionel Wickham (Crestwood: St. Vladimir's Seminary Press, 2002).

that it is *if* he wishes to hold to a consistent three-part concrete nature model of the incarnation. Well, suppose someone enamoured of much of Loke's model thinks this may be an avenue worth pursuing. What, if anything, does Loke's model bring to the table that augments the existing literature on a two-minds account of the incarnation? It seems to me that the answer to this involves a kind of cost-benefit analysis depending on wider theological commitments the particular theologian may have.

For instance, if one holds to a classical theistic picture of the divine nature, then the additions to a three-part concrete nature Christology that Loke brings may be unwelcome. For it requires substantive change to the divine life of the Word from the first moment of incarnation onwards in generating the divine preconscious, and it is incompatible with a doctrine of divine simplicity. So, on this way of thinking the cost of Loke's position probably outweighs its benefits.

However, if one is a theistic personalist[13] as many analytic theologians are, then Loke's way of understanding a three-part concrete nature model of incarnation may have much to offer. On this way of thinking, worries about 'amending' the doctrine of God in order to 'fit' with Loke's understanding of the incarnation are not necessarily problematic. For theistic personalists are quite happy to contemplate substantive change in the Godhead (for God is in time), and are not committed to a traditional doctrine of divine simplicity. So on this way of thinking, Loke's account has at least as many benefits as costs, and may be a functionalist kenoticism that many theistic personalists will find attractive.

Be that as it may, and despite his desire to maintain a theological position that is aligned with the classical Christology of Chalcedon, Loke's DPM is a revisionist understanding of the incarnation in important respects. Revision is not always a bad thing, of course, and I do not label it 'revisionist' in order to consign it to the scrapheap of ideas. Nevertheless, where it is most revisionist it appears to run into conceptual difficulties that can only be met by further revisions to the doctrine of God more broadly: revision upon revision. This too is a route many contemporary theologians are willing to countenance. But it is not a path that I am able to follow.

---

[13]For the distinction between classical theism and theistic personalism, see Brian Davies, *Introduction to the Philosophy of Religion*, Third Edition (Oxford: Oxford University Press, 2004 [1982]), ch. 1.

4

Colin Gunton's Christology

To understand the shape of Colin Gunton's theology, one must grasp the fact that he was a contrarian and a dissenter, in the English ecclesiastical sense of that term. This theological sensibility, I shall argue, shaped his Christology in a fundamental way. It meant that he engaged the tradition with passion and a real desire to understand and appropriate what he found useful there. But it also meant that he felt free to depart from the consensus where he believed it needed to be corrected or amended – and we shall see that he thought it needed to be corrected and amended in important respects. Only when we understand that both of these things are true of Gunton will we understand the puzzling tension in his thought between sympathetic, though eclectic, retrieval on the one hand and doctrinal revision and construction on the other.[1] This

---

[1] Others have suggested similar things about Gunton's theology. For instance, Bruce L. McCormack questions whether Gunton really counts as a Reformed theologian at all, despite his denominational affiliation (he was ordained and served as an associate minister in the United Reformed Church in Great Britain while teaching at King's College, London). It is 'a real question just how "Reformed" Colin's theology was – or was even intended to be', McCormack writes. His 'published criticisms of the Augustinian-Calvinist tradition on the one band, and of Barth on the other, on matters ranging from election and original sin to eschatology are so profound that it is not easy to make a case for the 'Reformed' character of Colin's theology. Instead, Gunton's theology is better characterizcd as a kind of older (pre-Roman) Catholicism.' McCormack, 'The One, the Three and the Many: In Memory of Colin Gunton', *Cultural Encounters* Summer (2005): 13–14. Similarly, John Webster judges that 'Gunton was seriously sceptical about aspects of classical Reformed Christology'. Webster, 'Gunton and Barth', in Lincoln Harvey, ed., *The Theology of Colin Gunton* (London: T&T Clark/Bloomsbury, 2010), 28.

may come as a surprise to some readers of Gunton. However, it is part of my contention about his being a dissenting theologian that Gunton was, in fact, much more revisionist in his theology than is sometimes believed.

Gunton is usually thought of as a theologian of the Trinity, and a contributor to the revivification of trinitarian theology in the last third of the twentieth century.[2] Nevertheless, he did in fact spend quite a bit of time thinking about matters christological, and had a fairly worked-out understanding of the person and work of Christ in the various places in which he developed his views over the course of his long and productive career. His Christology is of a piece with his broader dogmatic concerns about trinitarian theology, though there are important ways in which what he says about Christ also develops themes not present elsewhere in his work.

This chapter provides a critical engagement with four central dogmatic issues in Gunton's Christology. We shall not deal with his soteriology, which warrants a separate treatment.[3] Nor shall we consider his views on method in Christology, though he devoted some attention to these matters earlier in his career. There are two reasons for this latter omission. First, methodological questions raise meta-theological, not dogmatic, issues. That is, they are concerned with philosophical questions about how to go about the task of Christology, not about the substantive theological claims of Christology. In this chapter, I shall be concerned with the dogmatic issues in particular. The philosophical issues that arise are questions raised by the dogmatic issues, not questions about method as such.[4] Second, other recent discussions of Gunton's Christology

---

[2] For a sophisticated and nuanced account of Gunton's theological development by a student and colleague at King's College, London, see Stephen R. Holmes, 'Towards the *Analogia Personae et relationis*: Developments in Gunton's Trinitarian Thinking', in *The Theology of Colin Gunton*, 32–48.

[3] For helpful treatments of this topic, see Justyn Terry, 'Colin Gunton's Doctrine of Atonement: Transcending Rationalism by Metaphor', in *The Theology of Colin Gunton*, 1301–45, and Murray Rae, 'Gunton on Atonement', in Andrew Picard, Murray Rae and Myk Habets, eds, *T&T Clark Companion of Colin Gunton* (London: T&T Clark, 2021), ch. 6.

[4] The same is true of Alan Spence's recent treatment of Gunton's Christology, which is even more narrowly focused than mine. See Spence, Alan Spence, 'The Person as Willing Agent: Classifying Gunton's Christology', in *The Theology of Colin* Gunton, 49–64.

have provided some account of the methodological issues, making another such treatment otiose.[5]

We proceed as follows. The first section of this chapter considers Gunton's understanding of divine and human persons as these notions bear upon the person of Christ, and his understanding of kenosis. The second section deals with Gunton's Spirit Christology. The third section concerns his claim that Christ had a fallen human nature. The fourth section deals with his understanding of Christ's two wills. The chapter ends with a summary and conclusion in which I offer a brief assessment of the dogmatic shape and implications of these central theological structures in Gunton's Christology.

Divine Persons, Human Persons and Kenosis

It might seem strange to begin with Theology Proper in a chapter devoted to Christology. However, Gunton's theological project is driven by his doctrine of God, and what he says about divine persons, which he takes to be a kind of blueprint for understanding human persons. Given that Christ is the paradigmatic divine-human person, this has an important bearing on his Christology, as we shall see. Beginning with his views of divine persons, we will then consider some important aspects of his treatment of human persons before applying our findings to his Christology.

---

[5]See, for example, Uche Anizor, *Trinity and Humanity: An Introduction to the Theology of Colin Gunton* (Milton Keynes: Paternoster, 2016), ch. 5. Gunton's views on method in Christology can be found in his monograph, *Yesterday and Today: A Study of Continuities in Christology* (London: Dartman, Longman, and Todd, 1983). There is clear development in Gunton's work from his earlier understanding of Christology in his study *Yesterday and Today*, to his later work in *Christ and Creation: The Didsbury Lectures* (Grand Rapids: Eerdmans, 1992), and *The Christian Faith: An Introduction to Christian Doctrine* (Oxford: Blackwell, 2002). In between these works is a period of change in Gunton's thought that includes his engagement with the Scottish pastor-theologian, Edward Irving, and the great puritan divine, John Owen. Consequently, there are good reasons to focus on Gunton's mature thought, and especially on the dogmatic content of his Christology, which is what we shall do here. For discussion of Gunton's intellectual development, see Holmes, 'Towards the Analogia Personae et relationis'.

Gunton's views on divine personhood developed over the course of his career as part of a larger Harnackian polemic against the baleful effects of Greek metaphysics upon the development of Christian theology, and the derailing of fully trinitarian theology by Augustine and his epigone with their overemphasis upon divine unity at the expense of triunity. In *Act and Being*, which was one of his final works, he remarks, '[i]t is one of the tragedies – one could almost say crimes – of Christian theological history, that the Old Testament was effectively displaced by Greek philosophy as the theological basis for the doctrine of God.'[6] Here is not the place to discuss the merits or demerits of this larger theological metanarrative in detail. Suffice it to say that Gunton's views about the influence of Greek metaphysics, which he shared with his first *doktorvater*, Robert Jenson, have been subjected to serious challenge. And his views on Augustine are, to say the least, tendentious.[7] Nevertheless, it is important to understand that Gunton's view of the doctrine of God, and the Holy Trinity in particular, were part of a larger revisionist programme in which he saw himself, along with other representatives of the revival of trinitarian theology, as offering an important corrective to Western theology, which (so he thought) owed much to the insights of the theology of the Cappadocians, which preserved the right understanding of divine triunity over and against the Western predilection for a divine monad.

His mature position was a form of social trinitarianism. He maintained that the three divine persons are three distinct centres of will and action that are bound together via the relation of perichoresis or mutual indwelling. This perichoretic relation prevents

---

[6]Gunton, *Act and Being: Toward a Theology of the Divine Attributes* (Grand Rapids: Eerdmans, 2002), 3. For discussion of this point, see Anizor, *Trinity and Humanity*, ch. 2; Holmes, 'Towards the *Analogia Personae et relationis*'; and Christoph Schwöbel, 'The Shape of Colin Gunton's Theology. The Way Towards a Fully Trinitarian Theology', in *The Theology of Colin Gunton*, 182–208.

[7]See Lewis Ayres's forthright review of Gunton's book, *The Promise of Trinitarian Theology* (Edinburgh: T&T Clark, 1991), in *Journal of Theological Studies* 43.2 (1992): 780–2. More sympathetic critical accounts can be found in Bradley G. Green, *Colin Gunton and the Failure of Augustine: The Theology of Colin Gunton in the Light of Augustine* (Cambridge: James Clarke & Co., 2012), and Joshua McNall, *A Free Corrector: Colin Gunton and the Legacy of Augustine* (Minneapolis: Fortress Press, 2015).

the trinitarian persons from becoming distinct deities so as to avoid tritheism.[8] But the distinctions in the Godhead must be understood to be much more than merely subsistent relations, as with traditional Thomism. This is clearly on display in an essay engaging T. F. Torrance's reading of the Cappadocians. There Gunton writes: 'For Basil the persons are not relations; rather, persons are constituted by their relations to one another.' And later in the same passage, 'Without a distinction between persons – as the ones who are each particularly what they are by virtue of their relations (*schesis*) to one another – and the relations between them, the danger is that their particularity will be lost, as has been the case notoriously in the West with its excessive stress on the principle that the acts of God *ad extra* are undivided.'[9]

Gunton's account of human persons takes its theological cues from his views about divine personhood. For, as he writes in *Act and Being*, '[w]hat it is to be a human person in this case is identical with what it is to be a divine person, and therefore the word means the same at the levels of creator and creation.'[10] What is true of divine personhood is mirrored in creaturely persons. Thus, personhood is a univocal concept. Gunton understands this christologically. That is, he claims that it is because Christ is God incarnate that we can truly, if partially, and falteringly, understand things about God as Christ reveals them and as they are communicated to us by his Spirit. Earlier, in *Act and Being*, he writes, 'through him [Christ] and through him alone, the Spirit enables us to speak truly

---

[8]See Gunton, *The One, The Three and the Many: God, Creation and the Culture of Modernity*. The Bampton Lectures 1992 (Cambridge: Cambridge University Press, 1993), where he says that perichoresis 'enables theology to preserve both the one and the many in dynamic interrelations. It implies that the three persons of the Trinity exist only in reciprocal eternal relatedness . . . The three do not merely coinhere, but dynamically constitute one another's being'163–4.

[9]Gunton, 'Eastern and Western Trinities: Being and Person. T. F. Torrance's Doctrine of God', in *Father, Son and Holy Spirit: Toward a Fully Trinitarian Theology* (London: T&T Clark, 2003), 47. In an illuminating essay, Paul Cumin traces how Gunton's understanding of the ontological Trinity changed over time so that he ended up affirming the monarchy of the Father like his erstwhile colleague, the Orthodox theologian John Zizioulas. See Cumin, 'A Taste for Cake: Relation and Otherness with Colin Gunton and the Strong Second Hand of God', in *The Theology of Colin Gunton*, 77–8.

[10]Gunton, *Act and Being*, 147.

of God's eternal being.' And he goes on to say that it is on this particular matter 'that we find some purchase for a Scotist claim about the univocity of language in speaking of both the creator and the creation'.[11]

Because personhood is a univocal concept, and rooted in a particular understanding of the divine persons of the Trinity, it is natural for Gunton to think that personhood is essentially relational as well. Indeed, relationality is, as Paraskevè Tibbs puts it, a 'primary' and 'essential concept' for Gunton's theological anthropology.[12] Thus, Gunton maintains that '[t]o be a creature is to be constituted, to be made what one is, by and in a network of relationships'.[13] This constitutive relationally has both a horizontal and a vertical axis in relation to other creatures, and to God, respectively. Although he acknowledges that notions of personhood are fraught and contested, Gunton is willing to say that 'to be a person is to be distinct from other persons, and yet inextricably bound up with them; to be "other" only in "relation". Just as God is who he is in the extricable fellowship of the Father, Son and Spirit, so for us to be personal is to be what we are in relation to other persons'. And later in the same passage: '[w]e are what we each particularly and uniquely are in large measure by virtue of our particular connections with people, who have made and continue to make us who we are.'[14]

There seem to be (at least) two distinct claims being made here, which Gunton doesn't always clearly distinguish. The first of these is the thought that the relations persons have with others are formative in important respects, a notion that is difficult to contest. The second, and stronger, metaphysical claim is that being persons-in-relation is *constitutive* of who we are. This stronger claim is itself grounded in the idea that personhood is rooted in the Trinity, and then applied or extended to include creatures.[15]

---

[11]Ibid., 73.
[12]Paraskevè Tibbs, 'Created for Action: Colin Gunton's Relational Anthropology', in Lincoln Harvey, ed., *The Theology of Colin Gunton*, 126.
[13]Gunton, *Christ and Creation*, 36.
[14]Gunton, *The Christian Faith*, 43.
[15]'The roots of the notion lie in trinitarian theology.' Gunton, *The Christian Faith*, 43. Gunton's idea that (at least some) relations we have with other people are constitutive of who we are is a controversial notion, though it is characteristic of his

Having sketched out some salient aspects of his understanding of divine and human persons, let us now consider their application to Christology. In keeping with the tradition, Gunton is clear that Christ is a divine person with a human nature, although how he understands that this is unusual in various respects, as we shall see in due course. Nevertheless, this claim does pose a problem, to which Gunton addresses himself in several different contexts. This is the issue of how God may become human without relinquishing some of his divine prerogatives in order to do so. This is the challenge posed by *kenoticism*, the idea that (somehow) God the Son 'empties' himself in order to become human, based on the great Christ hymn of Philippians 2.

In order to understand his position on this matter, let us distinguish between ontological and functional kenoticism.[16] Ontological versions of kenoticism involve God the Son setting aside certain divine prerogatives in order to become human, like a monarch setting aside her royal status were she to abdicate the throne. Functional versions of kenoticism have to do with refraining from the use of certain prerogatives, but not abandoning them altogether. This is like the monarch deciding she will lay aside her power to dissolve parliament for some period due to political upheavals. The important thing to see here is that ontological kenoticism involves a substantial change to the divine person in question, whereas functional kenoticism need not involve a substantial change.

Gunton distances himself from ontological kenoticism, but seems willing to contemplate a weak version of functional kenoticism. Against ontological kenoticism, he writes '[t]he difficulties of such

---

broader trinitarian theology project. It is contentious for a number of reasons. For one thing, it appears to have counterintuitive consequences. Suppose that relations I bear to members of my immediate family are constitutive in the sense Gunton intends. Then it would appear that any world God created where, say, I didn't have a youngest brother would not be worlds that contained *me*. Rather, such a world would contain my *counterpart* – that is, some entity that looks and sounds like me, but who cannot be me on account of the fact that at least one of the constitutive relations he bears to another person (my youngest brother) is significantly different from mine. If that is right, then it seems to be a high price to pay for the kind of relational anthropology Gunton favours.

[16]A distinction I have elaborated elsewhere. See Crisp, *Divinity and Humanity: The Incarnation Reconsidered*. Current Issues in Theology (Cambridge: Cambridge University Press, 2007), ch. 5.

a theory have been much rehearsed. The chief of them only needs to be repeated. If it is not God, one fully God, but a depotentiated divinity that meets us, then the gospel is void, for that holds that in Christ the fullness of the Godhead dwells bodily.'[17] But, if the kenoticism in question is seen as 'the *expression* of the divine being rather than its *depotentiation*',[18] then that is a different matter. The incarnation is kenotic, he thinks, inasmuch as it is an expression of the fact that in Christ God acts in a fully human way.[19]

In this connection he also has something to say about the historic debate concerning the communication of idioms (*communicatio idiomatum*). This has to do with whether the attributes of Christ's humanity are communicated to his deity, and vice versa. Put concretely: Is Christ omniscient in his human nature? Is his human flesh omnipresent in creation in virtue of the hypostatic union? When his human body expires on the cross, does God die too? Gunton thinks that these questions are misplaced. He distances himself from the language of two distinct natures that interact or share qualities, preferring instead to speak of a *communication of actions*. Christ's actions are always the acts of God incarnate. So they are always fully divine and fully human actions.[20] However, language of the communication of actions doesn't really address the underlying issues. For one can still ask Gunton whether Christ is omniscient in his humanity, or whether his humanity is everywhere present. Claiming that Christ's actions are always wholly human and wholly divine does nothing to settle the substantive question, a question which is really about the relation between Christ's divinity and humanity.

But there are more significant questions in the neighbourhood that Gunton's views on divine and human personhood do not really address either. For instance, can a divine person whose relations are constitutive of who he is enter into new relations with creatures without changing in some substantive sense? Can such a divine person become human without changing in some substantive sense? Gunton does have a place for divine immutability in his Theology Proper, construing it in terms of a constancy of character that cannot

[17]Gunton, *Christ and Creation*, 83.
[18]Ibid. Emphasis original.
[19]Ibid., 85–6.
[20]See Gunton, *The Christian Faith*, 95.

be affected by action from without the Godhead.[21] But if that is right, then how can we affirm that (a) God is immutable in his character and being (in the relevant sense), (b) that God's relations are constitutive of his being, and (c) that God is able to enter in to new relations with creation and supremely in the incarnation in becoming human? The traditional Thomist way out of this triad of claims is to affirm that God has no real relation to creation.[22] But, given his relational ontology, that is not an option open to Gunton. On his view, God is really related to his creatures. But somehow, his relation to his creatures does not substantively change him – not even in the incarnation. It is difficult to see how both of these claims can be true, and, sadly, Gunton does not address himself to the question of their compossibility.

Spirit Christology

The Holy Spirit has a prominent place in Gunton's theology in general, and in his Christology in particular in what is often referred to as *Spirit Christology*. This is a rather plastic term, encompassing a variety of different views about the agency of the Holy Spirit in the life and ministry of Christ. For some, like Geoffrey Lampe, it provides a way of explaining how the human Jesus of Nazareth was empowered by the indwelling Holy Spirit so that he might perform his ministry.[23] The result is what is sometimes called a *degree Christology* because the Holy Spirit is said to indwell Christ to a greater degree than other human beings. What sets Christ apart from the mass of humanity is the extent to which he is empowered by the Spirit, not (or not necessarily) the fact that he is God incarnate.

---

[21]Ibid., 93.

[22]Thus, Thomas Aquinas: 'As the creature proceeds from God in diversity of nature, God is outside the order of the whole creation, nor does any relation to the creature arise from His nature; for He does not produce the creature by necessity of His nature, but by His intellect and will . . . Therefore there is no real relation in God to the creature; whereas in creatures there is a real relation to God; because creatures are contained under the divine order, and their very nature entails dependence on God.' *Summa Theologiae* 1. 28. 1. ad 3. (Translation of the Fathers of the English Dominican Province).

[23]See Geoffrey Lampe, *God as Spirit: The Bampton Lectures 1976* (Oxford: Oxford University Press, 1977).

Gunton was critical of the term 'Spirit Christology', which he associated with Lampe's position.[24] He was opposed to liberal theology and its anaemic understanding of the person and work of Christ, and appears to have associated Lampe with this sort of approach.[25] Gunton's understanding of the role of the Spirit in Christology was a substantive one, and was an aspect of his broader commitment to a much more robust pneumatology than he saw at work in some of his interlocutors – particularly, Karl Barth. It is this concern to recover a more prominent and thoroughgoing pneumatology that led Gunton in his christological work to read and appropriate ideas from Edward Irving and the puritan divine, John Owen.[26] But the position at which he arrived on the basis of this study was not a degree of Christology like Lampe. Instead, like Irving and Owen, he favoured a view according to which Christ was indeed God incarnate, but was empowered by the Holy Spirit to carry out his messianic mission.

Gunton is clear that Christ is a divine person incarnate. Appropriating the ancient theological distinction between the anhypostatic human nature of Christ (i.e. the idea that his human nature does not form a person independent of the incarnation) and the enhypostatic human nature of Christ (the idea that Christ's human nature is *personalized*, so to speak, in being assumed by God the Son in the incarnation), he argues that 'Jesus' humanity is the humanity of the eternal Son. Jesus is the eternal Son become incarnate.'[27] In other words, the human nature of Christ is united

---

[24]See Gunton, 'Two Dogmas Revisited: Edward Irving's Christology', *Scottish Journal of Theology* 41.3 (1988): 359–76; 373–4. Reprinted in Gunton, *Theology Through the Theologians: Selected Essays, 1972-1995* (London: T&T Clark/Continuum, 1996), 151–68. I will refer to the version in *Scottish Journal of Theology*..

[25]See Gunton, *Yesterday and Today,* ch. 8.

[26]See the concluding comments of Gunton, 'Two Dogmas Revisited' on this point. A useful comparison can be made in this connection with the work of Alan Spence, *Incarnation and Inspiration: John Owen and the Coherence of Christology* (London: T&T Clark/Continuum, 2007). Spence was one of Gunton's doctoral students at King's College, London, and this was the published version of his doctoral dissertation.

[27]Thus, Gunton: '*Anhypostasia* does not teach . . . the impersonality of Christ's humanity, but the fact that his hypostasis, his person, does not have its basis in the way that ours do in the processes of the finite world alone'. He goes on to say, '*Enhypostasia*, on the other hand, supplements the negative – not the same basis as

to the person of the Son; the Son is the person 'in' Christ, as it were (though Gunton does not use such language). His human nature is not a second person alongside the person of the Son.

To this traditional claim, Gunton adds an emphasis on the full humanity of Christ,[28] and on the agency of the Spirit in the virginal conception, incarnation, baptism and ministry of Christ.[29] The Spirit not only brings about the incarnation by means of the virginal conception of Christ. He also perfects the frail, *fallen* humanity of Christ (about which, more presently). 'Jesus, a man in need of divine support and guidance like all human beings, shares in human flesh in all its weakness and need.'[30] He is capable of sin, says Gunton, but is enabled not to sin by the agency of the Spirit.[31]

For those who are enamoured of this sort of pneumatological Christology, Gunton proves an ally even though his view is rather underdeveloped. Nevertheless, what he does say raises some concerns. As I have pointed out elsewhere[32] Spirit christologies

---

our persons – with a positive: that the person of Christ – his unity historic being – has its basis in the Son and in the new act of the Father in him.' Gunton, *Christ and Creation*, 47, 48. Compare, *The Christian Faith*, 79, where he makes the much-stronger claim that the heart of the Christian faith is that the historical Jesus is identical with the person of the Son of God.

[28]For example: 'unless Jesus is also fully human salvation is . . . not guaranteed.' And, 'For whatever reasons, and there have been a range of them, theology has found it difficult to do full justice to the humanity of Christ.' Gunton, *The Christian Faith*, 87, 98.

[29]See Gunton, *Christ and Creation*, 46–59. Compare *The Christian Faith*, 99, where he writes, 'If we are to understand what is going on first with Jesus and then with the human response to him, the central place of the Spirit cannot be ignored.'

[30]Gunton, *The Christian Faith*, 102. He goes on to say in the same passage that the Spirit renews and makes perfect the fallen humanity of Christ.

[31]Gunton, *The Christian Faith*, 105–6. Rather unhelpfully, Gunton goes on to say that Christ did have sinful impulses if being tempted to worship the devil is a sinful impulse. Nevertheless, he did not have an already-broken relationship with the Father out of which such temptation arose. Yet somehow he as redeemer does not need redemption from this state of affairs (*The Christian Faith*, 108). This form of words is unfortunate. For plainly, if Christ does have sinful impulses, then he is in a state of sin and does require redemption. Given Gunton's unequivocal commitment to the sinlessness of Christ, it may be most charitable to put this down to conceptual infelicity rather than clear theological conviction.

[32]See Oliver D. Crisp, 'John Owen (1616-1683) on Spirit Christology', in *Revisioning Christology: Theology in the Reformed Tradition* (Abingdon: Routledge, 2016 [2011]), 91–110. For criticism of my account, see Myk Habets, 'Spirit Christology:

like that of Gunton, which attempt to stick closely to the biblical tradition while giving more room for the agency of the Third Person of the Trinity, face a dilemma. God the Son takes a back seat in the incarnation because Christ is empowered and enabled to act in his human nature by the Third Person of the Trinity. In which case, the agency of God the Son in his human nature appears to be in jeopardy.[33] Or, both the Son and the Spirit are at work in the human nature of Christ simultaneously. This latter point might not be regarded as a problem. For, so it might be thought, there is nothing in principle objectionable about the claim that God in the persons of the Son and Spirit is at work in the human nature of Christ. For aren't all the works of God in creation trinitarian works? However, this is to mistake the nature of the concern. The worry is that this appears to overdetermine Christ's actions if, for any given act of Christ, the action in question depends on the agency of two divine persons. The doctrine of inseparable operations, according to which all the external works of God are trinitarian works, does not necessarily help Gunton in this regard. For many external works, the incarnation included, are said to be the particular preserve of one divine person, upon whom they terminate. In the case of the incarnation, this is God the Son. Although all three divine persons are involved in the incarnation, it is the particular work of God the Son to become incarnate. Claiming that the Holy Spirit is the agent that sustains the incarnation after God the Son assumes his human nature appears to jeopardize this.

But perhaps the thought is that the Spirit indwells Christ as he indwells the believer, where such indwelling is something distinct from the general agency of the Spirit in sustaining and conserving the creation. Suppose that is right. Even if it is, there are at least two problems with this. First, it suggests a kind of division in the

The Future of Christology?' in Myk Habets, ed., *Third Article Theology: A Pneumatological Dogmatics* (Minneapolis: Fortress Press, 2016), 207–32, and Lucy Peppiatt, 'Life in the Spirit: Christ's and Ours', in Oliver D. Crisp and Fred Sanders, eds, *The Christian Doctrine of Humanity: Explorations in Constructive Dogmatics* (Grand Rapids: Zondervan Academic, 2018), 166–82.
[33]Similarly, John Webster argues that Gunton's position rests 'on a separation of Word and Spirit that which gives little room to the Word's continuing activity in the history of the incarnate one'. Webster, 'Gunton and Barth', 28 .

external works of God that is unsustainable. It is not as if one divine person brings about the incarnation, and another sustains it independently of the first. Rather, *all* God's external works are triune works: the persons are inextricably united so that in acting in creation, all act.[34] Strange as it may seem, to claim that the Spirit indwells Christ in a manner similar to his indwelling of the believer fails to acknowledge the fact that the Spirit is not some entirely distinct agent at work in Christ in addition to the Son, but the Third Person of the one triune God.

A second and related problem with this claim about the indwelling of the Spirit in Christ is that it is difficult to see how the human Christ has more of the Spirit than any other creature if this is understood in quantitative terms. For the Spirit is everywhere present sustaining and conserving creation. That is just an implication of divine omnipresence. Thus, whatever analysis we give with respect to the indwelling of the Spirit in the believer or in the human nature of Christ, it cannot be one that implies some greater *quantity* of presence or some greater *amount* of the Spirit coagulated in a particular place. For the doctrine of omnipresence by definition excludes this option.[35] It seems theologically simpler, and more satisfactory to say that God the Son is incarnate by the fiat of the Father, and with the Spirit's help, though it is God the Son who is the divine person particularly at work, as it were, in and through his human nature. For although the incarnation, like all of God's external works, is a triune action, it terminates upon the person of the Son. (After all, it is the Son who is incarnate, not the Father, and not the Spirit.) This will not convince advocates of Spirit Christology like Gunton. But it does provide some theological reason to push back against this aspect of his Christology.[36]

---

[34]This is the notion that the external works of God are all trinitarian works (*opera trinitatis ad extra indivisa sunt*).

[35]A suggestion: indwelling is an epistemic matter, not an ontological one. That is, it is a matter of perceiving and understanding the agency of the Spirit in the life of the believer rather than in some ontological change in the believer.

[36]Gunton cites John Owen on this with approval in 'Two Dogmas Revisited', 375 n. 20. When one turns to the passage from which Gunton quotes, one is immediately confronted with Owen's formidable and dialectically agile intellect. He anticipates the worries I raise here, and has a ready response, namely that the trinitarian operations

A Fallen Human Nature?

The debate about whether Christ had a fallen human nature continues apace, though the lines of demarcation between the different views are at this point clearly drawn. Gunton was one of those who thought that Christ had a fallen human nature. Here too he was influenced by Edward Irving.[37] Gunton maintained that in becoming incarnate God the Son must assume a fallen human nature in order to identify with those whom he came to save, as a member of the same race, bound together through personal relations. He is clear that it is persons who sin, not natures.[38] Thus, Christ may have a fallen human nature and yet not sin if God the Son is the person 'in' Christ, so to speak (though this is probably not the language Gunton would have approved, since he did not like 'dividing up' Christ in this way). For, as Gunton puts it, 'the matter from which the Spirit builds a body for the Son is that same corrupt matter as that which constitutes the persons of other human beings.'[39] It is his *flesh* that is fallen, not his *person*. But, as is sometime true of other theologians who take this view, he is never entirely clear what he thinks fallenness refers to in his various forays into the topic.[40] For instance, if all he means to suggest is that the matter that composes Christ's human body is the same matter of which every other fallen human being is composed, this is a fairly tame theological claim, and one that defenders of the view that Christ's human nature is 'unfallen' could also make. (Though how matter is 'corrupt' is a little more difficult to understand.) But

---

safeguard rather than undermine Spirit Christology (though he doesn't refer to it as Spirit Christology). See John Owen, *Pneumatalogia* (originally published in 1674), in William Goold, ed., *The Works of John Owen*, vol. 3 (Edinburgh: Banner of Truth, 1966 [1862]), Bk. II. Ch. III., 160–2. There is not the space to pursue this here. But it is indicative of the fact that this is a complex and difficult area of Christology that raises important issues that are hard to nail down.

[37]See especially, Gunton, 'Two Dogmas Revisited'.
[38]See Gunton, *Christ and Creation*, 53 n. 13; *The Christian Faith*, 102.
[39]Gunton, *The Christian Faith*, 102.
[40]Thus, E. Jerome van Kuiken writes, 'Regarding the term "fallen", Gunton is even vaguer, affirming nebulously that Christ "in some way shares our fallen condition"'. (The reference here is to Gunton, *The Christian Faith*, 101.) See van Kuiken, *Christ's Humanity in Current and Ancient Controversy: Fallen or Not?* (London: T&T Clark, 2017), 47.

if there is something more substantive at issue – if, for example, the idea is that the human soul or mind of Christ is somehow tainted with original sin – then matters are more complicated. Unfortunately, it is not clear from what he does say which of these views (if either) he defends.[41]

Gunton does argue that Christ remains sinless through the agency of the Holy Spirit. The Spirit's work in the incarnation recapitulates or mirrors his work in the inner life of the Trinity as the one who enables the Son to be the Son by perfectly realizing the love that exists between Father and Son.[42] I am not entirely sure what this means, for it is not clear to me how any one divine person can *enable* another divine person to be that particular divine person. But perhaps this is no more opaque than the traditional trinitarian claim that the Son is eternally generated by the Father. Similarly, it is not clear to me how the Spirit enables Christ to be Christ unless what is meant is that the Spirit brings about the miracle of incarnation by means of the virginal conception – which Gunton explicitly endorses. But this is not sufficient to motivate the stronger claim about the Spirit enabling Christ to be Christ, or the Son to be the Son, unless this means something like: the Spirit is the means by which the Son becomes incarnate and in that sense 'enables Christ to be Christ' in the work of the virginal conception. But since (to repeat) all the external works of God are trinitarian works, this doesn't really amount to very much more than the idea that the manner by which the incarnation obtains is an external divine work that terminates upon the Holy Spirit in the virginal conception.

---

[41]This is a problem for the right interpretation of Gunton's views. For instance, Uche Anizor, in glossing Gunton's treatment of Edward Irving's Christology in his 'Two Dogma's Revisited' paper, writes that '[i]n his human nature Christ was subject to the effects of the fall. However, in his personhood, Christ was entirely sinless.' That seems true of Irving and Gunton. However, he goes on to say, 'Christ, then, took to himself the sin common to all humanity, creation even, and obtains victory over it by giving himself (and creation in him) fully over to the Father's will.' That may be true of Irving, but it is not clear that it is true of Gunton. See Anizor, *Trinity and Humanity*, 117.

[42]Gunton, *The Christian Faith*, 101–2.

Christ's Two Wills

We come to perhaps the most challenging aspect of Gunton's Christology, namely his account of Christ's two wills. After a brief preamble about classical Christology, which is the background against which Gunton develops his own position, we shall focus on three doctrinal claims Gunton makes about Christ's two wills. These are his apparent monothelitism, his unease about the two-natures doctrine, and whether he conflates divine and human action in the one theandric operation of Christ.

First, some background. Following the teaching of Maximus the Confessor, the Fathers of the Third Council of Constantinople in AD 681 canonized the view that Christ had two wills, one human (according to his human nature) and one divine (according to his divine nature). This is the doctrine of dyothelitism. The alternative, monothelitism, is the claim that Christ had only one will. The presumption was that wills are aspects of a person's *nature*, not the person as a hypostasis or fundamental substance. For, so the Constantinopolitan Fathers thought, without a human will Christ cannot be said to be fully human because wills are aspects of natures not persons. Christ is not a human person, strictly speaking, on pain of Nestorianism (roughly: the idea that there are two persons in Christ). But neither can he be a divine person with a divine will who wills as a divine person via his human nature (which is tantamount to Apollinarianism). He must have a human nature that has a human will as well.

Gunton denies this, affirming what appears to be a version of monothelitism.[43] His reasons for this are complex, and must be pieced together from various things he says across his writings.[44]

---

[43]This is puzzling. For in his 'Two Dogma's Revisited' essay on Edward Irving's Christology written in mid-career, Gunton writes with seeming approval, 'The radical self-involvement of the Son in the person of Christ thus enables Irving to share the rejection of monothelite christology, and to show why such an apparently obscure heresy must be resisted.' Gunton, 'Two Dogmas Revisited', 364. However, as we shall see presently, it may be that Gunton misconstrues dyothelitism in such a way that his position implies monothelitism, though he was not fully cognisant of this.
[44]I am indebted in this section to Alan Spence, 'The Person as Willing Agent: Classifying Gunton's Christology'. A more general account of Gunton's Christology

In *Act and Being*, Gunton makes the point that although a will is something a person is said to possess, 'to . . . hypostasize will as a kind of distinct entity *within* a person . . . has been the cause of insuperable theological difficulties in understanding the relation between the doctrine of the Trinity and christology'.[45] He focuses upon dyothelitism as a particular problem in this regard, using the example of Christ's prayer in Gethsemane (Matt. 26.36-56; Mk. 14.32-42; Lk. 22.39-46). Against the dyothelite position, Gunton argues two things. First, the traditional christological claim that the 'will is an attribute of nature and not of the hypostasis or person leads to saying that natures have wills, with an inevitably Nestorian outcome. A human nature and a divine nature cannot will anything. Only persons have wills, especially if by "will" we mean that which initiates or brings about action directed to an object or end.'[46] Second, he maintains that his own position is supported by Scripture. He writes, 'What we read in the gospel accounts of Gethsemane is an interaction between the will of the incarnate Christ – the eternal Son become man – and the will of the Father.' He goes on, 'Jesus is praying in the Spirit to the Father.'[47] This latter point is rather less clear, because it is consistent with more than one way of construing what is going on in the Gethsemane story. Matters are not helped by the fact that later in the same passage Gunton admits that some of the confusion has been caused by different conceptions of will. For, considered in terms of divine intention, God has one will for his creation, whereas (by implication, at least) considered in terms of an attribute, God has three wills: of the Father, of the Son and of the Spirit.[48]

Gunton approves of the modern psychological view that persons will actions; natures do not. But if that is the case, then it appears that on Gunton's reading of the Gethsemane narratives we have an interaction between the will of person of the eternal Son, and the will of the person of the Father. The reasoning seems to be this: wills belong to persons not natures; Christ is 'the eternal Son

---

is given in Anizor, *Trinity and Humanity*, ch. 5.
[45]Gunton, *Act and Being*, 28–9, emphasis original.
[46]Ibid., 29.
[47]Ibid.
[48]Ibid., 30–1.

become man'; Christ wills as a (divine) person; and Christ prays in the Spirit to the Father, concerning the will of the Father. Thus, we have two divine persons in conversation. Not only that, but Christ has only one will: his divine will, as a divine person. He does not also have a human will other than that of the divine Son of God willing as a human. This amounts to an eccentric understanding of the Gethsemane narratives.

Such a way of understanding Gunton is reinforced by what he says in *The Christian Faith*, another of his last works, and a short summary of Christian doctrine. There he seems to misconstrue dyothelitism in the context of the Gethsemane narratives of the canonical Gospels. 'Clearly, there are two wills involved' in Gethsemane, he avers. And 'one accepts the decision of the other'. But there are not two wills *within* Christ, but only 'two at work in his career, his will and the will of his Father'.[49] But this is clearly not the same as historic dyothelitism because it means Christ has only one will, namely, the will of God the Son. He has no human will in addition to his divine will as the Son.

In addition to this, as Alan Spence has recently pointed out, Gunton was rather uneasy about the Chalcedonian two-natures doctrine.[50] In *The Christian Faith*, he writes that the two-natures doctrine 'has sometimes led to the appearance of a kind of hybrid being, two contrary entities stitched together, like a centaur, suggesting two persons rather than one person in two natures'.[51] What he says next is also perplexing: 'That this teaching has since early times been labelled "Nestorianism" and officially rejected has not prevented some from speaking and writing as if it were true.'[52]

I take it that this is a case of Gunton being less careful than he ought to have been. A caricature of the two-natures doctrine might well lead a person to think that Christ is a hybrid entity. But no serious theologian would make that mistake. Even those with only a passing knowledge of the history know that the two-natures doctrine was developed at least in part in order to combat this sort of worry. Nor does the two-natures doctrine entail Nestorianism.

---

[49]Gunton, *The Christian Faith*, 109–10.
[50]Spence, 'The Person as Willing Agent', 52.
[51]Gunton, *The Christian Faith*, 78–9.
[52]Ibid.

Suppose we think of Nestorianism as the claim that in Christ co-exist two distinct persons, one human and the other divine. Plainly, this is *inconsistent* with the two-natures doctrine, because the two-natures doctrine *denies* there are two persons in Christ. It affirms one divine person subsisting in two natures. So if these were Gunton's reasons for being uneasy about the two-natures doctrine, they are not very good reasons because they are based on a straw man.

Spence provides a trenchant critique of Gunton on this topic in his essay on aspects of Gunton's Christology.[53] But I judge that he goes beyond the evidence when he claims that although Gunton affirms a single operation in Christ – one source of action – he appears to ascribe this one operation to both the human Christ, and to the Father. In support of this claim, Spence cites several key passages from *The Christian Faith*. Gunton writes that in Christ 'there are not . . . two natures in the sense of rival principles. His action is God's action only as the action of one who was fully human, and nothing must be said which might undermine that humanity.'[54] And, 'there are not two wills within Jesus, only two at work in his career, his will and that of the Father . . . The Father's will is fulfilled by the free human willing of the incarnate Son in the power of the Spirit.'[55] But against this must be set other passages (also cited by Spence) that seem to qualify these statements. For instance: 'we have a single personal action – that of Jesus Christ, the Son of God in the flesh – which is at once God's action and that of one who is fully human.'[56] This suggests that Gunton believed that there is one principle of action in Christ that is God the Son acting humanly. The language is unclear and at times unhelpful. But it does not amount to ascribing the one divine operation to two distinct agents.

Nevertheless, Gunton does seem to be confused about the metaphysics of Christ's agency, as well as mistaken about the implications of the classical christological consensus on the metaphysics of the incarnation, and these are not minor issues. At least part of the problem is that Gunton does not seem to think of

---

[53]Spence, 'The Person as Willing Agent'.
[54]Gunton, *The Christian Faith*, 105.
[55]Ibid., 109–10.
[56]Ibid., 95.

will as an attribute in the traditional sense, but as an action. He writes in *Act and Being*, 'underlying all this is the point which must be made: that will is not an attribute but a description of a personal agent engaging in a certain form of action.'[57] However, it is not clear to me how this more actualist-sounding account of Christ's will(s) is supposed to help Gunton avoid the charges of monothelitism and conceptual confusion about the two-natures doctrine. Those who are not independently motivated by a social account of the Trinity will find little in what Gunton says here that is attractive.

Summary and Conclusion

In the last paragraph of *Yesterday and Today*, which was his most sustained engagement with Christology, Gunton writes, 'Christology, like all theology, is a difficult and demanding discipline. In it, some attempt is made to think about the living Jesus of the Church's worship and of the New Testament confession. It cannot be done without the assistance of the past, nor without the great labour of exercising thought and judgement as to where the past was right and where it was wrong. But that is to reaffirm, not to deny, that it is the *same kind of discipline* as that engaged in by Ignatius, Athanasius and Anselm.'[58] This could almost be a summary statement of his approach to theology in general, and to Christology in particular. Gunton's attempt to wrestle honestly with the tradition, in critical engagement with the past in pursuit of a better theology for today represents much that is appealing. But his method did not prevent him from embracing conclusions about the person of Christ that must be troubling to those who are committed to a broadly classical, orthodox Christology.

In this essay I have offered a critical account of the dogmatic shape of Colin Gunton's Christology, according to four central dogmatic themes. For those committed to a social doctrine of the

---

[57]Gunton, *Action and Being*, 30. Gunton says similar things in *The Christian Faith*, 95. Compare Spence, who writes, 'I know understand him [Gunton] to be suggesting that he natures of Christ are to be viewed as actions or operations rather than substantial entities.' Spence, 'The Person as Willing Agent', 53.
[58]Gunton, *Yesterday and Today*, 208–9. Emphasis original.

Trinity, there will be much in Gunton's understanding of the person of Christ with which they can sympathize. And for partisans of moderate kenoticism, Spirit Christology, and the claim that Christ had a fallen human nature, Gunton proves an ally as well. But even for those who are sympathetic to these important aspects of Gunton's Christology what he says about the two-natures doctrine, and about the wills of Christ, are troubling if not (frankly) unorthodox.

Of course, this is just to express a view about Gunton's approach relative to a dogmatic standard, which, in this case, is the standard of classical Christology expressed in the canons of the great ecumenical councils of the undivided church. Taking the tradition seriously is certainly one aspect of Gunton's project. But it is not the only relevant aspect. As he says at the end of *Yesterday and Today*, there are places at which the theology of the past was *wrong* as well as places where it was *right*. Those who wish to emphasize the more critical and constructive aspects of Gunton's project can point to this with approval. According to this way of thinking, there are important ways in which classical Christology needs to be corrected. Gunton's reassessment of the person of Christ and the will(s) of Christ in the context of a fully social trinitarianism and (something like) an incipient actualist ontology is conducive to a revisionist project critically engaged with the great tradition of theology. This will not be to every reader's liking. But, importantly, such a revisionist-constructive way of thinking about Gunton's work is a view that – perhaps surprisingly – makes sense of his Christology. In this respect, and like his theology more generally, his is the work of a contrarian. And this is just what one might expect of an English systematic theologian who self-identified as a dissenter.

PART THREE

Applied Salvation

5

Anglican Hypothetical Universalism

It has long been believed that so-called 'four point' Calvinism is an inferior sort of thing – a kind of Reformed theology lite. The points held in common with the rest of the tradition are, of course, summed up in the acrostic TULIP, which is a modern, not an ancient, summary of the five central dogmatic claims of European Calvinism canonized at the Synod of Dordt.[1] These are Total depravity, Unconditional election, Irresistible grace and the Perseverance of the saints. The four-point Calvinist, we are told, believes all of the traditional five points of Calvinism, bar one: the claim that the atonement is limited to the elect (the 'L' of the TULIP acrostic). According to the 'four-pointer', the atonement is, in some sense, *unlimited* or *universal* in scope. Christ dies for the sins of the whole world, not merely for an elect. This, it is said, is a way of watering down traditional Calvinism to make it more palatable to those for whom the notion of a limited atonement is too much to stomach.

Caricatures come and go. Some have greater staying power than others. Yet even those that persist are still nothing more than cartoons that exaggerate certain features at the expense of others. This is certainly true of the persistent popular claim that four-

---

[1]The earliest record of the TULIP acrostic is from a periodical in 1913. Kenneth J. Stewart, discusses this in *10 Myths About Calvinism: Recovering the Breadth of the Reformed Tradition* (Downers Grove: IVP Academic 2011), ch. 3. See also Richard Muller, *Calvin and the Reformed Tradition: On the Work of Christ and the Order of Salvation* (Grand Rapids: Baker Academic, 2012), ch. 2.

point Calvinism is an inferior brand of Reformed theology. Recent work in the history of Reformed thought has shown that this is far from the truth, and that, in fact, the so-called four-point Calvinism was part of the fabric of Reformed theology from very early in its development.[2] Far from being a watertight theological 'system' that the Magisterial Reformers and their progeny developed and then passed on to succeeding generations, Reformed theology is a variegated and broad stream of Christian theology with different tributaries feeding into it, and different and discernible currents and eddies representing different schools of thought with their own particular doctrinal emphases and distinctive teaching.[3]

---

[2]The classic modern study is Brian G. Armstrong, *Calvinism and the Amyraut Heresy: Protestant Scholasticism and Humanism in Seventeenth Century France* (Madison, WI: University of Wisconsin Press, 1969). For more recent work, see, for example, Raymond Blacketer, 'Definite Atonement in Historical Perspective', in Charles E. Hill and Frank A. James III, eds, *The Glory of The Atonement: Biblical, Theological and Practical Perspectives* (Downers Grove, Il.: IVP Academic, 2004), 304–23; Alan C. Clifford, *Atonement and Justification: English Evangelical Theology 1640-1790. An Evaluation* (Oxford: Oxford University Press, 1990); Lee Gattiss, *For Us and for Our Salvation: 'Limited Atonement' in the Bible, Doctrine, History, and Ministry.* Latimer Studies 78 (London: The Latimer Trust, 2012); W. Robert Godfrey, 'Reformed Thought on the Extent of the Atonement to 1618', *Westminster Theological Journal* 37 (1975): 133–71; Michael A. G. Haykin, and Mark Jones, eds, *Drawn into Controversie: Reformed Theological Diversity and Debates Within Seventeenth-Century British Puritanism. Reformed Historical Theology,* vol. 17 (Göttingen: Vandenhoeck and Ruprecht, 2011); Anthony Milton, ed., *The British Delegation and the Synod of Dort (1618-1619).* Church of England Record Society, vol. 13 (Woodbridge: Boydell Press, 2005); Richard A. Muller, *Calvin and the Reformed Tradition;* Stewart, *10 Myths About Calvinism;* G. Michael Thomas, *The Extent of the Atonement: A Dilemma for Reformed Theology from Calvin to the Consensus (1536-1675).* Studies in Christian History and Thought (Milton Keynes: Paternoster, 1997); Jonathan D. Moore, *English Hypothetical Universalism: John Preston and the Softening of Reformed Theology* (Grand Rapids: Eerdmans, 2007); and F. P. van Stam, *The Controversy over the Theology of Saumur, 1635-1650: Disrupting Debates Among the Hugeonots in Complicated Circumstances* (Amsterdam: APA-Holland University Press, 1988).

[3]I have argued this at length in Crisp, *Deviant Calvinism,* and, more popularly, in Crisp, *Saving Calvinism: Expanding the Reformed Tradition* (Downers Grove, IL: IVP Academic, 2016). Stewart's book, *10 Myths About Calvinism,* is another recent example with a similar theme, as is Muller's *Calvin and The Reformed Tradition.* A recent compendium on Reformed theology that gives a good sense of the breadth of the tradition is Paul T. Nimmo and David A. S. Fergusson, eds, *The Cambridge Companion to Reformed Theology* (Cambridge: Cambridge University Press, 2016).

This includes different views on the nature and the scope of the atonement. That is hardly surprising given that Reformed theology represents a complex theological tradition that is 500 years old, and that reaches back to older ways of doing theology in resourcing itself. Nevertheless, the fact that Reformed theology is broader, and more catholic than is sometimes reported today – including the question of the scope of Christ's reconciling work – is an important claim worth pressing. It seems to me that redressing the balance so as to dispel the notion that 'four point' Calvinism is aberrant is an important contemporary theological task for those who care about the catholicity, as well as the integrity, of the Reformed tradition.

In previous work, I have given some historical-theological account of how what today is often called 'four point' Calvinism had more than one source and was a widespread early form of Reformed theology that was tolerated within the confessional bounds of Reformed thought.[4] This was even true of some of those who signed the canons of the Synod of Dordt, which is usually thought to be the ultimate source of the 'five points' of Calvinism. There are several discernible historic versions of something akin to the modern 'four point' Calvinism in the early period of Reformed theology, including the best-known version of Moise Amyraut (1596–1664), whose name is memorialized in the term *Amyraldism*, as well as the distinct version of moderate Calvinism that arose independently of its French cousin in the British Isles under the leadership of Archbishop Ussher of Armagh, John Preston and Bishop John Davenant, among others.[5] Amyraut's teacher was the Scot, John Cameron. So we might say that the two best-attested versions of moderate Calvinism in early Reformed thought were, in fact, British in origin: the Anglican and the Scots varieties, the

---

[4] See *Deviant Calvinism*. The best work on this topic is Moore, *English Hypothetical Universalism*. Richard A. Muller, *Calvin and the Reformed Tradition*, is also very helpful.

[5] I am aware of the fact that 'four point' Calvinism and 'five point' Calvinism are anachronisms when applied to early Reformed theology. As I have already intimated, they are modern heuristics that do not map onto the historic discussion. However, the fact is that these are the terms often used today in popular discussion of the topic of the scope of atonement in Reformed thought. So I have chosen to lead with these terms to set the scene, before critiquing the use of them in the next section.

latter of which was made famous once transmitted to Amyraut at the Reformed Academy in Saumur, France.[6]

Be that as it may, the task of this chapter is not to provide further historical-theological argument in support of the pedigree or distribution of versions of moderate Calvinism in early Reformed thought, let alone some historic precedent for the anachronistic four-point Calvinism, but rather to give a constructive account of a moderate Reformed doctrine on the scope of atonement for today. To that end, I will divide the chapter into several sections. In the first section, I make some important conceptual distinctions that will furnish the argument that follows. In the second section, I will set out one version of the doctrine that I think is theologically defensible. The third section considers some historic objections to this way of thinking. It also includes a comparison with a modern version of Reformed theology that is a kind of moderate Calvinism, namely Evangelical Calvinism.[7] The conclusion draws the different threads of the argument together.

Some Central Conceptual Distinctions

To begin with, let us put the misnomer 'four point' Calvinism to rest. Although I opened this chapter with the term because it is the way in which many people think of Amyraldism today, it is not a particularly helpful designation. Aside from being anachronistic when applied to historic Reformed theology, it is also question-begging. Naming a particular view 'the authentic doctrine' means that any variant on this will be treated as a deviation from a norm: 'the inauthentic doctrine,' or at least 'the revisionist doctrine' or

---

[6]The historical background is discussed at length in Moore, *English Hypothetical Universalism*. See also Crisp, *Deviant Calvinism*.

[7]Evangelical Calvinism takes its cues from the theology of the twentieth-century Scottish theologian, Thomas F. Torrance. The best single treatment of the scope of his thought can be found in his work, *The Mediation of Christ* (Colorado Springs: Helmers and Howard, 1992 [1984]). The development of Evangelical Calvinism was greatly assisted by the work of Myk Habets and Bobby Grow in their edited volume, *Evangelical Calvinism: Essays Resourcing the Continuing Reformation of the Church* (Eugene: Wipf and Stock, 2012), and its sequel, *Evangelical Calvinism, Vol. 2: Dogmatics and Devotion* (Eugene: Wipf and Stock, 2017).

something of that nature. But what is at issue here is the very idea that there is such a thing as *the* authentic version of Calvinism from which Amyraldism (or some other account of the scope of Christ's saving work other than that of the so-called limited atonement) is a deviation. Opening proceedings by claiming that authentic Calvinism just is five-point Calvinism begs the question at issue.

This in turn depends on a number of dubious popular assumptions about the nature of Reformed thought as well as about its development. For instance, it is often mistakenly thought that Reformed theology has one fountainhead, John Calvin. If Calvin held to a particular view, then, it is said, this is the Reformed view. But this is patently false. Reformed theology has never had a single source, and from the outset there were a plurality of leaders, with Calvin being a second-generation Reformer recruited into the fold by another Reformed pastor, William Farel. Not only that, Reformed theology is historically confessional in nature. That is, in making theological judgements Reformed Christians have always appealed to confessional documents as summaries of their faith, alongside the great catholic symbols of early Christianity. There are a number of such documents from the sixteenth century, and in many Reformed traditions confessions continue to be written into the modern era. These are thought of as subordinate norms, with Scripture as the norming norm. They are fallible and revisable, but nevertheless represent an important kind of theological standard in Reformed theology, and one that has more weight at least in ecclesiastical theology than, say, the teaching of any particular theologian – Calvin included.[8]

---

[8]As is well known, there is a debate about the dogmatic shape of Calvin's position on this matter. Some, like Paul Helm, have claimed that Calvin's position is consistent with the later doctrine of particular redemption, according to which Christ dies to effectually purchase salvation only for the elect. However, others have pointed out that there is material in Calvin's work that seems much more optimistic than this, and that Calvin himself speaks of the universal scope of Christ's saving work. For a summary of Helm's position, see his essay 'Calvin, Indefinite Language, and Definite Atonement', in David Gibson and Jonathan Gibson, eds, *From Heaven He Came and Sought Her: Definite Atonement in Historical, Biblical, Theological, and Pastoral Perspective* (Wheaton: Crossway, 2013), 97–120. For the view that Calvin's doctrine of the atonement is indefinite in scope, see Kevin Dixon Kennedy, *Union with Christ and the Extent of the Atonement in Calvin.* Studies in Biblical Literature (Bern: Peter Lang, 2002). More recently, Matthew S. Harding has argued that Amyraut's account

More fundamentally, language of 'four point' Calvinism fails to carve the issue at the joint. Often in popular reports of the doctrine, the claim is made that four-point Calvinists deny that the atonement is limited to the salvation of the elect. But this is at best a half-truth that obscures the real point at issue. The matter that divides these more moderate Reformed thinkers from their more conservative theological cousins is not whether the reconciling work of Christ is effectual for a particular number of fallen human beings but rather the nature of the mechanism by means of which this is brought about. Naming this helps dispel the conceptual fog surrounding this doctrine, and clarifies why language of four-point Calvinism should be set to one side.

Let me explain why. The question about the nature of the mechanism by means of which Christ's reconciling work is made effectual in the believer has two aspects. The first has to do with the scope of salvation brought about by the atonement. We might put it in the form of a question: *For whom does Christ's work bring about reconciliation?* The second has to do with the nature of salvation brought about by atonement. We could express it like this: *By means of what particular act does Christ bring about reconciliation?* If we want to know how Christ reconciles fallen human beings to Godself, then we are probably concerned with the *nature* of that reconciling work. The question of the *scope* of that saving work is distinct from this concern, however. Put crudely, it is the difference between asking *how* those saved from the fire were saved and asking *how many* were saved from the conflagration. We are concerned with the latter question: How many fallen human beings does Christ's reconciling work save? Those Reformed theologians who favour the 'limited' or 'definite' atonement option reply that Christ dies to save only the elect.[9] That is, the intention of God in

---

of the universal scope of atonement in fact parallels Calvin's in important respects. See Harding, 'Atonement Theory Revisited: Calvin, Beza, and Amyraut on the Extent of the Atonement', *Perichoresis* 11.1 (2013): 49–73.

[9] Many modern defenders of this view dislike the moniker 'limited' atonement, preferring instead 'definite' atonement or 'particular redemption'. The problem with the latter two terms is that they are ambiguous. Saying the atonement is limited in its scope to the salvation of some fraction of fallen humanity less than the total number of fallen humanity does get at what distinguishes this view from other accounts. Saying that the atonement is 'definite' or 'particular', does not. The reason is that

Christ is that his atonement be effectual only for the elect. There is no divine intention to bring about the salvation of those who are passed over by divine grace, and are damned as a consequence. However, this is not the only possible answer to the question of the scope of atonement. Some Reformed theologians appeal instead to a different sort of distinction, one that was introduced into theology by the great medieval theologian and bishop of Paris, Peter Lombard. In his famous work, *The Sentences*, which became the standard medieval textbook of theology in the ancient universities of Europe, the Lombard writes that Christ 'offered himself on the altar of the cross not to the devil, but to the triune God, and he did so for all with regard to the sufficiency of the price, but only for the elect with regard to its efficacy, because he brought about salvation only for the predestined'.[10] For our purposes, the important thing to notice here is the distinction he makes between the *sufficiency* of Christ's work in principle, and its *effectuality*, or actual distribution to the elect. We might put it a little more formally, thus:

SUFFICIENCY-EFFICIENCY DISTINCTION: Christ's reconciling work is sufficient in principle for all humankind, but efficient or effectual only for the salvation of the elect.

Compare the way in which there might be a vaccine developed to tackle a disease affecting a given population. Suppose there is enough of the medication to treat the entire population in principle. And suppose that it is offered to the whole population

---

the atonement could be for a definite or particular number of humanity for any number of fallen human beings. Those who are universalists, like the Reformed theologian Friedrich Schleiermacher, would affirm with enthusiasm the idea that the atonement is definite and particular in its scope, and would be right to do so: universalism entails the salvation of all humanity without exception. Thus, those who take this view of Christ's reconciling work believe it is particular, definite and universal in scope. Similarly, defenders of hypothetical universalism can agree that the atonement is definite and particular in one important respect. For these reasons, I shall retain the term 'limited' atonement in what follows to distinguish this position from alternatives like versions of hypothetical universalism, of which Amyraldism is a species.

[10]Peter Lombard, *The Sentences, Book 3: On the Incarnation of the Word*, trans. Guilo Silano (Toronto: Pontifical Institute of Medieval Studies, 2008), Bk. 3, Distinction 20, ch. 5 [66], p. 86.

by government proclamation. Still, we might think that there is an important difference between offering the medicine to the whole people and the question of whether or not the whole population avail themselves of this offer, and come to receive the medicine they need to recover. It is this point that the Lombard makes here. This distinction is at the heart of moderate Reformed soteriology. In the way in which it is taken up in the Scots-French strain of Amyraldism, it takes on a particular theological shape. As it is refracted through the work of the Anglicans headed up by the likes of Archbishop Ussher of Armagh, John Preston and Bishop John Davenant, it takes on a slightly different shape. But both share in common this way of thinking about salvation as dependent upon the sufficiency-efficiency distinction of Lombard.

Given that Amyraldism names only one species of this broader doctrine that sprang up in several different European centres of early Reformed thought, it would be a misnomer to label the larger whole by the smaller part. Instead, historians of doctrine like Andrew Moore and Richard Muller have adopted the language of *hypothetical universalism* because this characterizes the core theological claim shared in common between the different strands of this moderate Reformed understanding of soteriology. The hypothetical universalist embraces the sufficiency-efficiency distinction borrowed from the Lombard. This is said to be *hypothetically* universalist because it implies that Christ's saving work is in principle sufficient to save all of humanity. So there is one sense in which it is a universal work, in keeping with much of the New Testament witness, which reports that Christ is the saviour of the world (e.g. Jn 3.16). Defenders of the traditional limited or definite atonement doctrine must take the apparently cosmic passages in the New Testament (e.g. Colossians 1) as indicating that God saves examples of people from all nations, not literally that Christ's work saves the whole world, if by this is meant *every single member of the human race*. By contrast, the hypothetical universalist can simply say that Christ really does come to save the whole world, and mean it without caveat. Christ's work is in principle capable of saving every single member of the human race, and is sufficient to that purpose. How it is said to be effectually applied only to the elect is disputed among those who take this more moderate Reformed soteriology.

Consider, for example, our two candidate versions of hypothetical universalism, namely Amyraldism, and the Anglican strain of hypothetical universalism espoused by Ussher, Preston, and Davenant and their confreres – which I shall simply refer to as *Anglican hypothetical universalism* from here on in.[11] For the Amyraldians, there are two conceptual or logical stages in God's will regarding human salvation. The first stage is his conditional (and ineffectual) decree to save all humanity depending on their faith. In this sense, we might say that Christ's work is sufficient on the condition of the appropriate human response to this gracious divine act. However, knowing that fallen human beings will not turn to God in faith, there is a second, consequent and effectual divine decree that ensures that only the elect are given the faith necessary for salvation.

By contrast, the Anglican hypothetical universalists argued more simply on the basis of the Lombardian sufficiency-efficiency distinction to the claim that Christ's work is in principle sufficient to save every single fallen human being, but is effectual only for those to whom the gift of faith is given. On this version of hypothetical universalism, the divine will is not divided into an antecedent ineffectual conditional decree, and a consequent effectual unconditional one. Instead, the view turns on the claim that Christ's in-principle and sufficient work is made effective for those to whom God bequeaths the gift of faith.

All of this raises an immediate question: How do the two different versions of hypothetical universalism outlined here differ in substance from the majority Reformed position of limited or definite atonement? The difference lies in the way in which God's intention in the scope of salvation via atonement is connected to the efficacy of that atonement. To explain this more clearly, let us return to the example of the vaccine. In the case that is analogous to versions of hypothetical universalism, I distinguished between offering the medicine to the whole population with the proviso that there is a sufficient amount of the vaccine for all who desire it, and the question of whether or not every individual will avail themselves of this offer, and come to receive the medicine they need to recover.

---

[11]Moore's account in *English Hypothetical Universalism* gives references to the relevant primary sources. Perhaps the best and most comprehensive of these is John Davenant, *A Dissertation on the Death of Christ* in *An Exposition of the Epistle of St Paul to the Colossians*, 2 vols (London: Hamilton, Adams, and Co., 1832).

But this now needs some finessing given what we have just seen about the reasoning that motivates the Amyraldian and Anglican versions of hypothetical universalism, respectively. The supposition that informs both of these versions of hypothetical universalism is analogous to the idea that every member of the population refuses to avail herself or himself of the vaccine. So the vaccination has to be delivered directly to members of the population by medical personnel in order to vaccinate them. Those who are given the treatment are healed. Those who refuse the treatment perish.

Compare this thought experiment with a vaccine case analogous to the doctrine of limited atonement. In this case, a vaccine is concocted that is so potent that even one drop mixed into the drinking water of the whole populace would be sufficient to vaccinate them all. However, in point of fact, and for reasons undisclosed, only enough vaccine for a particular number of the populace chosen at random is actually formulated. Given that no one will voluntarily come to receive the vaccine, the medication is delivered directly to those who have been allotted a chance to survive, to whom it is administered. The rest of the population perishes.

There are structural similarities between these two vaccine stories, though there are also important differences as well. Both scenarios involve the effectual delivery of the vaccine for a particular number of the populace. However, an important difference is that in the first case there is in fact enough vaccine made available for the whole populace, whereas in the second scenario although one drop of the potent vaccine could in principle save the whole population, in fact only enough is made up and delivered for a fraction of those who live there. This helps us see where the nodal difference between hypothetical universalist and limited atonement doctrines really lies. It has to do with a subtle but important distinction regarding *the intention of God in salvation.*

In the hypothetical universalist case, although there are different stories told about how the will of God in salvation is expressed, they hold in common the idea that there is a sense in which Christ's atonement is actually sufficient for each and every human being. This is not merely a notional sufficiency. It is a real sufficiency. The same is not true of the limited atonement doctrine, which only holds to a notional idea of the sufficiency of Christ's atonement. The difference between a notional sufficiency and a real sufficiency is this. In the case of a notional sufficiency, what is in view is a conceptual distinction. Christ's reconciling work has the potency to save all of humanity because it is an atonement made by the God-man. In much traditional theology, there is an assumption, going back at least to Anselm, that the God-man has an infinite value because a divine person has an infinite value, and Christ is a divine person with a human nature.[12] Thus, any atoning work made by the God-man will be a work that has an infinite value in principle. We might say that it has that infinite value in abstraction, as it were, from the actual work of atonement just because it is the work of a person of infinite worth, whose work generates an infinite merit. In this way, God could have ensured that Christ's work brought about the effectual salvation of each and every fallen human being because any atoning work of the God-man would have a value sufficient to bring about the salvation of each and every fallen human being. But in point of fact, God has not done this. As the Apostle Paul points out in Romans 9, the purpose of God in salvation is for an elect. So, Christ's atonement actually saves only the elect and this is the particular number of fallen humanity for whom, in the purposes of God, it is actually intended. It is not intended for any other persons. Part of the reason for the insistence of those who adopt a doctrine of limited atonement on this point is that they think the purposes of God cannot be impeded or frustrated by creaturely action; they are irrevocable (Rom. 11.29). So whomever God deigns to elect must be elected according to his good purpose. If he deigns to elect a particular number through the atonement of Christ, then that particular number must be reconciled. The worry, from the point of view of the defender of limited atonement, is that hypothetical universalism posits a divine purpose that is frustrated or at least unfulfilled because of foreseen creaturely action. That is why the kind of sufficiency in view in the limited atonement doctrine can only be a notional or conceptual one.

Not so, hypothetical universalism. As we have seen, the kind of sufficiency in view there is a real, not merely notional, sufficiency. A real sufficiency is one that is, in fact, sufficient for the purpose. The hypothetical universalist can agree with the advocate of limited atonement that Christ's work has an in principle sufficiency for

---

[12]See Anselm, *Cur Deus Homo* in *Anselm: Basic Writings*, trans. Thomas Williams (Indianapolis: Hackett, 2009). I have discussed this in 'Salvation and Atonement: On the Value and Necessity of the Work of Christ', in Ivor J. Davidson and Murray A. Rae, eds, *The God of Salvation: Soteriology in Theological Perspective* (Aldershot: Ashgate, 2011), ch. 7.

the salvation of each and every fallen human being. But that is not enough. In addition, the defender of hypothetical universalism wants to say that God's purpose is to provide an atonement the actual value of which is sufficient to save each and every fallen human being. To return to our vaccination analogy, it is the difference between there being sufficient raw materials in the laboratory to make enough vaccine for each and every member of the population, and enough of the vaccine being actually made up from the raw materials sufficient to vaccinate each and every member of the population. The limited atonement doctrine is analogous to the first of these claims; the hypothetical universalist doctrine is analogous to the second. So, according to the hypothetical universalist, God intends to provide an atonement that is actually, really sufficient for the salvation of each and every fallen human being in keeping with those biblical passages that suggest that Christ dies for all of humanity (e.g. 1 Cor. 15.22; 2 Cor. 5.14-15, 19; Col. 1.20; 1 Tim. 4.10; Tit. 2.11; Heb. 2.9; 1 Jn 2.2, 4.14). Nevertheless, no fallen human being will avail herself or himself of the atonement offered independent of divine action in bringing about faith in the heart of the fallen human being so that she or he is able to receive the gift of salvation.

An Argument for Anglican Hypothetical Universalism

With these matters clarified, we may turn to the task of offering a constructive account of the doctrine.[13] We begin with the theological assumption culled from the Lombard:

> SUFFICIENCY-EFFICIENCY DISTINCTION: Christ's reconciling work is sufficient for all humankind, but efficient only for the elect.

In common with other accounts of hypothetical universalism, I shall take this distinction as the point of departure for my constructive

---

[13]In *Deviant Calvinism*, I offered another attempt at stating this doctrine, relying on the work of Bishop John Davenant to do so.

account of the doctrine. With this in mind, we can turn to consider these two claims about sufficiency and efficacy in turn. In the previous section we saw that there are several ways of construing this distinction in the Amyraldian and Anglican accounts of the doctrine. There are other versions of hypothetical universalism besides these, of course. It is just that these are perhaps the two that are best known, and the two that we are concerned with here. I favour the Anglican version. The reason is that (a) it is a simpler, more direct way of reasoning to substantially the same conclusion and (b) it does not require the questionable assumption – disputed by the defenders of limited atonement – that in the purposes of God there is at least one decree that is both conditional and ineffectual, namely the decree to save all humanity who turn to Christ in faith.

Regarding (a): When weighing up different arguments for substantially the same conclusion, or different hypotheses that explain the same evidence and provide substantially the same conclusion on the basis of different conceptual models, it is common to prefer the simpler explanation over the more complex. This is not a hard-and-fast theological rule, perhaps, but in general and other things being equal, where there are two competing explanations of the same data that reach substantially the same conclusion, it is preferable to have a simpler explanation rather than a more complex one – a principle that in theology is associated with Occam's Razor.[14] The Anglican version of hypothetical universalism is, so it seems to me, more elegant and more simple than the Amyraldian. This is not a sufficient condition for preferring one version of the doctrine over the others, but it is not weightless either.

Regarding (b): We have already noted that the second reason for preferring the Anglican view is significant because it seems problematic to think that anything can frustrate the will of God. Indeed, this is common coin in Reformed theology where a strong doctrine of God's absolute sovereignty and meticulous providence over creation means that it is difficult to see how any divine decree can be frustrated or impeded by a creaturely action. This problem does not arise on the Anglican version of the doctrine. On that view, the idea is that God's intention is to provide a means of human

---

[14]Occam's Razor is the principle that one should not multiply entities beyond necessity.

salvation that is, in fact, sufficient to atone for the sin of each and every fallen human individual, though it will only be effectual for those to whom the gift of faith is given. Christ's work is really sufficient, not merely notionally sufficient. But it is only efficacious for the elect. We could put the argument a little more formally in order to make its structure clearer, beginning with a minor revision to the sufficiency-efficiency distinction in order to disambiguate the notion of sufficiency in view here. Let us call this the *Ordained Sufficiency-Efficiency Distinction*:

> ORDAINED SUFFICIENCY-EFFICIENCY DISTINCTION: Christ's reconciling work is *ordained to be really* sufficient for all humankind, but efficient only for the elect.

On the basis of this distinction, the Anglican hypothetical universalist doctrine goes like this:

1. God intends and ordains that Christ's atoning work be really sufficient for the reconciliation of all humanity, by which is meant *actually* sufficient for the salvation of each and every fallen human being. (Call this *the ordained sufficiency of the atonement*.)
2. This ordained actual sufficiency normally requires faith as a condition in order to be made effectual. (*The efficacious condition of faith*.)
3. Faith is the gift of God (Eph. 2.8).
4. God normally provides the gift of faith to those whom he has predestined according to his good purposes (Deut. 29.29; Prov. 16.33; Eph. 1.4-5; Romans 9).
5. Those to whom God provides the efficacious condition of the gift of faith will infallibly be saved by means of the application of the saving benefits of the ordained sufficiency of the atonement.

This completes the argument. But it also raises an important question, having to do with limit cases that are counterexamples to the reasoning of the Anglican version of hypothetical universalism just sketched. These counterexamples comprise those individuals incapable of forming faith, such as those who die in utero, or before the age of reason, or who remain in a permanent vegetative state, or who are severely mentally impaired and incapable of decisions for which they can be held morally responsible. On the face of it, such persons seem to be excluded from salvation according to the Anglican hypothetical universalist argument because they are not fit subjects of the efficacious condition of faith. To put the point slightly differently, these kinds of individuals cannot act in the relevant sort of way that would render them appropriate candidates for praise or blame when it comes to failure to form faith. For they do not appear to be moral agents. On the face of it, this seems to pose a serious problem for the Anglican hypothetical universalist argument just given.

However, note the way in which the argument qualifies the scope of the gift of faith. Ordained actual sufficiency *normally* requires faith as a condition in order to be made effectual. It is *normally* the case that God provides the gift of faith to those whom he has predestined according to his good purposes. This qualification is deliberate. It leaves open the possibility that there are certain individuals, perhaps classes of people, who do not fall under the purview of these conditions because they are not appropriate candidates for the ascription of moral praise or blame.[15] For all we know, God ordains the salvation of such individuals as a class and independent of any condition of faith. That seems perfectly consistent with the logic of the Anglican hypothetical universalist scheme, and with God's gracious benevolence to his creatures.

Objections and Comparisons

This completes the constructive section of the chapter. We are now in a position to consider three of the most important objections to hypothetical universalism, as well as a brief comparison with another modern version of moderate Calvinism in the form of Thomas F. Torrance's soteriology. The objections have to do with how Reformed this doctrine actually is; with the supposed double payment objection it implies; and with whether it is theologically more satisfactory than the 'five-point' Calvinist alternative of

---

[15]I have argued for this in Crisp, *Analyzing Doctrine*, ch. 7.

limited atonement. Having considered these, we will briefly compare the hypothetical universalist view with that of Torrance and his theological heirs, namely the Evangelical Calvinists. This seems pertinent for two reasons. First, Evangelical Calvinism is another species of Reformed theology that posits a universal atonement. It is therefore in some respects a kind of theological cousin to hypothetical universalism, being another (contemporary) species of moderate Calvinism. Second, it is important to see how this more recent brand of Reformed soteriology, though universal in scope, is quite distinct from that of hypothetical universalism.

How 'Reformed' Is This Doctrine?

We begin with what might be the most pressing concern from the point of view of the majority voice in contemporary Reformed theology, though it is, in point of fact, the easiest concern to dispel. This has to do with whether the hypothetical universalist doctrine is truly a species of Reformed soteriology. As I indicated in the first section of the chapter, there should be no doubt about this. The very idea that hypothetical universalism is an aberrant Reformed doctrine depends on a tendentious reading of the history, and an anachronistic account of the shape of Reformed thought. Hypothetical universalism has been present from early in the development of Reformed thought, and has persisted as a minority report into the present. There are other moderate accounts of Reformed soteriology as well, which are distinct from hypothetical universalism, such as that of Thomas Torrance or Karl Barth. There is no good reason to think that moderate accounts of Reformed soteriology are less secure than more conservative accounts. Reformed theology is sufficiently broad that includes more than one way of thinking about this important theological matter. So this objection can be rebutted.

The Double Payment Objection

Next, we consider the double payment objection. This is often thought to be the single most significant conceptual objection to hypothetical universalism. It can be expressed as follows. If Christ dies for all humanity, then he pays for the sin of all humanity by his atonement. Yet some fallen humans die without faith and are damned as a consequence. How can this be? It suggests a kind of double payment for human sin, which is both unjust and immoral. For the sin of the damned is paid for by Christ's atonement and yet is paid a second time over in the suffering of the damned in hell. But we know that God does not act unjustly or immorally (Hab. 1.13; Jas. 1.13; Heb. 6.10). So there must be something amiss with the reasoning of the hypothetical universalist.

This is a well-crafted objection. However, for the objection to have teeth, it needs to be able to make good on the claim that (a) Christ's atonement *effectually* pays for the sin of all fallen humanity and that (b) those who die without faith and are damned also *effectually* pay for their sin in their everlasting punishment in hell. In other words, there must be a kind of symmetry between the efficacy of the payment for sin in Christ's atonement and in the punishment of the damned. Both must generate an actual and effectual payment for sin that is atoning. In the case of Christ, this would be actual and effectual, and completed in his sacrificial work on the cross. In the case of the damned, it would be actual and effectual and ongoing in their everlasting suffering in hell.

In the Anglican version of hypothetical universalism, there is an ordained sufficiency to Christ's work. It really generates a merit sufficient to atone for the sin of each and every fallen human being. But like the vaccine example, the generation of sufficient vaccine and its delivery are two different things. The ordained sufficiency of Christ's work means that Christ's work is truly sufficient for each and every fallen human being, nothing more. There is no question of an *effectual* atonement for all humanity here. It is perfectly possible for Christ to die for all humanity without this being effectual for all humanity just as it is possible to produce enough vaccine to save a whole populace without the vaccine being delivered to each and every member of the populace.

But once this much is clear, the objection begins to dissolve. Without the admission of an effectual atonement for each and every fallen human being the claim that Christ dies for all humanity no longer poses a problem. On the Anglican hypothetical universalist scheme, this just amounts to Christ providing an ordained sufficient atonement. The application of the benefits of this saving work are normally made via the gift of faith, and this is only given to the elect. Thus, the damned (if there be any such) are excluded from the benefits of salvation because they lack the faith by means of which they may appropriate the benefits of Christ's sufficient work. They die in their sin without those benefits. There is no *double* payment involved. There is just the consequence of sin without the interposition of divine grace in the gift of faith by means of which Christ's benefits may be accessed. Like the case of the vaccine, only those to whom the medication is delivered and administered may benefit from it.[16]

But we could reformulate the double payment objection to elide this counterargument. Suppose the objector replies as follows: even if we grant the claim that Christ's work has an ordained sufficiency as per the Anglican hypothetical universalist, this still means that Christ's work is infinitely more meritorious than the work to which it is put. And that seems to be a problem. For it means God massively overdetermines the merit of Christ's work. Indeed, it seems that there is a superabundance of merit that is otiose – never being put to use in atonement. To return to the vaccine analogy, it is like having a massive stockpile of the vaccine that is never deployed, and that remains in a warehouse unused. Such a state of affairs would be an enormous waste of resource. Just so in the case of the atonement, given the argument of the Anglican hypothetical universalist.

But this response can only succeed if the doctrine of limited atonement as most of its defenders understand it is, in fact, false. Here is why. We have already seen that the vast majority of those who defend limited atonement suppose that any atoning work performed by God incarnate will have an infinite value because it is performed by a person of infinite worth, namely the Second Person of the Trinity. Admittedly, on the limited atonement view God ensures that the atonement has a value commensurate to the number of those who are elect. But there is a kind of equivocation at the heart of this version of the limited atonement view. For, on the one hand, most defenders of this understanding of the scope of atonement want to say that any atoning work performed by a divine person will have an infinite value in abstraction, as it were,

---

[16]As I noted previously, for all we know those incapable of exercising the sort of agency consistent with moral praise and blame may be elected as a class and without faith. That seems plausible to me.

from the actual work to which it is put. But on the other hand, they want to claim that in fact the atonement only has the value to which God assigns it, that is, the effectual salvation of a fraction of humanity who are elect. Which is it? If the work of Christ is notionally sufficient for the salvation of all humanity because of the value of the person performing the work, then how is it that the actual work to which it is put has a value less than an infinite value? I suppose the defender of the limited atonement view might claim that God can ordain that an in-principle infinitely valuable thing will, in fact, save only the elect. In a similar manner, it might be that a vaccine potent enough to save a whole populace with one drop could be decanted into vials that are individually sufficient only to save a single individual, to whom they must be effectually administered. But even if that is the case, the defender of limited atonement can hardly use the same language of infinite merit against the hypothetical universalist. For on the limited atonement view it is also the case that Christ's work has an infinite value. It is just that the value in question is only thought to be notionally sufficient for the salvation of all humanity, not an ordained sufficiency. In both cases, though for different reasons, there is a superabundance of merit in the atonement of Christ.

But there is a third way in which the double payment objection could be reformulated. On this iteration, the concern is that Christ's atonement pays for all human sin in ordained sufficiency except for the sin of unbelief. Then, it appears that the hypothetical universalist is committed to the rather implausible theological claim that those who are damned suffer only for the sin of unbelief, not for other sins because other sins have been atoned for by the work of Christ. But, it could be argued, the damned cannot be held responsible for failing to believe the great things of the Gospel because faith is a divine gift. So the hypothetical universalist ends up holding a view according to which the damned suffer only because they lack saving faith, though they cannot be responsible for this lack of faith because faith is a divine gift. It would be like refusing medication to someone who lacks the ability to walk to a pharmacy to pick it up. Such a person can hardly be responsible for not being able to walk to pick up their medicine!

This is a stronger version of the objection. In response to the question of whether it is merely unbelief that damns a person, it is clear that all Christians would agree that such a condition is normally a reason to think a person is outside the bounds of salvation, other things being equal (i.e. excepting limit cases such as those discussed earlier). So that cannot be the problem. Rather, the concern is that it is this alone that damns a person because the rest of her sin has been atoned for in Christ. This the hypothetical universalist need not concede. As we have already seen, the idea of an ordained sufficiency to the atonement is like the idea of a bank of vaccination ready to be mobilized. It has a potency to deal with the disease affecting the populace. But it needs to be applied to them. This is what is meant by the ordained sufficiency of Christ's work. It has a merit sufficient in fact to atone for the sin of each and every human sinner. But it is only made efficacious upon being delivered to those to whom the gift of faith is given. So the real problem boils down to the question of the gift of faith. Now, all Reformed theologians agree that faith is a divine gift. So this is cannot be the point in dispute. Rather, the concern is that the hypothetical universalist is withholding salvation from those who lack the gift of faith, for which they cannot be held responsible. For the gift is not something that they can attain; its bestowal is an act of unmerited grace. But once again, this is a problem common to all Reformed (and more broadly, Augustinian) accounts of salvation. Now, a *tu quoque* response is not a decisive way of addressing the problem, and this is a *tu quoque* response. That said, it is a way of pointing out that those who defend a limited atonement doctrine have exactly the same problem to address since on the limited atonement doctrine only those given the gift of faith are able to receive the benefits of Christ's atonement, and faith is an unmerited divine gift. So this is not a difficulty peculiar to the hypothetical universalist, but a problem common to the sort of Reformed, and, more broadly, Augustinian scheme of salvation.

Is Hypothetical Universalism Theologically Less Satisfactory Than 'Five Point' Calvinism?

The third objection has to do with whether hypothetical universalism is a less satisfactory account of the scope of atonement than the sort of 'five point' Calvinism of the limited redemption doctrine that is more familiar to most people. By 'less satisfactory' in this context, I mean having less explanatory power, or having some explanatory deficit or difficulty not shared by the doctrine of limited atonement. It is often said that hypothetical universalism has a superficial appearance of being more kindly or gentle or 'softer' than the doctrine of limited atonement but that closer analysis demonstrates that appearance in this case is indeed deceptive. For, the objector claims, the hypothetical universalist view only *appears* to be more moderate. It is, in fact, as particular in its account of the salvation of the elect as any doctrine of limited atonement. Thus, there is no real theological gain in endorsing hypothetical universalism apart from the appearance of being more generous or more accommodating than limited atonement. And since this is a false appearance (for both doctrines entail the salvation of the elect alone), this is no more satisfactory than limited atonement. In fact, one might even think that the limited atonement doctrine is *more* satisfactory than hypothetical universalism because it is honest about its entailments, and makes them plain up front. By contrast, the hypothetical universalist appears to be more all-encompassing in its embrace of the sufficiency of a universal atonement. But, in fact, this does not necessarily yield a more optimistic account of the scope of atonement than the limited redemption alternative.

I have already made it clear that both limited atonement doctrines and hypothetical universalist doctrines are, in fact, particularist in their soteriology. Both sorts of view presume that God elects a particular number of fallen humanity and ensures that they are saved. They differ as to how this is brought about. So this much of the objection is on target, but is no threat to the hypothetical universalist because it is merely pointing out structural similarities between these two versions of Reformed soteriology. Similarly, the claim that the defender of hypothetical universalism employs a kind of conceptual sleight of hand in order to appear more moderate than the advocate of limited atonement is specious. The fact is, hypothetical universalism entails a hypothetically universalist claim about the scope of salvation. In the case of the Anglican doctrine I have defended here, potentially each and every fallen human being could be saved through the ordained sufficient atonement of Christ. The point is that no fallen human being will, in fact, be saved by the atonement without the gift of faith. And this is only given to the elect. So there is no underhand attempt to *appear* more moderate than is in fact the case. The sort of Anglican hypothetical universalism I have in mind is, *in fact*, more moderate in its claims about the ordained sufficiency of Christ's atonement than the limited atonement alternative of a notional sufficiency. Finally, there is the claim that hypothetical universalism is less satisfactory than limited atonement. Much here depends on the grounds on which the claim is staked. A debate could be had about the biblical adequacy of each of these views, and there are biblical texts that could be used in support of each. But if the debate is joined on the theological adequacy of each view, it is difficult to see how the Anglican hypothetical universalist view I have outlined is *less* satisfactory than the limited atonement alternative, unless one thinks that there is something axiologically better about a divine intention constrained by a notional sufficiency as opposed to one that is an ordained sufficiency. But I cannot see why one would think that. So, on balance, I think that the defender of limited atonement has not shown that hypothetical universalism is less satisfactory than the limited atonement alternative. And that is all that is needed to rebut this objection.

The Comparison with Torrance and Evangelical Calvinism

Finally, let us compare the logical form of hypothetical universalism to that of another species of moderate Reformed theology that includes the notion of a universal atonement, that is, Torrancean Evangelical Calvinism.

Earlier I mentioned that there is another, more recent strand of Reformed theology that might be thought to be a version of 'four-point' Calvinism, but which is different from the hypothetical universalism of early Reformed theologians in the British Isles and France. This is Evangelical Calvinism, which is a branch of Reformed theology indebted to the work of the twentieth-century Scottish divine, Thomas F. Torrance. (Another brand of moderate Scots Calvinism!) There is much about Evangelical Calvinism that is attractive, and it has generated a number of interesting and original lines of theological inquiry. But for our purposes, what is salient is the view these theologians have on the scope of Christ's saving work. The idea is this. Christ's atonement is not a single event on the cross, but a vicarious act that involves his assumption of human flesh in the incarnation. His whole life and ministry are aspects of this vicarious action, culminating in his death and resurrection. Christ's atonement is more than his identification with us in our fallen state. It is his adoption of our fallen state in order to redeem it from the inside-out, so to speak, as one of us. This, it is claimed, is the burden of the Pauline notion that Christ becomes sin for us (2. Cor. 5.21), and that he came in the likeness of sinful flesh (Rom. 8.3). The idea is not that he is a sinner, strictly speaking, but that he has a fallen human nature, and that by means of assuming that humanity, he heals not just his own individual human nature, but human nature as such – yours and mine included.

This way of thinking is closely related to the theology of Karl Barth, who took a similar view. It is also connected, in Torrance's mind, with the soteriology of some of the early Greek Fathers, especially Irenaeus and Athanasius. One of the consequences of this Torrancean position is the idea that all of humanity are included in the vicarious work of Christ. By his vicarious action he heals human nature as such, not just the human natures belonging to some fraction of the totality of humanity.[17] And by his vicarious action he *effectually* heals human nature as such. The vicarious action of Christ in atonement is not an 'in principle' saving act, but one that actually brings about the healing of all human natures. Torrance even goes as far as to say that Christ is the one justified on behalf of all humanity in his vicarious act, so that all humanity is vicariously justified by means of Christ's saving work.[18]

In many ways this is a very strong doctrine of the universality of Christ's atonement. It might be characterized as a version of 'four-point' Calvinism in that it affirms Christ's saving work is universal not merely in principle or in its sufficiency, as with hypothetical universalism, but in actuality. Christ's vicarious action (somehow)

---

[17]A very helpful account of Torrance's view on this can be found in Christopher Woznicki, 'The One and the Many: The Metaphysics of Human Nature in T. F. Torrance's Doctrine of Atonement', *Journal of Reformed Theology* 12 (2018): 103–26.

[18]Torrance, *The Mediation of Christ*, 86. I discuss this further in Oliver D. Crisp, 'T. F. Torrance on Theosis and Universal Salvation', forthcoming in *Scottish Journal of Theology* (2020). See also Myk Habets, *Theosis in the Theology of Thomas Torrance*. Ashgate New Critical Thinking in Religion, Theology and Biblical Studies Series (Abingdon: Ashgate, 2009).

heals and justifies all of humanity.[19] Nevertheless, Torrance and the
Evangelical Calvinists that have followed his lead are unwilling to
draw the conclusion that this view implies universalism, which is
viewed as a kind of abstraction that does violence to the tensions
present in Scripture. Although he is sympathetic to hopeful
universalism, which is the notion that we may hope to the salvation
of all humanity though we cannot affirm it dogmatically, Torrance
says that the true 'dogmatic procedure at this point' is 'to suspend
judgment . . . for here that is the most rational thing reason can
do. Whether all men will as a matter of fact be saved or not, in the
nature of the case, cannot be known.'[20]

It would be churlish not to take Torrance at his word on this
matter. Still, on the face of it, this does generate a problem with
the internal consistency of his position and that of the Evangelical
Calvinists who have followed his lead. For it appears inconsistent
to claim hold to both of the following:

1. In the purposes of God, Christ's vicarious act of salvation
   effectually redeems and justifies all of humanity; and

2. Possibly, at least one fallen human being is not effectually
   redeemed and justified by Christ's vicarious act of salvation.

However, Christopher Woznicki has recently pointed out that
Torrance emphasizes that the atonement is unanalysable because it
is ineffable. That is, it is literally a mystery that we cannot express
in words.[21] Perhaps that is true. Even if it is, it is difficult to escape
the conclusion that Torrance's position relies on a logical sleight of
hand. It is one thing to say with respect to a particularly thorny and
complex issue, 'we cannot fathom how these things are parts of one
consistent whole'. There are analogues to such concern in things
like the way light behaves like waves under certain observational
condition, and as particles under other conditions. But this is not

---

[19]A very readable recent account of the scope of salvation that draws on the
Evangelical Calvinist sensibility, written by one of the contributors to the *Evangelical
Calvinism* volumes, is Marcus Peter Johnson, *One With Christ: An Evangelical
Theology of Salvation* (Wheaton: Crossway, 2013).
[20]Torrance, 'Universalism or Election?' *Scottish Journal of Theology* 2 (1949): 310–
18; 314.
[21]Woznicki, 'The One and the Many', 125.

the same as affirming *both* 'we know that S is both x and y at one and the same time', *and* 'we cannot know whether S is both x and y at one and the same time'. That does seem inconsistent. Yet it appears to be the conclusion to which Torrance comes in the end.

Whatever we make of Torrance and Evangelical Calvinism, it should be clear that the version of hypothetical universalism I have set out in this chapter does not fall foul of such a worry. It may have other problems, of course. But the hypothetical universalist can consistently claim that there is one sense in which the atonement is universal in its sufficiency, and another sense in which the atonement is particular in its efficacy. Not only that, by elucidating the Evangelical Calvinist view of Torrance (and his followers) we can see that although both it and hypothetical universalism might be thought of as species of moderate Calvinism – in that both deny the claim that the atonement is 'limited' to the elect in an important sense – and although both are recognizably Reformed varieties of soteriology, they offer quite distinct, indeed incommensurate, accounts of how to understand universal scope of atonement.

Conclusion

In this chapter, I have attempted several things. First, to give some context to the complex discussion of Reformed soteriology. Second, to give some account of several strands of Reformed soteriology, particularly the French/Scots and Anglican versions of hypothetical universalism, and the doctrine of limited atonement. I have also given some account of a further modern moderate Reformed soteriology in comparison with hypothetical universalism, namely Torrancean Evangelical Calvinism. Third, I have offered an account of the nodal difference between limited atonement doctrines and hypothetical universalist doctrines of the scope of atonement, which has to do with divine intention in salvation. Fourth, I have provided a constructive version of Anglican hypothetical universalism, and defended it against three sorts of objections: that it is not Reformed; that it cannot overcome the double payment objection; and that it is less satisfactory than limited atonement. The version of the doctrine I have presented here seems to me to be defensible. It is thoroughly Reformed. And it is not, in the final analysis, less satisfactory than its cousin, the doctrine of limited atonement.

6

T. F. Torrance and Universal Salvation

Thomas Forsyth Torrance is without doubt one of the most important theologians of the latter half of the twentieth century. There was a time when he was thought of as principally the transmitter of Karl Barth's dogmatics to the Anglophone world, and as a churchman and ecumenist committed to 'theological science'. But with more work being done on his own dogmatic project in the last few decades, it has become clear that he is also an important and original systematic theologian in his own right. Perhaps his most significant contribution to modern theology, and especially modern Reformed theology, has to do with his account of the nature and scope of salvation in Christ – that is, his understanding of soteriology. There is an increasing amount of work being done on Torrance's theology, and much of that is focused on issues around his soteriology. This chapter is a contribution to that discussion.

The main task of the chapter is to offer an analysis and assessment of five of the main load-bearing structures in his soteriology with a view to assessing how they contribute to his understanding of two overarching themes in his thought, namely theosis and universal salvation. In a similar way, we might analyse the main structures that hold up the roof of a cathedral in order to assess whether they are sound, and, having done so, consider whether the roof itself is properly supported by the buttresses and pillars. What I am suggesting is that we treat Torrance's soteriology in a similar manner. We will look at some of the load-bearing structures, assess them and then step back to look at what it is that they support – to look, that is, at how these different structures together inform the broader themes of theosis and universal salvation. Although I shall be somewhat critical of Torrance's views, I hope it is clear that I consider myself a friendly critic. My own theological formation owes much to the theological sensibility of Torrance's theology, and even when I have departed from some of its central claims, it has often been in conversation with Torrance, or with Torrance in the back of my mind as an interlocutor. Over the course of the last fifteen years, the more I have thought about soteriology, the more I have returned to Torrance's work as a model. His work is steeped in the patristic and Reformation traditions, and has done much (I think) to press the bounds of Reformed theology in a more catholic direction, which I for one applaud.

We shall proceed as follows. First, I shall analyse five of the central structures in Torrance's understanding of soteriology. Having briefly considered some of the main issues in his soteriology, the second section provides a summary dogmatic statement of Torrance's soteriology, followed by a critical assessment of the overarching motifs of theosis and universal salvation as they are informed by the five soteriological themes. Torrance's soteriology clearly implies a doctrine of theosis, as other recent work on his theology has demonstrated.[1] I argue that it also implies universalism, though Torrance was adamantly opposed to universalism.

Five Central Structures in Torrance's Soteriology

Let us begin by considering five of the central dogmatic structures in Torrance's soteriology. These comprise: his account of the vicarious humanity of Christ; the notion of incarnation as atonement; his christological understanding of the divine image; his wholly objective view of the nature of justification; and his atonement mechanism mysterianism. These are not necessarily the only important aspects of his soteriology, but they are central dogmatic structures that are load-bearing. They are also characteristically Torrancean themes.

---

[1]There are a number of different studies relevant here. But the most comprehensive is Habets, *Theosis the in Theology of Thomas Torrance.*

(a) The Vicarious Humanity of Christ

This aspect of Torrance's soteriology has been important in the recent discussion of whether Christ had a fallen human nature.[2] There is a close connection between the question of whether Christ had a fallen human nature and Torrance's understanding of the vicarious humanity of Christ, that is, to the way in which the very act of incarnation is part of the salvific work of atonement in which Christ stands in for fallen humanity and acts on behalf of fallen humanity. Torrance writes that although Christ 'assumed our fallen and corrupt humanity when he became flesh', in this act of assumption 'he sanctified it in himself, and all through his earthly life he overcame our sin through his purity, condemning sin in our flesh by sheer holiness of his life within it. That is why death could not hold him even when he entered into and submitted to it, for there was no sin in him.'[3]

Recently, Jerome van Kuiken has argued that there is an important change in Torrance's theological anthropology that bears on this matter in his soteriology. Whereas in the earlier phase of his thought Torrance believed that sin was a property of persons, in his later thought he came to think that sin is a property of natures. This, as van Kuiken explains, 'allows him to affirm that in assuming fallen human nature, Christ assumed original sin, only to annihilate it upon assumption'.[4] Evidence for this can be found in Torrance's lectures on atonement. There he writes, 'it was not only our actual sins, but it was original sin and original guilt that the Son of God took upon himself in incarnation and atonement in order to heal, convert and sanctify the human mind and reconcile it to God.'[5] Elsewhere, in his lectures on the incarnation, he says, 'there is no doubt at all that by "human nature" the fathers wanted to stress the actuality of Christ's union with us in our true humanity, that

---

[2]Useful discussion on the background to this claim, as well as engagement with Torrance's position, can be found in van Kuiken, *Christ's Humanity*, especially 31–43.
[3]Thomas F. Torrance, *Space, Time, and Resurrection* (Grand Rapids: Eerdmans, 1976), 45.
[4]van Kuiken, *Christ's Humanity*, 38.
[5]Thomas F. Torrance, *Atonement: The Person and Work of Christ*, ed. R. T. Walker (Downer Grove, IL: IVP Academic, 2009), 440.

Christ was human in all points exactly like us, yet without sin.'[6] And in an essay on the doctrine of justification, he writes, 'In this union He both assumed our fallen human nature, taking it from the Virgin Mary, and sanctified it in the very act of assumption, and all through the holy Life He lived in it from the beginning to the end.'[7]

The idea seems to be this. The human nature assumed by the Son in its native state, that is, abstracted from the act of incarnation, as it were, is fallen and sinful, bearing original sin and original guilt. In the very act of assumption, the Son purges his human nature of sin as part of his vicarious action of atonement. This is rather like the way in which alcohol disinfects surfaces upon contact. When wine is poured into a chalice in, let us say, the celebration of the Eucharist, it cleanses the receptacle. Similarly, on this way of thinking, God the Son assumes his human nature at the first moment of incarnation, and, *in that very act of assumption*, purges it of sin. Thus, he is not personally united to a *sinful* human nature. Nevertheless, his human nature may still feel the effects of the fall, such as weakness, physical sickness, hunger and so forth.[8]

What then of the claim that Christ's vicarious action in the incarnation heals human nature as such? This is more difficult to understand. It appears that Torrance was influenced in this matter by the Eastern Fathers for whom human nature was a kind of universal that the Son somehow instantiates as a particular that, unlike my human nature or your human nature, is somehow able to causally affect and change the universal human nature that his particular human nature exemplifies.[9] In commenting on this view in the Eastern Fathers, Benjamin Myers says, 'The view that humanity is essentially one – that there is a universal human nature in which individuals participate – is so widely taken for granted in early

---

[6]Torrance, *Incarnation* (Downers Grove, IL: IVP Academic, 2009), 201.

[7]Torrance, 'Justification: Its Radical Nature and Place in Reformed Doctrine and Life', *Scottish Journal of Theology* 13 (1960): 231.

[8]I have argued that a view structurally similar to this is theologically defensible in Oliver D. Crisp, 'On the Vicarious Humanity of Christ', *International Journal of Systematic Theology* 21.3 (2019): 235–50.

[9]In a moment of scholarly understatement, in commenting on this problem in Torrance's theology, Christopher Woznicki says, 'The idea of a universal that is capable of being acted upon is unheard of in the philosophical literature.' Woznicki, 'The One and the Many', 123, n. 86.

Christianity that it is seldom discussed or defended.'[10] But this is a
difficult metaphysical claim to understand. Recently, Christopher
Woznicki has made a study of this problem in Torrance's theology.[11]
His suggests the best way to understand Torrance's view is as the
claim that Christ's human nature is an abstract universal: 'Christ
instantiates an abstract universal human nature and the rest of
humanity participates in an abstract universal human nature.'[12]
Thus, the difference between my human nature and Christ's
human nature turns on the fact that Christ's human nature is the
instantiation of the universal human nature – that is, a particular
human nature like mine. Yet it is (somehow) also able to causally act
upon, and change, the universal human nature that it exemplifies.
By contrast, my human nature is an instance of the universal human
nature, like Christ's human nature. But unlike Christ, my human
nature cannot causally affect the universal human nature of which
it is an instance. It is for this reason, according to Woznicki, that
Torrance says things like this: 'Since in Jesus Christ the Creator
Word of God has become man, in such a way that in him Divine
Nature and human nature are indivisibly united in his own Person,
the humanity of every man, whether he knows it or not, whether
he believes it or not, is ontologically bound up with the humanity
of Jesus.'[13]

Woznicki discerns two principles in Torrance's thought here. The
first of these is *the generality of Christ's human nature*, according
to which Whatever happens to Christ's human nature happens to
human nature in general. The second is *the particularity of Christ's
human nature*, which is that Christ must be able to act as a person
with an individual human nature.[14] This is linked to Torrance's
use of the an-enhypostasia distinction – a distinction culled from
patristic theology. It has to do with the way in which the human

[10]Benjamin Myers, 'The Patristic Doctrine of Atonement', in Oliver D. Crisp and
Fred Sanders, eds, *Locating Atonement: Explorations in Constructive Dogmatics*
(Grand Rapids: Zondervan Academic, 2015), 82.
[11]Woznicki, 'The One and the Many', 103–26.
[12]Ibid., 105.
[13]Torrance, T. F. Torrance, 'The Goodness and Dignity of Man in the Christian
Tradition', *Modern Theology* 4 (1988): 317, cited in Woznicki, 'The One and the
Many', 111.
[14]Woznicki, 'The One and the Many', 112.

nature of Christ is not a person independent of the incarnation, but is 'personalised', as it were, by being united to God the Son. Yet Torrance gives this distinction a particular metaphysical twist, investing it with rather more meaning than it sometimes has in traditional discussion of the topic. He writes,

> the anhypostasia and enyhypostasia taken together tell us that the incarnation was the union of the Word of God with mankind in solidarity with all men and women; yet it was union with one man or rather such a union with all humanity that was achieved and wrought out in and through this one man, Jesus of Bethlehem and Nazareth for all men and women.[15]

Somehow the assumption of human nature draws all human natures into a kind of union with his particular human nature so that what happens to his particular human nature has ontological effects that distribute to all other human natures via changes to the universal human nature of which they are instances, irrespective of whether the person in question is aware of these effects.

How are we to understand this? The controversial claim on which this whole picture hangs, and which Woznicki has helpfully clarified for us, is that Christ's human nature is both the instantiation of the universal human nature, and also somehow capable of causally affecting and changing the universal human nature of which it is an instance. That is very strange indeed, and a notion I struggle to comprehend. For it is one thing to say that a particular entity instantiates a universal, like the blue shirt instantiates the colour blue. It is quite another to say that the particular entity in question is capable of causally affecting and changing the universal it instantiates. For, as Woznicki points out, universals are usually thought to be part of the platonic horde, that is, forms that are causally inert and that are essentially unchanging. Yet, as he observes, strange though Torrance's idiosyncratic understanding

---

[15]Torrance, *Incarnation*, 230. Torrance says similar things about the an-enhypostasia distinction elsewhere. See, for example, his essay 'The Atonement. The Singularity of Christ and the Finality of the Cross: The Atonement and the Moral Order', in Nigel M. de S. Cameron, ed., *Universalism and the Doctrine of Hell* (Carlisle: Paternoster, and Grand Rapids: Baker, 1992), 225–56; 230.

of the generality and particularity of Christ's human nature claim might be, 'such a universal is needed if we are to make sense of Torrance's doctrine of atonement'.[16]

Not only is this a tall metaphysical order, it also has peculiar theological consequences. For it means that Christ's human nature is significantly unlike every other human nature – surely a result that Torrance would find objectionable. One of the most important things motivating Torrance's account of the vicarious humanity of Christ is his concern to ensure Christ's humanity is like ours in every respect, sin excepted (Heb. 4.15). Christ's vicarious act on our behalf is all about Christ taking on a particular human nature that is qualitatively similar to our own, sharing the same limitations. But if Woznicki is right, then the most plausible way of understanding the metaphysics underpinning Torrance's claims about the vicarious humanity of Christ require him to posit a human nature that is unique in very significant respects. That is surely a significant theological cost. It is ironic that the very notion of vicarious humanity Torrance utilizes in order to reinforce the solidarity of Christ with us in the assumption of human flesh ends up creating a significant ontological gulf between Christ's humanity and ours.

(b) Incarnation and Atonement

Some theologians, like Anselm of Canterbury, think that the atonement should be identified with the satisfaction of Christ on the cross. The incarnation is a necessary prerequisite to this act, but it is not in itself atoning or part of the act of atonement. Torrance appeals to an older way of thinking, especially that of patristic theologians like Athanasius and Irenaeus, for whom the incarnation is something like a phase or an aspect of Christ's atoning work. This is not the same as the physical doctrine of atonement. According to the physical doctrine of atonement, in virtue of becoming incarnate Christ atones for fallen humanity. Torrance argues, in effect, that this is a condition of atonement, but not a sufficient condition.[17] It must

---

[16]Woznicki, 'The One and the Many', 123, n. 86.
[17]This point is brought out well by Paul D. Molnar. See *Thomas F. Torrance: Theologian of the Trinity* (Aldershot: Ashgate, 2009), 142.

be by means of his vicarious action in healing human nature from the inside-out, so to speak, that we come to salvation. But Torrance also has an important place for the work of Christ on the cross and in resurrection. These are not incidental to the atonement, but express divine love to humanity as God works from both the Godward and human side in the sacrifice of Christ to atone for human fallenness. In this way, atonement is, as he puts it, an *internal* divine act, not an act *external* act directed from God to humanity independent of the incarnation. In other words, God brings about atonement through the incarnation. But he needs to become incarnate in order to heal human nature, and then to offer up a perfect sacrifice as a human being to God on behalf of humanity, while also acting as a divine person in doing so. In this way, it is God the Son as both God and human in the incarnation who brings about atonement on behalf of humanity. The whole act of atonement happens within the divine life, so to speak.

Some interpreters of Torrance seem to suggest something stronger than this, namely that the incarnation is where the atonement takes place.[18] But that seems to be at best a kind of half-truth. Torrance is sometimes rather effusive and unguarded in his language about the way in which the incarnation is (an aspect of) atonement, and sometimes does say things that seem to indicate something approaching a physical doctrine of atonement. But a charitable, and perhaps more expansive, reading of his work suggests the more rounded account given here.

(c) The Christological Image

Related to the questions of Christ's vicarious humanity, and Torrance's incarnation-focused doctrine of atonement is his understanding of the divine image. The way in which Torrance thinks of this matter, as with the previous soteriological themes we have considered, is dependent in important respects upon his appropriation of aspects of patristic theology, refracted through a

---

[18]This is how James J. Cassidy interprets Elmer Colyer's treatment of Torrance. See Cassidy, 'T. F. Torrance's Realistic Soteriology Objectivism and the Elimination of Dualisms: Union with Christ in Current Perspective', *Mid-America Journal of Theology* 19 (2008): 165–94; 167.

Reformation lens. Torrance thinks that we are made in the divine image, which is marred through the fall. Christ comes to restore the divine image to its properly functioning state in human beings by his vicarious action. As he puts it, 'God sent his only begotten Son into the world, that through him mankind might be restored to divine sonship, that is restored to the image of God. In the language of Paul, man was predestined to be conformed to the image of his Son.' Christ does this, he says, 'in order that he might restore mankind to the image of God'. He does this by being 'the perfect image of God on earth. . . . He was the perfect man and as such the perfect reflection of the glory and grace of God. Therefore in him our humanity is restored to its perfection in communion with God.'[19]

Elsewhere, Torrance writes about the way in which Christ is now the only true human–divine image because the fall all but obliterates the image in mere humans. Although fallen humans retain a capacity for union with the divine image, this must now be supplied by Christ.[20] He is the renewed divine image into whose likeness the redeemed will grow. Thus, the renewal of the divine image in fallen human beings through the agency of Christ as the true image is something that, as Torrance puts it, 'can be interpreted only in eschatological terms'.[21]

This is interesting, not least because Torrance seems to stop short of the patristic claim that Christ is the prototypical image of God in whose image we are created, and to whose image we are being conformed in the process of sanctification. Instead, what he says is that Christ perfects the image that is damaged in fallen humanity

---

[19]Torrance, *Incarnation*, 115–16.
[20]See the discussion of this in Habets, *Theosis in the Theology of Thomas Torrance*, 32–3. In *Theology in Reconstruction* (Grand Rapids: Eerdmans, 1996), Torrance sounds very Calvinian when he writes, 'Fallen man is utterly corrupt inasmuch as he is mastered by the contradiction of sin, which, just because it opposes the grace of God, means the obliteration of the *imago dei* in man . . . fallen man is utterly destitute of the *justitia originalis* or *imago dei*' (108, 109). Habets struggles with the tension in Torrance's thought here. Do fallen human beings possess the divine image or not? His solution is that Torrance's approach is perspectival: from a certain point of view the image in fallen human beings is effaced; but looking forward eschatologically to the image we have in Christ, we do possess the image.
[21]Torrance, *Theology in Reconstruction*, 108.

by being the perfect image. Christ's vicarious action restores the image to its fullness so that we may commune with God as our aboriginal parents did. But of course, being the perfect instance of a thing does not mean being the prototype in whose image all other instances of the thing in question are made. (To see the difference, just think of the difference between the perfect instance of a model T Ford automobile and the prototype model T Ford in whose 'image' all production line model T Ford cars are made.) It seems to me that Torrance could have said more on this score – more that would have made his account of the divine image more fully christological. Such a more developed account would also have the benefit of making clearer how it is that we may participate in the divine life. For if Christ is the hub between divinity and humanity, then it makes sense to think that his vicarious work in incarnation and atonement involves conforming us to his theandric image. Such a more completely christological account would also help explain how it is that Christ, as the hub between divinity and humanity, is the means by which we fallen human beings may be 'divinised'. For by being united to Christ in his divinized humanity, we too may be divinized. Although this falls short of being hypostatically united to a divine person, it could be that through the agency of the Holy Spirit we are joined to Christ and, via his theandric person, enabled to participate in God's life.[22]

(d) A Wholly Objective, Extrinsic and Effectual View of Justification

Torrance thinks that Christ's saving work objectively justifies all humanity. This is because he thinks that it is Christ who is justified by God, and it is Christ who, in his incarnation and atonement, redeems human nature. On Torrance's way of thinking, by assuming and healing fallen human nature, Christ heals human nature per se. That is, he heals the universal human nature of which his particular human nature is an instance. Not only that: because he heals and reconciles human nature in himself – in his own hypostatic union

---

[22]I have argued for this claim more fully in Crisp, *The Word Enfleshed: Exploring the Person and Work of Christ* (Grand Rapids: Baker Academic, 2016), ch. 4.

with fallen humanity – Christ is justified before God. But how? Because the atoning act of Christ (somehow) heals both his own particular human nature and human nature per se, the act of atonement that brings about the justification of Christ is also an act of justification that distributes to all of humanity. It would be like finding a water source that is brackish and undrinkable and adding some cleansing agent that clears the water and makes it potable again, so that as it flows downstream, it becomes a source of living water once more. Christ's vicarious action affects the 'water source'; of the universal human nature, which is then distributed 'downstream' to the rest of humanity.

Since this is a controversial claim that jars with much traditional interpretation of Reformed theology on the doctrine of justification, and has led to various different interpretations of what Torrance actually thinks about this topic,[23] it is worth letting Torrance speak for himself on the matter. In an important essay on justification in the *Scottish Journal of Theology*, he says things like this: 'justification means not simply the non-imputation of our sins through the pardon of Christ, but positive sharing in His divine-human righteousness.'[24] This happens through union with Christ. What is more, 'Once and for all we have been sanctified and consecrated in Christ's vicarious work . . . Christ has already consecrated or sanctified Himself for our sakes, so that we are already consecrated or sanctified in Him – therefore sanctification or consecration is imputed to us by His free Grace just like justification.'[25] Christ is the 'embodiment of our act of faith and trust and obedience toward God'.[26] He stood in our place, offering 'to God a perfect obedience and trust, a perfect faith and response which we are unable to offer, and he appropriated all God's blessings which we are unable to appropriate'.[27] We share in Christ's justification, says Torrance, because through union with him we are incorporated into his faithful act of contrition and penitence on our behalf. Thus, he can say, 'Justification has been

---

[23]This is documented in Cassidy's article, 'T. F. Torrance's Realistic Soteriology Objectivism'.
[24]Torrance, 'Justification', 231.
[25]Ibid., 233–4.
[26]Ibid., 235–6.
[27]Ibid., 236.

fulfilled subjectively as well as objectively in Jesus Christ, but that objective and subject justification is objective to us'.[28] His is a doctrine of justification by Christ alone.[29]

Put in the language of dogmatic theology, it is a *wholly objective, extrinsic and effectual doctrine of justification*. It is wholly objective because it is wholly on the basis of Christ's justification that all of humanity is justified. So there is no subjective component. Union with Christ by the secret working of the Holy Spirit simply provides me with access to the objective act done on my behalf. For this reason, it is also extrinsic. That is, it is performed outside of me, and for me, by Christ. But it is also effectual. The justification of Christ, and consequent justification of all humanity is not merely potentially effective. It is not just that because of Christ's justification I may appropriate the benefits of Christ's justification by faith. Rather, Christ's act of justification through the incarnation immediately and effectually justifies all humanity. Thus, according to Torrance, 'Because in Jesus Christ human nature is perfectly and indivisibly united to God the Creator, he constituted in his humanity the ontological source and ground of being of every man and woman, whether they know him or not, but to those who receive and believe in him he is the One in whom and through whom they may be born anew as sons and daughters of the heavenly Father.'[30] One important – indeed, momentous – consequence of this view is that all human beings have already been made new creatures in Christ. Torrance writes, 'He died for all men, the good and the bad, and all alike come under the total judgment of His Death and Resurrection; all alike have to be born again in Him, and made new creatures.'[31] As Woznicki summarizes it, the 'regeneration of human nature is not a subjective act; rather, it has occurred objectively in Christ at the moment of incarnation.'[32]

Even faith is vicarious, on Torrance's way of thinking. 'He has believed for you, fulfilled your human response to God, even

---

[28]Ibid.

[29]Ibid., 237. This is Torrance's phrase.

[30]Torrance, *The Mediation of Christ* (Colorado Springs: Helmers & Howard, 1992 [1983]), 72.

[31]Ibid., 239.

[32]Woznicki, 'The One and the Many', 109.

made your personal decision for you', says Torrance, 'so that he acknowledges you before God as one who as already responded to God in him, who has already believed in God through him, and whose personal decision is already implicated in Christ's self-offering to the Father, in all of which he has been fully and completely accepted by the Father, so that in Jesus Christ you are already accepted by him.'[33]

Torrance writes this in a moving passage in his little book, *The Mediation of Christ*, focused on the need for evangelical, heartfelt penitence on the part of the believer. But it is odd that he does so. For the implication of his view is surely that human faith as a response to Christ's vicarious action on our behalf, including justification and faith, means that Christ has already responded to God on behalf of all humanity. As James Cassidy points out in commenting on this passage in *The Mediation of Christ*, although Torrance wants to stress that personal faith is still important, 'it is in no way essential to being united to Christ. Furthermore, it is not necessary to salvation. Salvation is accomplished by Christ for us *in his faith*, not ours.'[34]

To better understand what Torrance means here, imagine a situation in which a group of laptop computers are linked via radio signals to a wireless internet hub.[35] Their connection to the World Wide Web is solely via the hub. All these computers have a qualitatively identical fault in their operating systems that can only be corrected by receiving an update from the internet via the hub. Now, imagine that the connection that hardwires the hub to the internet is faulty. However, an engineer is called and he corrects the fault, hooking up the hub to a high-speed fibre-optic cable connection. Once this is achieved, the hub works perfectly, and the computers that are virtually linked to the internet via the radio signals sent and received from the hub have their operating systems automatically updated and fixed. This is akin

---

[33]Torrance, *The Mediation of Christ*, 94.
[34]Cassidy, 'T. F. Torrance's Realistic Soteriological Objectivism', 182–3. Emphasis original. He goes on to say, 'Christ unites us to God in the incarnation and he unites us to himself through pouring out the Holy Spirit upon the church at Pentecost. There is then no need to speak about a work of the Holy Spirit regenerating the hearts of people today in the subjective life of the believer' (184).
[35]This is an analogy I have used for similar purposes in Crisp, *The Word Enfleshed*.

to Torrance's understanding of the way in which the vicarious humanity of Christ is not only particular, that is, having to do with the assumption of a particular human nature (like the hub), but also general, that is, having to do with the transformation of all human natures as a consequence of what happens to the particular human nature of Christ (via the hardwired link to the internet).[36] Notice that according to the laptop story, the operating systems are *automatically* updated and corrected; the same is true according to Torrance's doctrine of justification. The change brought about through the incarnation immediately and effectually distributes to all humanity. That is important. It is for this reason that critics like Cassidy worry that Torrance's account of justification makes human faith entirely redundant.

Nevertheless, despite his views about the way in which Christ is justified and all of humanity is justified by means of Christ's justification, Torrance rejects universalism. He argues that universalism, like the doctrine of limited atonement, is a kind of blasphemy that attempts to reduce Christ's saving work to a formula that, once understood, infallibly generates certain results. It is, as he puts it, the 'recourse to a logic-causal explanation of why the atoning death of the Lord Jesus Christ avails or does not avail for all people'.[37] For anyone who comprehends Torrance's doctrine of justification, such an emphatic rejection of universalism must appear baffling. For, on the face of it, universalism seems to be implied by the claim that Christ is justified and through his justification all humanity is justified, objectively, extrinsically and effectually. When set alongside his views about election, this becomes an even more pressing concern. Thus, Torrance says:

> The great fact of the Gospel then is this: that God has actually chosen us in Jesus Christ in spite of our sin, and that in the death

---

[36]Torrance elaborates on this later in the same passage of his *Incarnation* lectures: 'The doctrine of enhypostasia insists here that within that anhypostatic solidarity of Christ with our common human nature, he came also as an individual human being in our humanity, seeking in addition a solidarity in terms of the interaction of persons within our human social life, in personal relations of love, commitment, responsibility, decision, etc.' (p. 213).
[37]Torrance, 'The Atonement. The Singularity of Christ and the Finality of the Cross: The Atonement and the Moral Order', 248.

of Christ that election has become a *fait accompli*. It means too that God has chosen all men, in as much as Christ died for all men, and because that is once and for all no one can ever elude the election of His love. In as much as no one exists except by the Word of God by whom all things were made and in whom all things consist, and in as much as this is the Word that has once and for all enacted the eternal election of grace to embrace all men, the existence of every man whether he will or not is bound up inextricably with that election – with the Cross of Jesus Christ.[38]

In light of such passages, Kevin Vanhoozer has recently asked, 'Are the elect "in Christ" simply by virtue of being human (ontology) or because they have somehow become beneficiaries of his life and work (soteriology)?'[39] It would seem that, for Torrance, the former, rather than the latter, is the case. Not only that, but given his views about justification, it would seem that the 'elect' number of human beings is the total number of human beings.

Before leaving this theme, it might be worth briefly considering one option that might at first glance be thought to offer a possible way for the Torrancean to avoid universalism. In traditional doctrines of hypothetical universalism, a distinction is made between the sufficiency of the atonement and its effectuality. Christ's reconciling work is said to be sufficient for the salvation of all humanity because of its infinite value, but it is only effectual to those who appropriate the benefits of Christ's work by faith. Hence, *hypothetical* universalism. Could Torrance's position be structurally similar to this, implying only a *potential* or *hypothetical*, but not *actual*, universalism? Unfortunately, no. Torrance's position cannot appeal to a similar distinction between the sufficiency and efficacy of Christ's work because his doctrine of justification entails that all humanity is justified objectively, extrinsically and effectually. If that is the case, then it is difficult to see how anyone is excluded from the ambit of

---

[38] Torrance, 'Universalism or Election?', 310–18; 315.

[39] Kevin J. Vanhoozer, 'The Origin of Paul's Soteriology: Election, Incarnation, and Union with Christ in Ephesians 1:4 (with Special Reference to Evangelical Calvinism)', in Benjamin E. Reynolds, Brian Lugioyo, and Kevin J. Vanhoozer, eds, *Reconsidering the Relationship between Biblical and Systematic Theology in the New Testament: Essays by Theologians and New Testament Scholars* (Tübingen: Mohr Siebeck, 2014), 182.

salvation – universalism is the inevitable outcome.[40] This seems to be a serious problem of consistency in Torrance's thought that neither he nor his defenders have been able to effectively address.[41]

(e) Atonement Mysterianism

In the matter of the mechanism of atonement, Torrance is what in philosophical circles would be called a *mysterian*. By mechanism of atonement, I mean the specific kind of action by means of which Christ brings about human reconciliation with God. Torrance does not have a clear view on this matter. By mysterianism, I mean the view that we are not in the kind of epistemically advantageous position needed in order to have a settled view on a particular matter. Thus, it remains mysterious. 'The saving act of God in the blood of Christ,' he writes, 'is an unfathomable mystery before which the angels veil their faces and into which we dare not and cannot intrude, but before which our minds bow in wonder, worship, and praise.'[42]

Consider the case of a medieval physician to whom Harvey's discovery of the circulation of the blood is unknown because modern anatomy and physiology postdates him. When asked why it is that blood appears to be pumped around the human body so that human beings bleed upon having their skin punctured, and bleed profusely when veins or arteries are severed, the physician

---

[40]It is also worth pointing out that Torrance rejects the sufficiency-efficacy distinction, which he (mistakenly) attributes to Alexander of Hales. He thinks that the distinction arbitrarily restricts God's grace in Christ. See Torrance, 'The Atonement', 245–6. Yet in his lectures on the atonement, he uses the language of sufficiency and efficacy and applies it to the atonement in this way: 'Objectively, then, we must think of atonement as sufficient and efficacious reality for every human being – it is such sufficient and efficacious reality that it is the rock of offence, the rock of judgment upon which every sinner who refuses the divine love shatter himself or herself and is damned eternally.' *Atonement*, 189.
[41]Perhaps the most sustained attempt to address this can be found in the work of the Evangelical Calvinists. See the essays in Myk Habets and Bobby Grow, eds, *Evangelical Calvinism: Essays Resourcing the Continuing Reformation of the Church* (Eugene, OR: Wipf and Stock, 2012).
[42]T. F. Torrance, *Karl Barth: Biblical and Evangelical Theologian* (Edinburgh: T & T Clark, 1990), 239.

may have views about how this comes about, but at some point he is likely to admit defeat. He just does not have access to the explanations of modern medicine provided by the scientific method. We might say that he is a mysterian about blood circulation. One way of characterizing Torrance's way of thinking is as a similar case of mysterianism. The idea is that we are not in a position this side of the grave to know exactly how Christ's atonement reconciles us to God. So we should adopt a kind of mysterianism towards mechanisms of atonement as they are presented to us in particular models or doctrines of atonement.

Having said that, Torrance does employ a lot of the traditional terminology with respect to the atonement, including language of sacrifice, expiation and even propitiation – although he reinterprets propitiation so that it is a two-way divine action from the human and Godward side internal to the divine life, rather than a matter of the placating of divine wrath by some human act of sacrifice.[43] But he eschews any particular mechanism of atonement. These different atonement terms feature themes or motifs in his understanding of the atonement, without commitment to a particular mechanism above and beyond the incarnation and vicarious work of Christ.

Critical Engagement with Torrance's Soteriology

Let us take stock. We have considered five load-bearing structures that are central to Torrance's soteriology. If we were to summarize these different themes in one dogmatic thesis, it might look like this:

THESIS: *In Christ, God assumes a human nature in order that we might be able to participate in the divine life.* This can be understood as follows. At the first moment of incarnation, God

---

[43]Thus, Torrance says, 'Propitiation has nothing to do with propitiating God as though he needed to be placated in order to reconcile us to himself, but with the two-way movement on the part of God who in his prevenient love freely draws near to us in order to draw us near to himself on the ground of the atoning self-sacrifice of Christ offered for us'. From 'The Atonement. The Singularity of Christ and the Finality of the Cross: The Atonement and the Moral Order', 242.

the Son acquires a fallen human nature, which he sanctifies in the very act of assumption. Throughout his life, ministry, death, and resurrection, Christ acts vicariously in order to heal our fallen humanity in atonement. This vicarious action is entirely objective in nature: his redemptive act brings about the actual justification of all humanity. Those who by faith appropriate this saving work are able to enjoy the benefits of union with Christ and participate in the triune life of God.

Put differently, when considered synoptically, the five central structures of Torrance's soteriology yield a doctrine of theosis. Like several other Western theologians, Torrance seldom uses the language of *theosis* or *theopoiesis*, let alone 'divinization' or 'deification', because of its unhelpful associations in much Western thought with the loss of personhood in the divine, or the admixture of humanity and divinity.[44] Nevertheless, his position implies a doctrine of theosis.[45] For instance, in *The Mediation of Christ*, Torrance writes, 'The hypostatic union took on the form of a dynamic atoning union which steadily worked itself out within the structures of human existence all through the course of our Lord's vicarious earthly life from his birth to his crucifixion and resurrection.' Later in the same passage, he goes on to say, 'Yet it is not atonement that constitutes the goal and end of that integrated movement of reconciliation but union with God in and through Jesus Christ in whom our human nature is not only saved, healed and renewed but lifted up to participate in the very light, life an love of the Holy Trinity.'[46]

---

[44]He does use this language on occasion. But in general he seems reluctant to name his doctrine a version of theosis as such presumably because of its associations in Western theology of the period in which he was writing. For discussion of this point, see Habets, *Theosis in the Theology of Thomas Torrance*, ch. 1. Habets cites a notable case where Torrance uses the term 'theosis' in his address to the World Alliance of Reformed Churches in Frankfurt on 5 August 1964. See the conclusion of ch. 1 of his book.

[45]Habets concurs. In the conclusion to his study of Torrance's doctrine of theosis, he writes, 'although the formal language of theosis may appear rather infrequently in Torrance's work, its material content is pervasive'. Habets, *Theosis in the Theology of Thomas Torrance*, 193.

[46]Torrance, *The Mediation of Christ*, 65 and 66, respectively.

There are two crucial claims here. First, Christ's vicarious work in the incarnation and atonement are penultimate actions that are directed towards the ultimate goal of participation in the divine life. Second, the hypostatic union is the means by which we are placed in a position to be able to participate in the divine life. Without the incarnation there could be no participation because without the incarnation there would be no means by which our humanity could be united with divinity: an unbridgeable ontological gulf would exist. As Torrance glosses this elsewhere in his monograph, *Space, Time, and Resurrection*,

> [T]he staggering thing about this is that the exaltation of human nature into the life of God does not mean the disappearance of man or the swallowing up of human and creaturely being in the infinite ocean of divine Being, but rather that the human nature, remaining creaturely and human, is yet exalted in Christ to share in God's life and glory.[47]

In this connection, it is important to understand precisely that to which Torrance is committed. The idea is not that human beings are 'made divine' in some general sense, as if our human natures could simply be exalted by divine fiat independent of the work of Christ. Rather, Torrance's claim is that the fallen humanity that we each suffer and instantiate is taken up and reschematized in Christ's hypostatic work, so that by being united with Christ our humanity may be renewed through union with Christ's renewed humanity. As Myk Habets puts it, riffing on a Torrancean theme, theosis is 'the re-creation of our lost humanity in the dynamic, atoning interaction between the divine and human natures within the one person of Jesus Christ, through whom we enter into the triune communion of God's intra-trinitarian life'. Indeed this, he says, 'is what distinguishes *theosis* in Reformed thought from other expressions of deification or divinization'.[48] Torrance would surely agree with that.

---

[47]Torrance, *Space, Time, and Resurrection*, 135. Cf. *The Mediation of Christ*, 62–7.
[48]Myk Habets, 'Reformed *Theosis*? A Response to Gannon Murphy', *Theology Today* 65 (2009): 489–98; 491 and 492, respectively. In an almost identical passage, Habets imputes the same sentiment to Torrance in *Theosis in the Theology of Thomas Torrance*, 137–8.

One common criticism of the recent interest in Western accounts of theosis is that they make of theosis a theme in a broader scheme of salvation. The worry for such critics is that theological *motifs* in a person's thought are not the same as theological *doctrines*.[49] Doctrines are comprehensive; motifs are features of some larger theological framework. But clearly Torrance does think of the whole of soteriology in terms that are recognizably a doctrine of theosis. In a recent introduction to Eastern Orthodox theology, Andrew Louth writes:

Orthodox theology insists on the doctrine of deification, theosis, because recovering the fullness of the image will involve real change in ourselves, changes that mean the image of God in which we are created becomes more and more evident . . . deification, as St Maximos makes so clear, is the restoration of our true humanity, not its diminishment or abandonment. And it is a change grounded in the amazing change that God himself embraced, when he became human for our sakes, not abandoning what he is – divinity – but assuming what he is not – humanity.[50]

This sets theosis in its broader soteriological context, and, in particular, highlights the way in which theosis is linked to a particular theological anthropology and understanding of the order of salvation (*ordo salutis*) as it is understood in Western theological nomenclature. If some Western theologians cherry-pick the notion of union with Christ or participation in the divine life leaving behind the anthropological context in which these notions are set, the same cannot be said for Torrance. In fact, Louth's characterization of theosis in this passage could have been written of Torrance's soteriology. There are significant differences from some later strands of Orthodox thought that depend on the distinction between the divine energies and essence, but Torrance clearly does hold that our

---

[49]For this concern, see Gösta Hallonsten, 'Theosis in Recent Research: A Renewal of Interest and a Need for Clarity', in Michael J. Christensen and Jerrfry A. Wittung, eds, *Partakers of the Divine Nature: The History and Development of Deification in the Christian Tradition* (Grand Rapids: Baker Academic, 2007), 281–93.
[50]Andrew Louth, *Introducing Eastern Orthodox Theology* (Downers Grove, IL: IVP Academic, 2013), 95.

transformation through the reconciling work of Christ involves our being united with his theanthropic person. His central focus on the vicarious humanity of Christ; the notion of incarnation as atonement; his christological understanding of the divine image; his Christically focused view of the nature of justification; and his atonement mechanism mysterianism – all fit together as aspects of his Reformed version of theosis.

What, then, of universal salvation? As I have already indicated, this a real problem in Torrance's theology. His soteriology seems to imply universalism, but he refuses to draw this conclusion. A similar difficulty has afflicted interpreters of Torrance's *doktorvater*, Karl Barth. However, there is an important difference between the two that is salient for our analysis. The difference is this. For Barth, Christ as the Elect One brings about the derivative election of all humanity who are elect in him, provided they do not reject that status – which he thinks of as an 'impossible possibility'. For this reason, we cannot presume to know whether all are finally reconciled to God. Hopeful universalism is the best option.[51] But, despite its name, hopeful universalism is not in fact a species of universalism. For to hope for the reconciliation of all humanity based on the gracious work of God in Christ is not the same as asserting that all humanity will be saved.

This is something Torrance cannot affirm, though he may wish to do so. For his soteriology commits him to the view that all humanity is reconciled to God through Christ's vicarious action in incarnation, and atonement, including our justification. Because Christ's vicarious action brings about the effectual justification of all humanity, there is no theological wiggle room for hopeful universalism. Though Torrance is very clear that faith is needed to appropriate the benefits of Christ's saving work, this seems, at best, to be a kind of evangelical residue in his thought that is inconsistent with his wholly objective, extrinsic and effectual soteriology.

But is this really a problem for Torrance? Clearly, he would have thought so. After all, he was implacably opposed to universalism.

---

[51]The discussion of this topic in Barth's theology is enormous. My own thinking has been changed by reading David Congdon's essay, 'Apokatastasis and Apostolicity: A Response to Oliver Crisp on the Question of Barth's Universalism', *Scottish Journal of Theology* 67.4 (2014): 464–80.

However, someone enamoured of Torrance's soteriology may feel that what I am calling the evangelical residue of Torrance's emphasis on personal faith could be dropped as a requirement for salvation given the other load-bearing structures in Torrance's soteriology. Such a person might think that Torrance would have been better advised to have the courage of his convictions and embrace a doctrine of universalism, according to which all humanity is destined to participate in the triune life of God.

7

Regeneration Reconsidered

In the garden, Augustine famously heard children singing the words *'tolle lege, tolle lege'* ('take up and read, take up and read'), and, picking up and reading a copy of the epistles of Paul, was spiritually transformed. He writes:

> I snatched it up, opened it, and read in silence the passage that first caught my eye: 'not in revealing and drunkenness, not in debauchery and licentiousness, not in quarrelling and jealousy, but put on the Lord Jesus Christ and make no provision for the flesh in its lusts.' [Rom. 13.13-14] I had no desire read further; there was no need. As soon as I reached the end of this sentence the light of assurance was poured into my heart and all the clouds of doubt melted away.[1]

In the language that Laurie Paul has recently made familiar, Augustine underwent a paradigmatic transformative experience.[2] Put in the nomenclature of traditional theology, we would say that he was *regenerated*.

But what do we mean by regeneration? What do we think happened to Augustine in the garden if we regard this famous passage from the *Confessions* as a record of his conversion to the Faith? In recent analytic theology, there has been some interest in the indwelling of the Holy Spirit in the believer, and (to a lesser

---

[1]Augustine, *Confessions*, translated with an Introduction by Thomas Williams (Indianapolis: Hackett, 2019), Bk 8. 12.29, pp. 137–8.
[2]See L. A. Paul, *Transformative Experience* (Oxford: Oxford University Press, 2014).

extent, and often by implication) the transformation that this brings about in regeneration. The work of Jonathan Edwards and William Alston have featured prominently in this discussion as offering important models for thinking about regeneration, and we shall come to their respective contributions in due course. However, as my rendition of the Augustine story indicates, I want to focus on how we should understand the doctrine of regeneration as one aspect of what Reformed theologians call the *ordo salutis* or order of salvation that is brought about by the Holy Spirit in his application of the benefits of Christ's reconciling work to the believer. We might put the concern like this: *What is regeneration, and how should we understand this aspect of the doctrine of salvation in Christian theology?*

To this end, I begin by outlining one particular account of regeneration, drawing on the theology of Jonathan Edwards in particular in order to do so. Although the account I have in mind is broadly Edwardsian in shape, it is not exactly the same as Edwards's view in certain important respects, and my aim in enlisting Edwards's help is not to follow his position slavishly, but to retrieve certain ideas from Edwards in pursuit of a constructive account of regeneration. Following recent work by Ray Yeo and Kimberley Kroll, I shall call the view I have in mind the infusion account, since its central claim is that in regeneration the Holy Spirit is directly infused into the believer the upshot of which is the gift of a new disposition or habit by means of which the believer may live a life pleasing to God.[3] Having outlined the infusion account, I discuss some of its central claims in the second section. The third section focuses on several objections to this account that have recently been raised in the literature by Yeo. In a concluding section, we shall consider the upshot of this analysis for contemporary theology.

---

[3]See Ray S. Yeo, 'Towards a Model of Indwelling: A Conversation with Jonathan Edwards and William Alston', *Journal of Analytic Theology* 2 (2014): 210–37, and Kimberley Kroll, 'Indwelling without the Indwelling Holy Spirit: A Critique of Ray Yeo's Modified Account', *Journal of Analytic Theology* 7 (2019): 124–41. Cf. Steven L. Porter and Brandon Rickabaugh, 'The Sanctifying Work of the Holy Spirit: Revisiting Alston's Interpersonal Model', *Journal of Analytic Theology* 6 (2018): 112–30. The most comprehensive treatment of these matters of which I am aware is Kroll's unpublished PhD thesis, 'The Condescension of the Spirit: the nature of the relation of the indwelling Holy Spirit' (University of St Andrews, 2020).

The Infusion Account of Regeneration

As the Augustine story intimates, regeneration is that divine action by means of which fallen human beings are inwardly morally and spiritually renewed and transformed so that they are able to live a life pleasing to God.[4] In some of the recent analytic-theological literature on indwelling, this is not always clearly distinguished from the indwelling presence of the Holy Spirit consequent upon the act of regeneration that brings about human sanctification.[5] But whether regeneration occurs in the work of Christ, which is then applied to the whole of humanity (which is the view of Thomas F. Torrance[6]), in the womb (as, apparently was the case with John the Baptist), at the moment of baptism (as with the doctrine of baptismal regeneration found in many Christian communions), or at some later point in a person's life (as in the morphology of conversion associated with traditional evangelical theology), it marks off the moment at which a person is changed from being in a state of alienation from God, to being in a state of reconciliation. What happens thereafter is distinct and consequent upon this, and is usually understood to involve the sanctifying work of the indwelling Holy Spirit. Though we shall have to say something about the indwelling of the Spirit and about sanctification, my main concern here is to have a better understanding of what is meant by regeneration.

There are different ways in which regeneration might be construed. But common to most ways of thinking about regeneration is the idea that it is a kind of transformative experience. In her work on transformative experiences, Laurie Paul distinguishes between *epistemic* transformation and *personal* transformation.[7]

---

[4]At least, that is how regeneration is commonly understood. If one thinks, like Thomas Torrance, that regeneration happens vicariously in the reconciling work of Christ that is applied to all humanity, then this moral and spiritual transformation has already occurred, and what happens in the life of the individual is more like an epistemic change as the individual comes to understand the regenerate state she already enjoys as a result of Christ's saving work on her behalf. For a helpful discussion of this, see Christopher Woznicki, 'The One and the Many', 103–26. We will return to Torrance's views in the conclusion.

[5]See, for instance, Porter and Rickabaugh, 'The Sanctifying Work of the Holy Spirit: Revisiting Alston's Interpersonal Model'.

[6]For discussion of this point, see ch. 6.

[7]Paul, *Transformative Experience*, 17.

An experience is epistemically transformative if you can only know what it is like by undergoing the transformation yourself. For instance, seeing a particular colour for the first time. A personal transformation is one in which your view on an issue that is fundamental to who you are is changed. For example, reading *The Communist Manifesto* and having one's political views changed forever as a consequence. When a transformative experience includes both an epistemic and personal aspect, it is truly transformative. A good example of this is becoming a parent. Those who have become parents often say that it is a transformative experience that they could not have prepared themselves for, and (often) did not fully understand, prior to actually having a child. Something about undergoing the experience of becoming a parent for oneself changes a person, in a way that no textbook could explain adequately. Religious conversion or regeneration is another example of a truly transformative experience that has both epistemic and personal aspects. In addition to the example of Augustine, paradigmatic examples of regeneration as a truly transformative experience can be found scattered throughout ecclesiastical history in the testimonies of leaders of the various Christian churches.

Here are two well-known examples from the key leaders of the Arminian and Calvinist branches of the evangelical Great Awakening. John Wesley's famous report of his conversion goes like this:

> In the evening, I went very unwillingly to a society in Aldersgate Street, where one was reading Luther's Preface to the Epistle to the Romans. About a quarter before nine, while he was describing the change which God works in the heart through faith in Christ, I felt my heart strangely warmed. I felt I did trust in Christ, Christ alone for salvation; and an assurance was given me that he had taken away my sins, even mine and saved me from the law of sin and death.[8]

Edwards's account has striking similarities:

> The first that I remember that ever I found anything of that sort of inward, sweet delight in God and divine things, that I have

---

[8]From *John Wesley*, ed. Albert Outler (New York: Oxford University Press, 1964), 66.

lived much in since, was on reading those words, I Tim. 1:17. 'Now unto the King eternal, immortal, invisible, the only wise God, be honour and glory for ever and ever, Amen.' As I read the words, there came into my soul, and was as it were diffused through it, a sense of the glory of the Divine Being; a new sense, quite different from any thing I ever experienced before. Never any words of scripture seemed to me as these words did. I thought with myself, how excellent a Being that was; and how happy I should be, if I might enjoy that God, and be wrapped up to God in heaven, and be as it were swallowed up in him.[9]

But what does the sort of truly transformative regenerative religious experience reported by the likes of Augustine, Wesley and Edwards consist in? How should we characterize it? Taking my cue from Jonathan Edwards, I shall understand regeneration as the infusion or transmission of the Holy Spirit to the believer, one consequence of which is the gift of a new disposition or habit by means of which the believer is able to live a life pleasing to God. This is *the infusion account of regeneration*. We might say that it involves the provision of a new or at least *renewed* or *revitalized* spiritual sense, something like the sense of the divine (*sensus divinitatis*) about which Calvin writes in his *Institutes*.[10] This spiritual sense is distinct from our five natural senses, which may be why it is sometimes conflated with the indwelling presence of the Spirit. My claim is not that the testimonies of Augustine, Wesley, Edwards or whomever *imply* an infusion account of regeneration, but only that they are *consistent* with it as a kind of model that may account for the phenomenology reported by these (and other) great Christian thinkers of the past, whose testimonies have become something of a pattern or paradigm for thinking about regeneration going all the way back to the Apostle Paul on the road to Damascus.[11] Something akin to the idea that the divine grace given in salvation is an infused habit or

---

[9]Jonathan Edwards, 'Personal Narrative', in John E. Smith, Harry S. Stout, and Kenneth P. Minkema, eds, *A Jonathan Edwards Reader* (New Haven: Yale University Press, 1995), 283–4.

[10]See Calvin, *Institutes of the Christian Religion*, 1. 1–4.

[11]Although I shall not discuss the biblical basis for this doctrine in detail, there are a number of biblical passages one could point to as indicative of something like the infusion account. Take, for example, the report of Christ's famous conversation

disposition can be found in both Catholic and Protestant thought. For instance, in the *Summa Theologiae*, Thomas Aquinas writes:

> man is helped by God's gratuitous will, inasmuch as a *habitual gift is infused* by God into the soul; and for this reason, that it is not fitting that God should provide less for those He loves, that they may acquire supernatural good, than for creatures, whom He loves that they may acquire natural good. Now He so provides for natural creatures, that not merely does He move them to their natural acts, but He bestows upon them certain forms and powers, which are the principles of acts, in order that they may of themselves be inclined to these movements, and thus the movements whereby they are moved by God become natural and easy to creatures, according to Wisdom 8:1: 'she . . ordereth all things sweetly.' Much more therefore does He infuse into such as He moves towards the acquisition of supernatural good, certain forms or supernatural qualities, whereby they may be moved by Him sweetly and promptly to acquire eternal good; and thus the gift of grace is a quality.[12]

Such grace is, he says, a formal cause that inclines the believer to gracious acts.[13]

It may be surprising to some that the notion of grace as an infused disposition or habit can be found in the work of some Reformed thinkers as well.[14] Nevertheless, Jonathan Edwards is a clear example of this. He refers to regenerating grace as a 'new simple idea'[15] transmitted directly the soul and, at other times,

---

with Nicodemus about being born again in John 3 or the Ethiopian eunuch Philip encounters in the Book of Acts.

[12]Thomas Aquinas, *Summa Theologiae*, 5 vols, trans. Fathers of the English Dominican Province (New York: Benziger Brothers, 1911), 1a. Q. 110, Art. 1.

[13]Ibid. A formal cause in the Aristotelian sense Aquinas has in mind is a cause that provides the form or structure of an act or a thing, such as the whiteness of the white thing (to use Aquinas' example).

[14]This is surprising because some theologians seem to think that Reformed theologians eschew language of infused grace, preferring instead the forensic language of imputation.

[15]John Locke maintained that there are certain new simple ideas that we commonly have such as the redness of a particular patch of our visual field prior to understanding it as the redness of a particular tomato. Edwards adopted Locke's terminology to

as a 'spiritual sense'. He writes, 'this new spiritual sense is not a
new faculty of understanding, but it is a new foundation laid in
the nature of the soul, for a new kind of exercises of the same
faculty of understanding. So that new holy disposition of heart that
attends this new sense, is not a new faculty of will, but a foundation
laid in the nature of the soul, for a new kind of exercises of the
same faculty of will.'[16] Elsewhere he makes it clear that this 'new
foundation' is, in fact, the Holy Spirit himself. In other words, God
communicates *himself* to the believer in regeneration in the person
of the Spirit, so that the disposition provided by the new or renewed
spiritual sense is consequent upon this divine action and arises out
of the moral reordering of the human person brought about by the
communication and indwelling of the Spirit.[17]

Edwards often uses the language of altered perception with
which to describe this new spiritual sense. It is as if the regenerate
person acquires a new sense in addition to her five natural senses,
a kind of extrasensory perception, that enables her to perceive God
and that provides her with a new motivation to live a holy life. The
idea is something like this. Human beings are morally disordered
as a consequence of sin. What is lacking in fallen human beings
is a principle by means of which the various aspects of human
moral nature can be rightly ordered. This principle is, in fact, the
indwelling Holy Spirit, whose presence in pre-fallen human beings
ordered the various moral and spiritual aspects of our aboriginal
parents in such a way that they were able to be rightly related to
one another and to God. On this Edwardsian account, the fall has
two consequences both of which are deleterious for human nature.
The first is that, in sinning, the immediate indwelling presence of

---

describe the 'new sense' brought about by regeneration. For discussion of Locke and
Edwards in this regard, see Paul Helm, 'Regeneration and the Spirit', in Marc Cortez,
Joshua R. Farris, and S. Mark Hamilton, eds, *Being Saved: Explorations in Human
Salvation* (London: SCM Press, 2019), 246–61.

[16] Jonathan Edwards, *Religious Affections, The Works of Jonathan Edwards*, vol. 3,
ed. John E. Smith (New Haven: Yale University Press, 1959), 206.

[17] See Edwards, *Religious Affections*, 205, 262, 398, 469, and Edwards's comment
that 'there is no other principle of grace in the soul than the very Holy Ghost
dwelling in the soul and acting there as a vital principle'. Edwards, *Writings on the
Trinity, Grace and Faith, The Works of Jonathan Edwards*, vol. 21, ed. Sang Hyun
Lee (New Haven: Yale University Press, 2002), 196.

the Holy Spirit is withdrawn. The second, consequent upon the first, is that human nature without the ordering indwelling presence of the Spirit becomes morally and spiritually disordered.[18]

Now, once the Holy Spirit is communicated to the fallen individual, healing the alienation from God and renewing and reordering her vitiated moral nature, the Spirit is reintroduced as the ordering principle that enables the human individual to rightly relate to others and to God. This divine act also provides the new habit or disposition by means of which the regenerate individual may live a life pleasing to God. This marks an important difference between the Edwardsian and Thomist account of divine grace in salvation. For it appears that on the Edwardsian picture, *God himself* is the means by which the new habit is formed in the believer, one which provides the individual with a new or renewed spiritual sense.[19] This is not true on the Thomist account, where created grace is something distinct from God that is superadded to the creature.[20] On the Edwardsian account, it is as if there is a kind of malfunctioning circuit in the moral nature of fallen human beings, and God provides the junction box and electrical connection needed to complete and power the circuit, thereby hooking up the fallen creature directly to the divine power source so that the creature may begin to function properly once more. We could put the Edwardsian account of regeneration like this:

REGENERATION: the divine action by means of which the Holy Spirit is communicated to the believer, indwelling the believer, and infusing a new supernatural disposition or habit into a fallen human person that provides a spiritual sense by means of which the regenerate person may begin to live a life pleasing to God.

Moreover, in addition to being in this state of moral and spiritual renewal, on the Edwardsian way of thinking consequent upon the first moment of regeneration the believer is on a trajectory of further

---

[18]I have discussed this at greater length in Oliver D. Crisp, *Jonathan Edwards and the Metaphysics of Sin* (Aldershot: Ashgate, 2005).

[19]As I have already intimated, there are echoes of Calvin's notion of the repaired *sensus divinitatis* here, but I shall leave the exploration of that theme for another occasion.

[20]See *Summa Theologiae* IIa IIae q.23 a.2.

transformation in the process of sanctification on the way towards ever greater and more intimate union with God in Christ by the power of the Holy Spirit. This process of ongoing sanctification and ever more intimate union with God is like a mathematical asymptote: we move closer to union, participating ever more intimately with the divine, but never reaching a point of total loss of the self like a drop of water in the ocean. This process of sanctification and union with God in ever greater asymptotic intimacy and participation in the divine life is *theosis*. Although he doesn't use the language of theosis, Edwards makes use of the concept. He says:

> The creature is no further happy with this happiness which God makes his ultimate end than he becomes one with God. The more happiness the greater union: when the happiness is perfect, the union is perfect. And as the happiness [of the creature] will be increasing to eternity, the union will become more and more strict and perfect; nearer and more like to that between God the Father and the Son; who are so united, that their interest is perfectly one. If the happiness of the creature be considered as it will be, in the whole of the creature's eternal duration, with all the infinity of its progress, and infinite increase of nearness and union to God; in this view, the creature must be looked upon as united to God in an infinite strictness.

And,

> I suppose it will not be denied by any that God, in glorifying the saints in heaven with eternal felicity, aims to satisfy his infinite grace or benevolence, by the bestowment of a good infinitely valuable, because eternal: and yet there never will come the moment, when it can be said, that now this infinitely valuable good has been actually bestowed.[21]

Elsewhere, I have attempted to build upon this Edwardsian understanding of theosis, finessing it with a christological account

---

[21]Jonathan Edwards, 'Dissertation on God's End in Creation', in *Ethical Writings: The Works of Jonathan Edwards*, vol. 8, ed. Paul Ramsey (New Haven: Yale University Press, 1989), 533–4; 536.

of the divine image into which believers are being conformed in sanctification, which appears to be missing in Edwards's understanding of the matter. (In short: Christ is the prototypical divine image in whose image believers are being formed by the Holy Spirit.[22]) For present purposes I will simply stipulate that the sort of doctrine of theosis I am interested in here, which draws upon Edwards's account as a source, but which is distinct from Edwards's position, goes like this:

> THEOSIS: The doctrine according to which redeemed human beings are conformed to the image of Christ in his human nature. By being united to Christ by the power of the Holy Spirit, redeemed human beings begin to exemplify the qualities of the human nature of Christ and grow in their likeness to Christ (in exemplifying the requisite qualities Christ's human nature instantiates). This process of transformation and participation goes on forevermore. It is akin to a mathematical asymptote.

One could consider regeneration dogmatically, as a topic in systematic theology. In Reformed accounts of this matter, which is the tradition with which I am most familiar, this would fall under the doctrine of the order of salvation (*ordo salutis*), which has to do with how the benefits of Christ's reconciling work are applied to particular individuals so that they become the beneficiaries of his action. Normally, this is discussed in terms of the particular agency of the Holy Spirit, the person of the Godhead upon whom this application of Christ's salvific work terminates. The thought is this: Christ reconciles estranged fallen human beings to Godself by means of his salvific work. We might say that his work reconciles fallen humanity *in principle*. But the benefits of this work must then be applied to particular fallen human beings by means of the agency of the Holy Spirit. Only by means of this additional work of the Spirit are the benefits of Christ's work *effectually applied* to the individual. Similarly, setting up a wireless hub that can connect

---

[22]See Crisp, *The Word Enfleshed*, and idem, *Analyzing Doctrine*. Ray S. Yeo criticizes Edwards's understanding of salvation at just this christological point. See Yeo, 'Towards a Model of Indwelling: A Conversation with Jonathan Edwards and William Alston'. Yeo's account is itself the subject of criticism on this score in Kroll, 'Indwelling without the Indwelling Holy Spirit: A Critique of Ray Yeo's Modified Account'.

a person's laptop computer to the internet via radio signals, and switching the hub on, are both necessary for the laptop computer to be connected to the internet wirelessly. But the laptop itself must have its wireless capability switched on in order for it to emit and receive the radio signals so that it may be connected wirelessly to the internet. It is not sufficient for the hub to be in working order and switched on. The laptop must also have its wireless capability switched on so that it can emit and receive the radio signals that connect it up to the hub. These are two distinct things. In much traditional Reformed theology in particular, and in much Christian theology more broadly (the relevant changes having been made), the reconciling work of Christ and the salvific work of the Holy Spirit in applying the benefits of Christ's work to the individual are only jointly necessary for regeneration.[23]

To this a further point must be added – a point that may distinguish Reformation theology from the theology of other branches of Christianity in some respects, depending on one's theological sensibilities. This is that the fallen human individual upon whom the Holy Spirit works is entirely *passive* in this action. This is the doctrine of *monergism*, according to which *the application of the benefits of Christ's reconciling work is entirely a work of divine grace*. Apostle Paul says that even the faith exercised by the fallen individual in receiving the gift of salvation in regeneration is a gift of God (Ephesians 2). Fallen human beings contribute nothing to this change. Indeed, they are incapable of contributing anything to this change because they are, as the New Testament says, 'dead in their sins' (Eph. 2.1). That is, fallen human beings are so blighted by the moral and noetic effects of sin that they are incapable of acting so as to receive the gift of salvation offered by God independent of divine grace. There are different ways in which Protestant theologians have understood this passivity of the human will in the face of divine regenerative grace. Calvin says things like this in his *Institutes of the Christian Religion*[24]:

I say that the will is effaced; not in so far as it is will, for in man's conversion what belongs to his primal nature remains

---

[23]As I noted earlier, Thomas F. Torrance's position is an exception to this general trajectory in Reformed thought. I have discussed this in Chapter 6 of this volume.
[24]Calvin, *Institutes*, 2 vols.

entire. I also say that it is created anew; not meaning that the will now begins to exist, but that it is changed from an evil to a good will. I affirm that this is wholly God's doing . . . God not only assists the weak will or corrects the depraved will, but also works in us to will [Phil. 2.13]. From this, one may easily infer, as I have said, that everything good in the will is the work of grace alone. . . . Not a whit remains for man to glory in, for the whole of salvation comes from God.[25]

Not only is grace offered by the Lord, which by anyone's free choice may be accepted or rejected; but it is this very grace which forms both choice and will in the heart, so that whatever good works then follow are the fruit and effect of grace; and it has no other will obeying it except the will it has made.[26]

Man is so held captive by the yoke of sin that he can of his own nature neither aspire to good through resolve nor struggle after it through effort.[27]

By contrast, Edwards developed a view, found in earlier French Reformed theology of the Academy of Saumur that there is no natural impediment to fallen human beings acting so as to receive the gift of salvation offered by God in Christ. It is just that they are morally incapable of doing so absent divine grace because of the noetic effects of sin. This distinction between natural and moral (in) ability is at the heart of his account of regeneration. In a memorable (though lengthy) passage, he writes of two hypothetical cases:

the one, that of a man who has offended his prince, and is cast into prison; and after he has lain there a while, the king comes to him, calls him to come forth to him; and tells him that if he will do so, and will fall down before him, and humbly beg his pardon, he shall be forgiven, and set at liberty, and also be greatly enriched, and advanced to honor: the prisoner heartily repents of the folly and wickedness of his offense against his prince, is thoroughly disposed to abase himself, and accept of the king's offer; but is confined by strong walls, with gates of brass,

---

[25]Calvin, *Institutes* 2. 3. 6.
[26]*Institutes* 2. 3. 13.
[27]*Institutes* 2. 4.1.

and bars of iron. The other case is, that of a man who is of a very unreasonable spirit, of a haughty, ungrateful, willful disposition; and moreover, has been brought up in traitorous principles; and has his heart possessed with an extreme and inveterate enmity to his lawful sovereign; and for his rebellion is cast into prison, and lies long there, loaden with heavy chains, and in miserable circumstances. At length the compassionate prince comes to the prison, orders his chains to be knocked off, and his prison doors to be set wide open; calls to him, and tells him, if he will come forth to him, and fall down before him, acknowledge that he has treated him unworthily, and ask his forgiveness; he shall be forgiven, set at liberty, and set in a place of great dignity and profit in his court. But he is so stout and stomachful, and full of haughty malignity, that he can't be willing to accept the offer: his rooted strong pride and malice have perfect power over him, and as it were bind him, by binding his heart: the opposition of his heart has the mastery over him, having an influence on his mind far superior to the king's grace and condescension, and to all his kind offers and promises.[28]

A more recent account of these matters that bears on our discussion in important respects is that developed by Eleonore Stump. She adopts a Thomist-inspired account of human moral agency, according to which humans have three moral configurations or 'settings', rather like the different gears in an automatic car gearbox.[29] The car has a first setting, which is 'Drive'. When in this configuration, the car will move forward. It also has a second setting, which is 'Reverse'. When in this configuration, it will move backwards. There are other settings of course. A third is 'Neutral'. In this configuration the car will move neither forward nor back. It remains stationary. On Stump's way of thinking, fallen human beings are in a similar moral state. We have a configuration where we are capable of obeying and pleasing God. We have a configuration where we are incapable of pleasing God, but instead actively resist God. And we have a third configuration

---

[28]Jonathan Edwards, *Freedom of the Will*, IV. 4, pp. 362–3.
[29]See Stump, *Aquinas* (New York: Routledge 2003), 389–404. See also the discussion of this in Simon Kittle, 'Grace and Free Will: Quiescence and Control', *Journal of Analytic Theology* 3 (2015): 89–108.

wherein we are in a kind of morally neutral state with respect to divine agency. This she calls *moral quiescence*. The quiescent person is not actively resisting God; nor is she actively seeking to please God. She is neither acting to please or reject God. Instead, she is in a passive but receptive state, capable of being acted upon by a divine agent. The qualification 'passive but receptive state' is important here, and indicates a difference between Stump's account and that of both Calvin and Edwards. For on Stump's way of thinking, the individual who is morally quiescence is in a state that is receptive to divine grace. This is not true of the fallen individual in need of salvation according to the accounts given by Calvin or Edwards. In the case of Calvin, the fallen individual is in a morally corrupt state and actively resists God's agency until and unless the Holy Spirit acts directly upon the individual to graciously regenerate them. And in the case of Edwards, the fallen individual is naturally capable of turning to God, but morally incapable due to the noetic effects of sin that have rendered the individual morally disordered without the indwelling agency of the Spirit. The result is the same: in both Calvin and Edwards, fallen human beings are rendered incapable of turning towards God, or making themselves receptive to God's action, or even to cease resisting God's susurrations, without divine grace.

Suppose we think of the fallen human being on analogy with a drug addict. The addict is incapable of reforming his own behaviour without intervention. He is in the thrall of the substance he abuses, that is, he is physically and psychologically dependent upon it. Now, we might say that there is, in fact, no natural impediment to him kicking his habit even though he is an addict. It is not physically or psychologically impossible for him to do so. He could simply refuse to imbibe the drug henceforth, and go through withdrawal, eventually conquering his dependence. But, for all practical purposes, this is impossible without some intervention. He needs help, and (let us suppose) without it he is not able to bootstrap himself out of his parlous circumstances. Borrowing a notion from the work of Harry Frankfurt, we might say that our addict has conflicted first- and second-order desires. He desires the drug, and most of the time he desires to desire the drug. But sometimes he desires to desire to be rid of its influence. Occasionally, he desires to be rid of it as well. But his first- and second-order desires do not line up, as a consequence of which he is morally conflicted. In other words, as Frankfurt would say, he does not will to be rid of the drug addiction *wholeheartedly*. He does not desire to be rid of it and at the same time desire to desire to be rid of it. So he remains an addict.

In the language of Edwards, the addict has no natural impediment to kicking his habit, but he has a moral impediment to doing so. He is morally and noetically disordered as a consequence of being in a state of sin, and requires some act of divine grace to be able to will in an ordered way so as to be regenerated. The requisite act of divine grace is, of course, the communication of the Holy Spirit.

Let us sum up our findings thus far. I have outlined a kind of Edwards-inspired or Edwards*ian* account of regeneration, namely the infusion account. According to this view, regeneration can be expressed like this:

REGENERATION: the divine action by means of which the Holy Spirit is communicated to the believer, indwelling the believer, and infusing a new supernatural disposition or habit into a fallen human person that provides a spiritual sense by means of which the regenerate person may begin to live a life pleasing to God.

Following Edwards, as I understand it regeneration is intimated related to theosis. Although the two doctrines are conceptually distinct, and regeneration does not entail theosis, there is a certain fittingness to the idea that the communication of the Spirit in regeneration yields theosis understood in the following manner:

THEOSIS: The doctrine according to which redeemed human beings are conformed to the image of Christ in his human nature. By being united to Christ by the power of the Holy Spirit, redeemed human beings begin to exemplify the qualities of the human nature of Christ and grow in their likeness to Christ (in exemplifying the requisite qualities Christ's human nature instantiates). This process of transformation and participation goes on forevermore. It is akin to a mathematical asymptote.

To these two claims, I would add the caveat, expressed in a more dogmatic register, that regeneration is wholly a divine work. As intimated previously, this is the doctrine of *monergism*, according to which the application of the benefits of Christ's reconciling work is entirely a work of divine grace; human beings contribute nothing to this work. We might express it thus:

> MONERGISM: the doctrine according to which the application of the benefits of Christ's reconciling work by the agency of the Holy Spirit in REGENERATION is wholly a work of divine grace; in this process the human agent is entirely passive, but not quiescent.

It seems to me that MONGERGISM is distinct from the Thomist understanding of moral quiescence favoured in the recent literature by Eleonore Stump. For, on the monergist view, fallen human beings are not even capable of getting themselves in a quiescent state in order to be receptive to divine grace. The very act of being quiescent is itself an act of divine grace, not a human act on this Reformed way of thinking.

Discussion of the Infusion Account

In his classic paper, 'The Indwelling of the Holy Spirit', William Alston distinguishes three models of indwelling.[30] These are *the fiat model, the interpersonal model* and *the sharing model* respectively. According to the fiat model, God directly ordains moral and spiritual change independent of human action just like he ordains the creation of the world. According to the interpersonal model, the change in the human subject is brought about by a kind of receptivity to the presence of the Spirit, and interaction with the Spirit. According to the sharing model, spiritual and moral change is brought about through participation in the divine life. Although these are three distinct ways of thinking about what Alston calls the indwelling of the Spirit, he sees that they might also be repurposed as three aspects of one model of indwelling. Our concern is more narrowly focused on regeneration, but the essential point remains the same: the three models can be combined as aspects of an infusion

---

[30]William P. Alston, 'The Indwelling of the Holy Spirit', in Thomas V. Morris, ed., *Philosophy and the Christian Faith* (Notre Dame: University of Notre Dame Press, 1988), 121–50.

account. To see this, let us consider each model in relation to the infusion account, beginning with the fiat model.

The infusion account involves divine fiat because, given monergism, it is entirely a work of divine grace and involves the communication of a divine person to the believer. However, it should also be clear from the foregoing that the infusion account does not entail God creating something de novo in the believer. Some Reformed theologians seem to think that regeneration does involve a kind of creation or recreation (think, for example, of Calvin's position in his *Institutes* and what he says about the effaced divine image in fallen human beings[31]). But if regeneration implies the creation of an entirely new disposition in the believer this may raise concerns about personal identity across time, for it would seem to suggest that the person prior to the act of regeneration is significantly different from the person after the act of regeneration. Before regeneration the individual is fallen and incapable of pleasing God; after regeneration the person is morally and spiritually renewed and able to please God by the introduction of a new disposition or habit. There is an intrinsic change to this person that also appears to be an essential change to the person in question.[32] But we do not want to say that in regeneration the individual is transformed from having one nature to having another nature, for that is tantamount to saying the change involves the transformation of one person to another. Rather, we want to say that in regeneration the individual is transformed in relation to the God from whom she or he is alienated by sin.

One way to avoid this worry raised by the dispositional aspect of the infusion account is to make clear that Spirit's work is not to create a new intrinsic and essential disposition in the believer ex nihilo, but rather to reorder the vitiated moral nature of the fallen individual. This is an intrinsic change, but not necessarily an essential one. It is the difference between saying the radio needs a replacement transistor and motherboard in order to work properly (intrinsic, essential change), and saying that the radio transistor

---

[31]See Calvin, *Institutes* 1. 15.
[32]An *intrinsic change* is a change that happens to a particular entity itself independent of context and circumstance. An *essential change* is a change that alters the very essence or nature of a thing.

needs to be repaired and the motherboard recalibrated so that the radio is able to detect and transmit radio waves in audible sounds once more (intrinsic, non-essential change). So it would seem that there is something right about the fiat model: God does ordain human salvation and this is brought about in regeneration solely by divine action. But the action in question is not necessarily a creative act, strictly speaking. It does not involve the generation of a de novo nature in the human person. Rather, it is more like healing or repairing the noetic and moral damage caused by sin. Just as the broken radio cannot receive radio signals until it is repaired, so fallen human beings are incapable of rightly detecting and processing divine 'signals' until such time as the Holy Spirit repairs the damage caused by sin. But clearly, repairing a broken radio transmitter is not the same as creating a new radio transmitter de novo or replacing one transmitter with another. Just so, repairing the noetic effects of sin in the provision of a renewed spiritual disposition in regeneration is not the same as creating such a disposition or replacing it with another disposition.[33]

Let us turn next to the interpersonal model discussed by Alston. Here too there is something that this gets right. Although God ordains the salvation of the individual and brings this about through the agency of the Holy Spirit in regeneration, it is by means of an act that is interpersonal in nature. God acts upon the person, he regenerates the person and so on. However, given monergism, there must first be some divine act in regeneration before the human individual is capable of relating to God in such a personal way. We might say that the interpersonal model is a good way of thinking about the work of the indwelling Spirit, but a poor way of thinking about regeneration. For regeneration is wholly a divine work, and must be wholly a divine work because human beings are totally depraved and incapable of turning to God let alone relating to him without the interposition of divine grace. It is this grace that is provided through the renewing work of the Spirit's presence in the act of regeneration.

---

[33]Edwards would probably dissent from my account of the kind of dispositional change involved in the infusion account outlined here. It is closer to a more Calvinian account of regeneration.

What about the sharing model? Recall that according to the sharing model, moral and spiritual change is brought about through participation in the divine life. This is certainly true of the version of the infusion account outlined in the previous section. It is the divine life that is communicated to the believer in the person of the Holy Spirit, who brings about the repair of the spiritual sense, and this is commensurate with the idea that the regenerate person is set on a trajectory of theosis. Participation is at the heart of the expanded version of infusion that includes theosis. What the infusion account provides is a clearer way of modelling what we mean by the act of regeneration and how it relates to subsequent indwelling and sanctification.

Objections to the Infusion Account

We are now in a position to consider some objections to the infusion account. Ray Yeo offers several objections to Edwards's account of regeneration, which are also relevant to the version of the infusion account I have set out here. I will tackle these objections in ascending order of seriousness, beginning with those that seem least problematic, and leading towards those that seem most difficult to address.

First, Yeo argues that the Edwardsian view raises *the spectre of monism*. The worry can be put like this. Edwards affirms divine simplicity. Thus, in communicating the Spirit to the believer in regeneration, God communicates himself. Yet Edwards is clear that this does not mean God communicates his *essence* to the believer, which would imply a very strong doctrine of union indeed, one that jeopardizes the distinction between the creature and the creator (hence the worry about monism). Instead, Edwards maintains that what is communicated to the believer in the act of infusion is *divine holiness*.[34] But, says Yeo, this is disingenuous because if he is committed to a traditional doctrine of divine simplicity, then the communication of holiness *just is* the communication of the divine essence, for divine attributes are identical with the divine essence.[35]

---

[34]See Edwards, *Ethical Writings*, 638–40.
[35]See Yeo, 'Toward a Model of the Indwelling', 220.

For, by Edwards's own admission, what is communicated to the redeemed human is Godself.

The traditional way around this concern is to deny that God has a real relation with the created order. When we speak of God relating to his creatures, we mean that there is some change in the creature relative to God, not that there is some change in God relative to the creature. The relation in question is only a conceptual one, just as a merely Cambridge change is one that does not really affect both relata. The fact that my son was smaller than me, and is now bigger than me implies no change in me. Similarly, on this way of thinking, the change brought about by communicating holiness to the soul of the believer is not a real change in God, but is a real change in the believer. However, Edwards cannot avail himself of this distinction in explaining his account of the infusion of holiness to the believer because he thinks that God communicates *himself* in regeneration, not merely some created effect.[36] So Yeo is right to put his finger on this vulnerability in Edwards's account. However, this is not necessarily a problem for all versions of the infusion account. For, as I have outlined it here, the infusion account is independent of the traditional doctrine of divine simplicity. One could hold to the infusion account and deny or amend the traditional doctrine of divine simplicity accordingly.[37] In which case, Yeo's objection doesn't go through.

Second, there is a concern about the connection between the Spirit on the infusion account, and union with Christ – what we might call *the pneumatic union worry*. Are we united to God through the humanity of Christ? On the Edwardsian account, it looks like believers are united to the Spirit in the first instance, and logically subsequent to this are united to Christ – but to his divine, not his human nature. As Yeo puts it, 'the way in which' Edwards 'makes the connection from Spirit-union to vital union with Christ is to equate the Holy Spirit with the Spirit of Christ. The saints enjoy vital union with Christ via infusion because the Holy Spirit

---

[36] I have discussed this further in Oliver D. Crisp, 'Jonathan Edwards on God's Relation to Creation', *Jonathan Edwards Studies* 8.1 (2018): 2–16.
[37] Here I have in mind something like the moderate version of divine simplicity I defend in *Analyzing Doctrine*.

is also the Spirit of Christ.'[38] By collapsing the Spirit into the Spirit of Christ, Yeo worries that Edwards fails to attend to the way in which the humanity of Christ is traditionally thought to be the conduit of union with God (recall the hub example, used earlier when discussing theosis). There are real problems with Edwards's Christology which is, it seems to me, underdeveloped in important respects. But there is nothing about the version of the infusion account I have outlined here that requires this particular aspect of Edwards's project. Recall that on the infusion account, as I have construed it, regeneration amounts to the following:

> REGENERATION: the divine action by means of which the Holy Spirit is communicated to the believer, indwelling the believer, and infusing a new supernatural disposition or habit into a fallen human person that provides a spiritual sense by means of which the regenerate person may begin to live a life pleasing to God.

This does not address the way in which the Spirit unites the believer to Christ; but that is deliberate. In much Reformed theology, union with Christ is a distinct theological topic. Though it is intimately related to the notion of regeneration in the *ordo salutis*, it is that aspect of salvation that connects up regeneration to the benefits of Christ. We might say that regeneration is the divine act that applies the benefits of Christ's redemptive work to the believer, and, in so doing, unites the believer to Christ via the agency of the Holy Spirit. The infusion of the Spirit, and the renewing and healing of the spiritual sense in the believer, enables the believer to be united to Christ via his human nature. In other words, it enables the redeemed human to begin to participate in the divine life, which comes about through union with Christ. But this is accounted for in the way in which we construed theosis. Taken together, these two aspects of a complete infusion account are sufficient to rebut Yeo's worry about union with Christ as it arises in Edwards's version of the infusion account.

Third, there is a worry about the way in which Edwards understands the infusion of the Spirit into the believer and the agency of the Spirit in the believer thereafter in indwelling. Call this

---

[38]Yeo, 'Toward a Model of the Indwelling', 221.

the merger worry. This has to do with whether infusion of the Spirit implies participation in the perichoretic life of God, and, if it does, how this is possible for finite, fallen minds. In outlining the concern, Ray Yeo writes:

> According to Edwards (WJE 13:367-368), the minds of the regenerate participate in the same intra-Trinitarian divine love or delight (i.e., the Holy Spirit) that the Father has towards his perfect idea of himself (i.e., the Son). However, it is difficult to see how a finite and often sinful human mind could bear a disposition for a divine psychological state. As mentioned, the divine mind seems to be utterly distinct in kind from regenerate human minds in its perichoretic trinitarian psychological structure and being. As far as we can tell, sincere Christians throughout the history of the church do not possess a trinitarian mind in the same way that God does. Thus, on what grounds can we hold that regenerate human minds are able to bear the same divine psychological states that God does in his trinitarian divinity? Edwards attempts to force a kind of direct meshing of the divine mind with the human mind in a very strong and literal way. But can his conception of infusion be ultimately coherent given the drastically different kinds of minds between divinity and humanity?[39]

He concludes, 'finite and unperfected human minds, even when regenerated, simply do not have the required trinitarian kind of mind, divine resources and cognitive environment to bear the load of a triune and divine psychological life of love. The chasm of divine transcendence cannot be bridged.'[40] Once again, it is not clear to me that the version of the infusion account outlined here falls foul of this concern. Yeo writes that 'the minds of the regenerate participate in the same intra-Trinitarian divine love or delight (i.e., the Holy Spirit) that the Father has towards his perfect idea of himself (i.e., the Son)' and that 'it is difficult to see how a finite and often sinful human mind could bear a disposition for a divine psychological state'. Presumably, the thought here is that God cannot communicate

---

[39]Ibid., 219.
[40]Ibid.

to his creatures the love that he has within his own divine life. But why think that? The answer seems to be that human beings are incapable of bearing the sort of love God has for Godself. But why think that the infusion account requires *that*? Surely all that it requires is a relation of love between God and the creature that is sufficiently intimate that the creatures may begin and continue to enjoy the benefits of participating in the divine life. Now, suppose that the Spirit is the bond of love between the Father and the Son as many classical theologians have thought. The infusion of the Spirit into the believer, and the union of the believer with the Spirit, is a union with the self-same divine person who is the bond of love in the divine life. But why does that require that human minds bear a disposition for a *divine* psychological state? Suppose you have a small child, whom you love dearly. Must the child enjoy the fullness of an adult loving relationship with you as a parent in order for the child to love in a real, complete way? Surely not. There will be ways in which you love the child that are appropriately different from the way in which you love, say, your spouse. Yet both loves are human loves, and both are truly expressions of your love.

Note that the new sense or disposition generated by the infusion of the Spirit into the believer is not a divine sense. It is not as if, in infusing himself into the believer, the Spirit heals human nature and enables the redeemed person to participate in the divine life *as if that person were an additional divine person*. How could that be? It is impossible for finite creatures to become divine persons.[41] The massive ontological gulf that exists between God and creation can never be spanned. But why think that is what is required here? All that the infusion account requires is that the Spirit himself is infused into the believer, and heals human nature by the provision of a new disposition or habit, by means of which the believer may begin the

---

[41]Edwards does say some incautious things in this regard that Yeo picks up on, and that suggest he thinks all that distinguishes humans from God is a matter of degree: we could in principle become divine beings if sufficiently enlarged. But in that speculation Edwards was wrong. See Edwards, 'Miscellanies' notebook entry 135, where he writes 'if we should suppose the faculties of a created spirit to be enlarged infinitely, there would be the Deity to all intents and purposes, the same simplicity, immutability, etc'. *The 'Miscellanies': Nos. a-z, aa-zz, 1-500, The Works of Jonathan Edwards Vol. 13*, ed. Thomas A. Schafer (New Haven: Yale University Press, 1994), 295.

process of participating in the divine life. It is just a confusion of what this entails to suggest that this is tantamount to a bridging of the ontological divide between God and humans. For the infusion of the Spirit is the means by which the redeemed individual is united to Christ and ,via Christ, is able to participate in the divine life. Although, as we have already seen, Edwards does not make this last christological claim, and may even have had a deficient account of union with Christ, this is not a deficit shared by the infusion account outlined here. Once more, Yeo's concerns can be met by an infusion account that draws deeply on Edwards, but that corrects or amends his theological shortcomings.

Conclusion

The doctrine of regeneration is a transformative experience at the heart of the Christian understanding of salvation. This is true however we understand the moment of transformation that regeneration brings about. To see this, let us briefly consider the example of Thomas Torrance, mentioned in passing earlier. We might think of his view as a kind of limit case to the sort of broadly Reformed understanding of regeneration I have offered here. He thinks that regeneration occurs vicariously in the redeeming work of Christ, which is then applied to all humanity so that, from a certain point of view, it is Christ who is regenerated in his vicarious humanity for our sake. Yet, even if Torrance is right about this, there must still be some additional divine act by means of which the benefits of Christ's saving work are applied to those to whom the gift of faith is given. This is true whatever one thinks about the scope of salvation (whether universal or less than universal), unless one holds that the application of Christ's benefits to the individual via the gift of faith is somehow otiose. But it is difficult to see how that could be the case – at least, in regard to those capable of exercising the gift of faith. If the vaccine I need to be returned to full health is universally available, it still needs to be administered to me in order for me to feel its benefits. If Torrance is right about regeneration being part of Christ's vicarious reconciling work, then presumably the Spirit enables us to see and understand that we are already included in the ambit of the Faith because of Christ's vicarious work. Though this isn't regeneration, it is still a work of epistemic transformation that may be momentous, and that is consequent upon regeneration. Transformation is still part of the equation, so to speak. Relegating regeneration to the vicarious work of Christ does not obviate the need for a transformative experience.

The account of regeneration I have defended here is a version of the infusion account that owes its origins to the work of Jonathan Edwards, though it is distinct from Edwards's position. It is truly transformative, including both epistemic and personal aspects. To recap, the three main doctrinal claims at the heart of this view are as follows:

REGENERATION: the divine action by means of which the Holy Spirit is communicated to the believer, indwelling the believer, and infusing a new supernatural disposition or habit into a fallen human person that provides a spiritual sense by means of which the regenerate person may begin to live a life pleasing to God.

THEOSIS: The doctrine according to which redeemed human beings are conformed to the image of Christ in his human nature. By being united to Christ by the power of the Holy Spirit, redeemed human beings begin to exemplify the qualities of the human nature of Christ and grow in their likeness to Christ (in exemplifying the requisite qualities Christ's human nature instantiates). This process of transformation and participation goes on forevermore. It is akin to a mathematical asymptote.

MONERGISM: the doctrine according to which the application of the benefits of Christ's reconciling work by the agency of the Holy Spirit in REGENERATION is wholly a work of divine grace; in this process the human agent is entirely passive, but not quiescent.

Clearly, this infusion account is inconsistent with Torrance's position. It presumes that regeneration is a divine work that is not included in Christ's vicarious redemptive act, but is consequent upon it. Nevertheless, the infusion account is consistent with a range of views about *when* regeneration occurs other than the limit case provided by Torrance. It could obtain in utero, as with John the Baptist; in baptism, as with many historic Christian communions;

or at some point after baptism, as evangelicals have historically understood matters.

I have also clarified and defended the infusion account against three objections raised against in the recent literature by Ray Yeo. It seems to me that it represents a way of thinking about this vital topic in the doctrine of salvation that is plausible, and that commends itself to a wide range of theological approaches to the Christian doctrine of salvation that understand it as a truly transformative experience.

PART FOUR

Christian Life

8

Eucharistic Presence

One of the perennial problems for sacramental theology has been the question of Christ's presence in the Eucharist. All Christians affirm that Christ is *somehow* present in the celebration of the Eucharist. Even if we suppose that the Supper is merely a memorial feast, Christ is present by his Spirit. This is true even if that presence is not a peculiar or special presence distinct from his omnipresence in creation.[1] Controversy is joined in discussion of the *manner* in which Christ is said to be present in the celebration of the Lord's Supper. What is meant by the dominical words of institution, given in the New Testament? How are the eucharistic elements actually the body and blood of Christ (if they are, indeed, the body and blood of Christ)? These questions were at the heart of early Reformation debates such as the Colloquy of Marburg in 1529, which cemented the differences between Zwingli and Luther. Luther refused to budge from his own consubstantial understanding of the dominical claim '*hoc est corpus meum*' (Lk. 22.19). Zwingli appealed to Jn 6.63, and the claim was that 'the flesh profits nothing' (τὸ πνεῦμά ἐστιν τὸ ζῳοποιοῦν, ἡ σὰρξ οὐκ ὠφελεῖ οὐδέν). It has been a running sore in ecumenical discussions ever since. And it remains one of the most significant theological questions that divides Christians of different communions today. It is nothing short of a scandal that adherents of, say, Presbyterian or Anglican or Lutheran traditions still cannot imbibe the Eucharist with Roman Catholics or Orthodox

---

[1]Thus, there is an interesting research project yet to be developed on how God's general omnipresence is to be analysed and distinguished from his peculiar presence in the Eucharist. But that is for another day.

Christians after 500 years of (often vituperative) debate.[2] The issue of the manner of Christ's presence in the Eucharist is not the only important issue for discussion of this sacrament. But it can fairly be described as a central and difficult one. For it is a question about what we might call the metaphysics of the eucharistic presence of Christ.

No mere theological essay is likely to transform the discussion for the better. Yet constructive and irenic proposals that take steps towards full rapprochement between the historically separate communions of Christianity are surely something to be welcomed. Who knows? Perhaps they may even have some (small) positive effect in the long-standing attempt to heal these divisions in the one, holy, catholic and apostolic church.[3]

This chapter represents one attempt by a theologian in the Reformed tradition to provide a constructive account of the Lord's Supper as a contribution to the wider discussion of the theology of the Eucharist. It is not the last word on the subject[4]; but the hope is that it may be a modest positive contribution to this discussion. The assumption is that different Christian communions may have something important to bring to the theological discussion of the Lord's Table, including those in the Reformed tradition.

---

[2]Over the centuries, there have been many attempts at rapprochement between different Christian communions. George Hunsinger's work is one notable recent contribution to this ecumenical literature. See George Hunsinger, *The Eucharist and Ecumenism: Let Us Keep the Feast*. Current Issues in Theology (Cambridge: Cambridge University Press, 2008). At the heart of his work is a careful and nuanced ecumenical proposal for the celebration of the Eucharist. A useful recent textbook on sacramental theology is Justin S. Holcomb and David A. Johnson, eds, *Christian Theologies of the Sacraments: A Comparative Introduction* (New York: New York University Press, 2017).

[3]Of course, assuming that different communions all belong to one holy, catholic and apostolic church is itself a theological statement that will be disputed by those communions who claim that they alone have the full expression of the sacraments requisite for the life of the church. But a working assumption of this chapter is that no ecumenical progress will be made where a given communion refuses to contemplate the possibility that 'separated brethren' may, in fact, have something important to contribute to this discussion.

[4]In many ways this chapter represents footnotes to the important studies of Hunsinger and Arcadi. It is an extension of ideas to be found in their work.

The argument proceeds as follows. In the first section, I draw on the recent work of the Anglican theologian James Arcadi, augmented by Reformed theologians George Hunsinger and Brian Gerrish to provide an abbreviated taxonomy of different eucharistic views as a kind of conceptual framework that informs the later sections of the chapter. Then, having surveyed some of the live options in eucharistic theology, in the second section I consider three recent proposals in more detail. These are the views expressed by George Hunsinger in his understanding of what he calls Reformed transelementation, Marilyn Adams's defence of hypostatic impanation, and James Arcadi's attempt to find a kind of middle way between these two views in his sacramental impanation doctrine. With this discussion in mind I then turn to outline the beginnings of a constructive Reformed account of impanation, which draws on a broadly Reformed sensibility though it is not a piece of confessional or even dogmatic theology in the strict sense of that term, but more of a *theologoumenon* or theological opinion presented to my peers for their consideration and critical feedback. The third section briefly considers the ecumenical upshot of this reasoning.

An Arcadian Eucharistic Taxonomy

To begin with, it is important to situate the constructive proposal I shall defend in the broader theological context of eucharistic theology. Happily, in the recent theological literature this job has been made much easier by the scholarship of George Hunsinger and James Arcadi.[5] Hunsinger gives a helpful précis of the ecumenical background to eucharistic debate, and then proposes a constructive linguistic account of the Eucharist in light of that survey. And James Arcadi gives a comprehensive taxonomy of different eucharistic views before developing his own preferred account of the Eucharist, which is a version of the doctrine of impanation (about which, more presently).

---

[5]See Hunsinger, *The Eucharist and Ecumenism*; and James M. Arcadi, *An Incarnational Model of the Eucharist*. Current Issues in Theology (Cambridge: Cambridge University Press, 2018). See also Arcadi, 'Recent Philosophical Work on the Doctrine of the Eucharist', *Philosophy Compass* 11.7 (2016): 402–12.

Arcadi distinguishes between different *modes* of eucharistic presence and different *manners* in which these particular modes are construed.[6] The mode of presence concerns the metaphysics of the Eucharist, that is, *how* it is that the elements of bread and wine are said to become the body and blood of Christ (assuming they do, in some sense, become the body of Christ). Yet there may be more than one *manner* in which the particular mode is understood in a given eucharistic tradition. Thus, there are *corporeal, pneumatic* or spiritual, and (with a rather cumbersome turn of phrase) *no non-normal* modes of eucharistic presence doctrine, and different versions of each mode.

In the case of the corporeal mode, the idea is that after the consecration of the eucharistic elements the *substances* of Christ's body and blood become present in some way that is related to the elements. One manner in which the corporeal mode has been understood is the doctrine of transubstantiation, according to which the substance of the eucharistic elements are transformed into the body and blood of Christ, although the accidents or perceptible properties of the elements remain the same. In this way, those masticating and imbibing the eucharistic elements are eating and drinking the real body and blood of Christ, although they appear to remain bread and wine because the perceptible properties of the elements are unchanged. Another sort of corporeal mode is the Lutheran doctrine of consubstantiation. On this view, the body and blood of Christ come to be present in with and under the elements of bread and wine so that there is no transformation or annihilation of the substance of the bread and wine, but rather the addition of the body and blood alongside the eucharistic elements.

At the other end of the eucharistic spectrum are what Arcadi calls no non-normal views about the mode of Christ's presence in the elements. Accounts that fall under this description entail no change to the elements after consecration. As Arcadi puts it, for views consistent with this mode, 'the elements are of little concern'.[7] The reason is that the elements are merely a means by which the worshipper may be drawn to 'intensify their thoughts

---

[6]Arcadi, *An Incarnational Model of the Eucharist*, ch. 1.
[7]Ibid., 22.

about Christ'.[8] They act as a kind of cypher or symbol or focus of attention that aides the worship of the communicant. The best known example of such a view falls within the Reformed tradition, namely, Zwinglian memorialism.[9] The idea here is that the elements remain the same after consecration, and the body of Christ remains locally present at the right hand of the Father in heaven. Partaking in the Lord's Supper is about remembering Christ 'until he comes', not about the conferral of some special sacramental grace by means of the corporeal presence of Christ's human body in the eucharistic elements. Indeed, as Arcadi points out, on this view a similar concentration of the communicant's focus upon Christ could be had by listening to a powerful sermon, scriptural meditation or prayer. There is nothing uniquely sacramental about participating in the Eucharist for the Zwinglian memorialist. Indeed, there is nothing sacramental about it at all since the elements are not, on this view, *outward and visible signs of an inward and invisible grace* (to borrow Augustine's famous definition of a sacrament).[10] Instead, they are ordinances to be observed.

Arcadi also includes the eucharistic abstinence of members of the Society of Friends and the Salvation Army as a kind of limit case of no non-normal views of the Eucharist. Perhaps that is right, although I am inclined to think of such views as theologically aberrant in the sense of departing from an accepted standard, rather than as a limit case of a particular category of thing. Although I will not argue for this claim here, there seem to be good theological reasons for thinking that eucharistic abstinence as an established practice (because, say, Christ did not intend the church to continue the practice, or did not intend to establish a particular ecclesial meal distinct from ordinary meals, or whatever) deprives the community

---

[8]Ibid.

[9]For present purposes, it is sufficient that this view is often associated with the name of Huldrych Zwingli even if, in fact, Zwingli's mature view was somewhat different from this. Arcadi is interested in mapping the conceptual terrain of eucharistic views, and not in ascertaining which view a particular historic theologian actually held. I have followed his lead in this respect.

[10]For useful discussion of Augustine's view, see Thomas L. Humphries, Jr., 'St. Augustine of Hippo', in Holcomb and Johnson, eds, *Christian Theologies of the Sacraments*, 41–58.

that adopts such practices of one of the central rites of Christianity. In this way, such practices are surely aberrant.[11]

In any case, we need not spend time on such views given the focus of this chapter. Our concern is with those accounts of the Eucharist that fall within the bounds of the Reformed tradition, which clearly excludes eucharistic abstinence, just as it excludes most corporeal modes of understanding the Eucharist.[12] Aside from Zwinglian memorialism, most Reformed accounts of the Eucharist fall in the middle of Arcadi's eucharistic spectrum, under the pneumatic mode. Arcadi mentions several manners of this mode that fall within the bounds of Reformed theology. The first is *Genevan instrumentalism*, the second is *Canterbury parallelism*.[13] Let us consider these two manners of the Reformed pneumatic mode in more detail, beginning with Genevan instrumentalism.

Although the connection with Calvin is implicit in the name Genevan instrumentalism, Arcadi distances himself from Calvin exegesis and sticks to the matter of setting out a particular view. On this way of thinking, the faithful who partake of the blessed elements are united by the power of the Holy Spirit to Christ, whose human body remains locally present at the right hand of the Father. As Arcadi puts it, 'the bread and wine become instruments used by the Holy Spirit to intensify the connection between the faithful and the body and blood of Christ.'[14] This link is an instance of metonymy, where the eucharistic elements are related to the body

---

[11]It may even be true to say that such communities are not churches, strictly speaking, because they lack an essential sacramental expression of the life of the church.

[12]Hunsinger is frank in his admission that he has no clue what to say about eucharistic practices of churches in the anabaptist, pentecostal, and charismatic traditions (see *The Eucharist and Ecumenism*, 11). For, as he points out at the end of his study, 'Ecumenical convergence does not seem possible without affirming Nicene Christianity, a high view of the eucharist, and some sort of episcopal polity' (Ibid., 314). I am not in a more advantageous position on this matter, though I hope that the proposal offered here might also be acceptable to some of my anabaptist, pentecostal and charismatic comrades – for a proposal that excludes these numerous communions in principle clearly cannot be an ecumenical one.

[13]The terms 'memorialism', 'parallelism', and 'instrumentalism' are culled from B. A. Gerrish's excellent article, 'The Lord's Supper in the Reformed Confessions', *Theology Today* July (1966): 224–43.

[14]Arcadi, *An Incarnational Model of the Eucharist*, 20.

and blood of Christ without becoming substantially the body and blood of Christ.

Canterbury parallelism is named after the great Anglican Reformer, Archbishop Thomas Cranmer. Although it is similar to Genevan instrumentalism, the role played by the eucharistic elements is slightly different. On this view there is an analogy between partaking of the elements and consuming the body and blood of Christ, but the elements themselves are not necessary for the communicant to obtain the spiritual benefit of feeding on Christ inwardly. Whereas Genevan instrumentalism has the elements as the means by which the Spirit really, mystically, but non-corporeally unites the believer to Christ, Canterbury parallelism focuses upon the inward spiritual transformation of the believer who partakes of the Lord's Supper. Arcadi comments, 'Cranmer even states that if one cannot receive the bread and wine – perhaps due to illness – that person is merely to think deeply on the fact that Christ feeds that person spiritually and that person can receive the same benefits.'[15]

Now, Arcadi is not specifically interested in demarcating which views of eucharistic presence are consistent with Reformed theology. Nevertheless, discerning which of the views he outlines are within the bounds of Reformed theology is a relatively easy task. Reformed accounts of eucharistic presence are usually thought to be instances of what he calls the pneumatic mode, or the no non-normal mode.[16] They are not usually thought to be consistent with the corporeal mode because they do not presume that Christ is somehow corporeally locally present in, with, under or even *as* the eucharistic elements.[17] Rather, Christ is either not really present in any special or unusual sense, as with memorialism, or he is really but not corporeally present. Importantly, for memorialism and the Genevan and Cantaurian manners of the pneumatic mode,

[15]Ibid., 21.
[16]Thus, Gerrish in 'The Lord's Supper in the Reformed Confessions'.
[17]The notion that the eucharistic elements simply become the body of Christ – bread and wine *as* the corporeal body and blood Christ – is a kind of limit case to corporal modes, which Hunsinger calls the Capernaitic position. (See Hunsinger, *The Eucharist and Ecumenism*, 52–4.) This, as Arcadi explains, comes from those confused auditors of Jesus's words in Jn 6, who thought he was indicating a literal manducation of his flesh. See Arcadi, *An Incarnational Model of the Eucharist*, 15–16.

Christ is not locally present in the elements. Instead, he is either no more present in the Lord's Supper than anywhere else in creation (memorialism), or the believer is united to Christ by the Holy Spirit either by means of the instruments of the eucharistic elements, or by some other action that has the same result, namely a spiritual feeding upon Christ in the heart (Genevan and Cantaurian accounts).[18]

Adams, Arcadi and Hunsinger on Eucharistic Presence

So much for taxonomy. Let us now turn to consider three recent, and related, proposals about eucharistic presence in more detail. These are the doctrines defended by George Hunsinger, Marilyn Adams and James Arcadi. We will consider each of them in turn. I will argue that they all make valuable and helpful contributions to the question of eucharistic presence that are grist to the mill for the constructive proposal I will set forth in the third section of this chapter.

In his constructive proposal for the metaphysics of eucharistic presence, Arcadi specifically engages Hunsinger's work, which, being a study borne out of a more postliberal sensibility, fights shy of the language of the metaphysics of the Eucharist. Nevertheless, both make contributions that bear on the metaphysical question. Hunsinger proposes a version of *transelementation* or *metastoicheiosis* as an ecumenical proposal on the theological question of 'the bread we break', as he puts it. At the conceptual heart of his account is the claim that the Reformed view of 'the relationship between Christ's life-giving flesh and the consecrated elements is one of mutual indwelling (*koinonia*)'.[19] It is a view

---

[18]For many who adopt a corporeal mode, Christ is not locally present in the eucharistic elements *in the same manner* as he is at the right hand of the Father in heaven either. Of course, defenders of a corporeal mode do often think that Christ is somehow locally corporeally present in the elements. The point is that they also usually maintain that he is not locally present in the same way in which he is locally present in heaven – a point made in order to avoid concerns about the integrity of Christ's body in heaven, as we shall see.

[19]Hunsinger, *The Eucharist and Ecumenism*, 315. Cf., 77.

borrowed from some of the Magisterial Reformers, such as Thomas Cramner and Martin Vermigli, who in turn appropriated it from Eastern Orthodox theology. On this way of thinking, the elements are elevated and objectively converted so as to become the body of Christ by their mystical union with Christ's flesh and the power of the Holy Spirit, but without the implication that their substance is destroyed, the accidents of bread and wine remaining, as with, say, transubstantiation.[20] Christ is really present in the eucharistic elements, Hunsinger avers, but the presence is by means of the *mystical participation* of the consecrated elements with the body of Christ, locally present in heaven. Although this participation is real, it is not one that entails the transmutation of the elements into Christ's flesh and blood, or the addition of the flesh and blood of Christ to the elements.

Whether this constitutes a corporeal presence doctrine or not is difficult to say – and the metaphysical ambiguity at the heart of this proposal may also speak to its ecumenical valence from Hunsinger's point of view.[21] He cites Orthodox theologian Alexander Schmeman with approval in this connection when he says that 'The [eucharistic] symbol does not so much "resemble" the reality that it symbolises as it participates in it and therefore it is capable of communicating it in reality'.[22] It is this notion of the elevation of the consecrated eucharistic elements and their mystical participation in Christ's real presence that is at the heart of this proposal. The eucharistic elements are somehow capable of such participation without any loss of substance – a kind of eucharistic philosophers' stone if ever there was one!

In many ways, Arcadi takes up where Hunsinger leaves off. Whereas Hunsinger regards his transelemention proposal as rhetorical, that is, as a proposal about the language of eucharistic presence that prescinds from judgements about the metaphysics

---

[20]Ibid., 315.
[21]This is not meant as a slight to Hunsinger's work. Like the language of diplomacy, which has to strike a difficult balance between competing parties, Hunsinger's rhetorical proposal is concerned to address the matter of the 'bread we break' in a way that is sufficiently ambiguous that it may appeal to more than one party in the debate. That is no mean theological feat.
[22]Alexander Schmeman, *The Eucharist* (Crestwood: St Vladimir's Seminary Press, 1988), 38, cited by Hunsinger in *The Eucharist and Ecumenism*, 63.

of the Eucharist, Arcadi presents his work as providing a kind of metaphysical underpinning (what he calls a 'metaphysical infrastructure'[23]) to some of the central notions with which Hunsinger concerns himself. The idea is not to provide explanation that dispels the mystery. Rather, it is to offer a theological model that may help us have a better conceptual grip on what is meant by the mystical union of the eucharistic elements with the person of Christ. This is important because, as both Hunsinger and Arcadi point out in different ways in their respective studies, confusion about what is entailed by particular eucharistic proposals have been the bane of ecumenical discussion of this topic.

Arcadi's model is a version of the medieval doctrine of impanation. As Marilyn Adams has put it, impanation is the doctrine according to which 'just as the Divine Word becomes in-carnate (en-fleshed) when it assumes a particular human nature into hypostatic union with itself, so the Divine Word becomes im-panate (em-breaded) when – at the moment of consecration – it hypostatically assumes the eucharistic bread nature on the altar'.[24] So the idea is this: at the epiclesis, when the eucharistic elements are consecrated, God the Son hypostatically unites himself to the elements. He literally assumes them, so that he acquires a bread-body and a wine-body. In fact, he acquires multiple bread-bodies and wine-bodies since he acquires all eucharistic elements once they are consecrated in the many locations at which the Eucharist is daily celebrated across the globe. They become personally or hypostatically united with him in a way analogous to the manner in which his human body is personally united to him in the incarnation. Thus, there is a real, corporeal union with God the Son. But it is by means of hypostatic union with the matter of the eucharistic elements, not by means of some union of the hypostatic elements with the human nature of Christ, which is locally present in heaven.

As Adams points out, this is a very neat, economical way of obtaining the desiderata of a corporeal presence view without some of the obvious costs that trouble those (like the Reformed) attracted to pneumatic or no non-normal modes of presence. The

---

[23]Arcadi, *An Incarnational Model of the Eucharist*, 250.
[24]Adams, *Christ and Horrors: The Coherence of Christology*. Current Issues in Theology (Cambridge: Cambridge University Press, 2006), 296.

doctrine preserves a full-blooded account of corporeal presence in the Eucharist, but without the need for change to the elements themselves in order that they may become the flesh of Christ. And it preserves a clear distinction between the corporeal presence of Christ in the eucharistic elements and the physical integrity of his corporeal presence in heaven, which the Reformed were particularly concerned about.[25]

There is more than one way to construe the mode of impanation.[26] One could argue, like Adams, that God the Son hypostatically unites himself to the eucharistic elements each time they are consecrated. But one might opt for a more semi-detached relationship between God the Son and his bread- and wine-body, in a way analogous to a three-part model of the incarnation, according to which in the incarnation God the Son unites himself to a human body and a human soul, rightly configured.[27] This is the approach adopted by Arcadi. On this way of construing impanation, God the Son remains united to his human nature, which is locally present in heaven. But he assumes a bread-body and wine-body in the eucharistic elements that are united to his human nature or some part of his human nature (e.g. his soul, or his body), and via his human nature, to his divine nature.[28] In expounding this sort of view, Arcadi writes, 'the

---

[25]The worry is that a corporeal account of Christ's presence in the Eucharist runs the risk of compromising the integrity of Christ's body, which is locally present in heaven. For a body that can be locally present in one region of space-time, and also locally presence in many other locations simultaneously – as happens in the celebration of the Eucharist on a daily basis – is a body that is compromised in some important fashion (or so it is thought).

[26]See Arcadi, *An Incarnational Model of the Eucharist*, ch. 6. Cf. Arcadi, 'Recent Philosophical Work on the Doctrine of the Eucharist'.

[27]This is also discussed in detail by Arcadi. Three-part models of the incarnation hold that the incarnation comprises three 'parts': God the Son plus his human nature, which is composed of a human body and human soul, rightly configured. Thus, there are three 'parts' in Christ: God the Son, his human body, and his human soul. For elaboration of this sort of view, see Crisp, *Divinity and Humanity*.

[28]I am conflating two different models of imputation here. These are what Arcadi calls *natural impanation* and *sacramental impanation*, respectively. Natural impanation 'posits a natural union between the elements or the human soul and Christ'. Sacramental impanation 'proffers a sacramental union between the elements and the human body of Christ' (Arcadi, *An Incarnational Model of the Eucharist*, 209). Both models presume that the union in question is between the God the Son, via (one or other substance of) his hypostatically united human nature, and the

entirety of the human body in Christ does not become bread, nor – like a piece of cod going into the frying pan – does it become merely coated with bread. Rather, the body is extended to include the bread as a part'. What is more, 'This is much more like the incorporation of the bread into the body. The bread participates in the body, and, as St. Paul states, is a participation in the body of Christ.'[29] Thus, on Arcadi's approach we want a doctrine of impanation that implies participation but not hypostatic union.

In order not to lose track of the differences here, let us call the version of impanation discussed by Adams *hypostatic impanation*, and the version mooted by Arcadi in some of his work, *instrumental impanation*. For, so it seems to me, the relevant difference between the two views has to do with whether God the Son is immediately and personally united with the eucharistic elements (as per Adams), or whether he is mediately and indirectly united to them via his human nature on analogy with an instrumental union – like the union of the person and the knife he uses to chop up an apple. Attractive though versions of the instrumental model may be, they lose something of the economy Adams remarks upon in her exposition of the hypostatic view. They also reintroduce the worry about mystical union that we had with Hunsinger's account. For on the instrumental approach, we still have to say something about how it is that Christ's human nature locally present in heaven is also present in the sacraments once consecrated. How does the bread and wine participate in Christ's humanity exactly? What sort of relation is envisaged here? Arcadi suggests a kind of instrumentalism: the elements are taken up as sacramental instruments and participate in Christ's human nature (or some part thereof) in order to do so. The affinities with Hunsinger's transelementation proposal should be

---

eucharistic elements. But I presume the relation could be between God the Son via his human nature taken as a whole concrete particular, and the eucharistic elements (though Arcadi doesn't explore this option in detail). In any case, for my purposes it is not necessary to make these further distinctions, though they are certainly metaphysically possible options. The main take away is that in each of these cases discussed by Arcadi, the union between Christ and the eucharistic elements is not hypostatic but *instrumental*. He uses them as instruments that he joins or that participate in (some substance of) his human nature.

[29]Arcadi, *An Incarnational Model of the Eucharist*, 251.

clear.[30] But equally, the fact that we are left, like Hunsinger, with an unexplained relation of mystical union at the heart of the Arcadi's instrumentalist approach to impanation should also be apparent.

Such a worry doesn't arise for the hypostatic impanation account in the same way. This is because it simply assumes that the consecrated elements are directly and immediately hypostatically united with God the Son. Communicants are literally 'biting and chomping their salvation', as Adams memorably puts it.[31] Thus, on the hypostatic impanation account Christ's human body remains intact and locally present in heaven, whereas his eucharistic body is distinct, and locally present in the celebration of the sacrament. There is no infringing of Christ's local heavenly session, and no reason to think that the integrity of his human nature is compromised, or gerrymandered in order to provide some metaphysical just-so story about real corporeal eucharistic presence. Nevertheless, there is a kind of sacramental entanglement going on here,[32] whereby God the Son may be simultaneously multiply incarnate in his human body in its heavenly session, and in the scattered eucharistic elements as they are celebrated in liturgies around the world. But I suggest that this is to be expected because any claim about the real corporeal presence of Christ in the eucharistic elements will have some strange implications given that it is a metaphysically exotic thing.

Let us take stock. I have reviewed some aspects of proposals on eucharistic presence mooted by Marilyn Adams, James Arcadi and George Hunsinger. Hunsinger suggests a Reformed transelementation, which he takes to be a rhetorical proposal about the language of eucharistic presence not about the metaphysics of eucharistic presence. And transelementation is not, he thinks, the

---

[30]Nevertheless, Hunsinger is clear that his doctrine 'is not a matter of "impanation", because it does not hold that the substance of the bread is hypostatically united to Christ, or that christ's body has "become bread" (for the reverse is true), or (as was sometimes said) that "God has become bread."' Hunsinger, *The Eucharist and Ecumenism*, 77.

[31]Adams, *Christ and Horrors*, 311.

[32]I mean entanglement in the sense used in physics for two particles that are mysteriously entangled or linked even though they may be in discrete regions of space-time that are at a great distance from one another. A similar sort of view is implied by direct impanation, *mutatis mutandis*.

same as impanation. Adams defends a version of impanation, which we have called the hypostatic account. God the Son hypostatically unites himself to the eucharistic elements at the moment epiclesis in the liturgy by the agency of the Holy Spirit. Arcadi, attempting in good Anglican fashion to be a voice of mediation, adopts a middle way, which I have dubbed instrumental impanation. Christ makes the eucharistic elements an instrument of his corporeal presence, yet without evacuating the elements of their bread- or wine-natures or otherwise transmuting them in the process.

A St Andrean Reformed Impanation

In light of the foregoing, we may turn in this third section to set out a constructive account of eucharistic presence from within the Reformed tradition. In particular, I want to suggest a way in which Reformed theologians may appropriate a version of hypostatic impanation. I will set out this view in a series of numbered statements so as to make its structure clear. I will then provide some hermeneutical glosses on these statements in order to explain the theological import of each one as necessary. In a bid to continue Arcadi's conceit of connecting particular eucharistic doctrines with cities, I will dub it *Saint Andrean Reformed Impanation* or just the Saint Andrean account. Let us begin with a kind of dogmatic sketch of the view in numbered statements:

1. When consecrated by an appropriate authority (e.g. a minister of Word and Sacrament), the eucharistic elements of bread and wine become hypostatically united to God the Son via the agency of the Holy Spirit.

2. This union does not alter the perceptual properties or the nature of the eucharistic elements. The substance and accidents of the bread and wine remain bread and wine.

3. Nevertheless, these elements become the bread-body and wine-body of Christ.

4. Thus, God the Son is really, corporeally present in the consecrated eucharistic elements, not in a 'fleshly' manner (via his human nature), but in the nature of bread and wine, which is personally, spiritually united to God the Son.

5. The eucharistic elements are, therefore, instruments used by God the Son as a means of grace and as the conduits used by the Holy Spirit to unite the believer to God (the Son).

6. This union also preserves the integrity of the human nature of Christ, which remains wholly locally present at the right hand of the Father in heaven.

This completes our dogmatic sketch. Now, we may consider several hermeneutical glosses on these statements in order to meet certain potential problems raise by the account as it stands.

(a) Concerning the Real Presence of Christ in the Eucharistic Elements

Perhaps the most pressing concern raised by the Saint Andrean account is what it implies about the corporeal (or other) presence of Christ in the eucharistic elements. There is good reason to zero in on this matter. First, it is the central concern of this chapter, which is to give a metaphysical account of this particular eucharistic matter. But, second, on the face of it the Saint Andrean account seems to be somewhat ambiguous about the manner of Christ's real presence in the eucharistic elements, which would certainly tarnish its explanatory appeal. Third, there is the worry that the sort of real presence implied by this doctrine runs contrary to the typical spiritual or no non-normal modes of eucharistic doctrine defended by Reformed theologians. In other words, there is a worry that the Saint Andrean doctrine is not a Reformed doctrine at all.

On the question of the ambiguity of the Saint Andrean understanding of divine presence in the eucharistic elements, we can say this: the view certainly implies a doctrine of real presence. God the Son is really present in the bread and wine because once consecrated they are hypostatically united to him. They become his bread-body and his wine-body. It is also true to say that this is a corporeal presence doctrine because what is manducated is literally the body of Christ. It is just that the body in question is a bread-body rather than a body of flesh. Of course, God the Son is not present by means of his human nature, or even in a fleshly manner (i.e. by means of some parcel of flesh). But that cannot be an objection to the *corporeal* nature of the presence entailed by this view, since there is a body in view. It is just that the body in question is not a human body. In fact, for the Reformed, the body in question cannot be his human nature because his human nature remains wholly present at the right hand of the Father in heaven.

Nevertheless, there may be another worry in the neighbourhood of this one: if we are united to God the Son via his bread-body, are we united to Christ? This is a more difficult objection to turn back. It certainly seems to be true that on this account we are not directly united to Christ's human nature, and are not manducating his flesh. But it may be that this is less of a concern if, in addition to saying that the bread and wine become God the Son's bread-nature and wine-nature, we say that these are used as sacramental instruments by Christ – along the lines suggested earlier in our look at Hunsinger and Arcadi's accounts of sacramental presence. Then God the Son is hypostatically united to his bread-nature and wine-nature, and this is a hypostatic union *in addition to* the union he already has with his human nature, which remains locally present in heaven. His bread-nature and wine-nature are instruments used by Christ in order to unite us to Godself.

What about the matter of a doctrine of real presence undermining the sort of Reformed view typical in the tradition? How does the Saint Andrean account sit alongside other Reformed views that usually presume some version of a spiritual or no non-normal manners of presence? It is true that most Reformed doctrines are wary of any notion of corporeal presence. But the traditional worries motivating Reformed divines about re-sacrificing Christ, and about jeopardizing the integrity of Christ's human nature as it is locally present with the Father in heaven can all be met on the Saint Andrean view. Christ is not re-sacrificed in the consecration of the elements: a new union obtains. And Christ's human nature is not compromised but remains intact and locally present in heaven. What is more, the sort of union envisaged in this sacramental scheme, though both real and corporeal in nature, is bloodless. We are not left having to find sophisticated metaphysical schemes by means of which to avoid the charge of theological cannibalism. For the body we manducate is not a human body at all.[33]

---

[33]Compare Hunsinger, *The Eucharist and Ecumenism*, 48–51, who shows from a number of early Reformed confessions that the Reformed were not leery of real

(b) Concerning Christ's Local Presence

We have already touched upon the matter of the local presence of Christ's human nature, a vexed matter in Reformed thought. But it is worth taking a little more time to explain this more thoroughly if it is a Reformed version of impanation that is in view, given Reformed squeamishness about jeopardizing the local presence of Christ in heaven. For Reformed theologians, it is imperative that the body of Christ, and his human nature more generally, remain wholly locally present at the right hand of the Father in heavenly session. For he acts there as our great high priest (as the author of the Epistle to the Hebrews puts it). Any account of the Eucharist that jeopardizes that is unacceptable, and (so it was thought) this included most real corporeal presence doctrines like transubstantiation and consubstantiation. As Hunsinger puts it, 'The Reformed did not wish to *deny real presence absolutely*. But they could affirm it only insofar as it seemed compatible with Christ's integral body in its heavenly state.'[34]

However, note that, on the Saint Andrean account the body of Christ remains wholly locally corporeally present in heaven at the right hand of the Father. He is not partially or wholly locally corporeally present in the eucharistic elements as well. Note also that although from one point of view the Saint Andrean account implies the real presence of God the Son in the eucharistic elements, this real presence is not corporeal in the conventional sense often found in textbook accounts of the real corporeal presence of Christ in the eucharistic elements. For no change takes place in the consecrated bread and wine. What changes is not the nature of the elements or their accidents, but their relation to a divine person. They come to be personally united to the Second Person of the Trinity as his bread-body and wine-body. Thus, the Reformed concern about the local presence of Christ does not even arise on this account.

---

presence in the Eucharist, just of a particular way of construing corporeal presence.
[34]Hunsinger, *The Eucharist and Ecumenism*, 50. Emphasis added.

(c) Concerning the Manducation of Eucharistic Elements

According to the Saint Andrean view, all who eat the consecrated elements eat the bread-body of Christ and imbibe the wine-body of Christ. Doesn't this fly in the face of the Reformed concern to distinguish conventional manducation of the elements from the spiritual feeding of believers united by the Spirit to Christ? Answer: Not necessarily. The reason being that there is still a difference between those who eat with faith and those who eat without. Those who eat with faith are indeed united to God via the bread-body of God the Son by the agency of the Holy Spirit. Those who eat without faith do, as the Apostle says, 'eat and drink judgment on themselves' because they eat the bread or drink the cup of the Lord in an unworthy manner' and are therefore 'guilty of sinning against the body and blood of the Lord' (1 Cor. 11.27). Specifically, they are guilty of not discerning the body of our Lord (1 Cor. 11.29) – which makes sense if what is to be discerned is the real presence of Christ in the eucharistic elements.

(d) Concerning Multiple Incarnations

A final metaphysical concern is that the Saint Andrean account implies that God the Son has multiple bodies to which he is simultaneously hypostatically united. Some may find this odd. But it is hardly metaphysically impossible: a divine person may personally unite himself to one or more particular hunks of matter.[35] In this case, the hypostatic union in question is a union with something inert rather than with an organism. But in one respect this is a point in favour of the Saint Andrean account because it has no whiff of cannibalism about it. And in another respect (though this is ad hominem) it strikes me as *no more peculiar* than the idea that somehow the flesh of Christ is in, with, and under, or exists, as the eucharistic elements.

---

[35]I have discussed this elsewhere. See Oliver D. Crisp, *God Incarnate: Explorations in Christology* (London: T&T Clark, 2009).

The Upshot

In this chapter I have set out to defend one version of a hypostatic union doctrine of impanation. I have argued that this might be an ecumenical contribution from a Reformed perspective. There is much more that could be said about these matters. But this is a proposal. It is not a complete account of the Eucharist, let alone a complete account of divine presence in the eucharistic elements. Nevertheless, I think enough has been said for us to conclude that the Saint Andrean account provides one way of thinking about eucharistic presence that does, it appears, fit within the Reformed tradition broadly construed, and that does offer one version of a doctrine of impanation that addresses a number of the traditional concerns Reformed theologians have had with other real, corporeal presence doctrines of the Eucharist. Though this is a modest conclusion as far as ecumenism goes, if I am right, then there is at least one doctrine that, in one important respect, constitutes a real corporeal presence doctrine of the Eucharist that is consistent with the Reformed tradition, and that may be a step towards rapprochement with those communions for whom the corporeal presence of Christ in the Eucharist is a sacramental sine qua non.

9

Prayer as Complaint

Often prayer in the Christian tradition is thought of as a solution to a problem – or, at least, as a means by which a person may find a solution to a problem. We pray in order to get a particular sort of result, one that (we hope) will ameliorate, if not entirely satisfy, some felt need or concern. Here is a hypothetical example. Smith's spouse is in a critical condition in hospital as a result of a road traffic accident. She prays that her spouse may be saved from death and fully recover in time. She prays that the medical doctors will be successful in their treatment. She prays that God will intervene in some way, or ensure that her desired outcome is the one that actually obtains.

Such prayer is a commonplace in Christian piety. It is, in fact, intercessory prayer, or what theologians call prayers of impetration because it involves actively requesting something of the Deity in the hope that the request will be met. Often, such prayers seem to presume that there are several possible outcomes with respect to a particular set of circumstances, and that a prayer offered up in order to secure one particular outcome rather than another may be efficacious, or at least partially constitutive of God directing events in that direction, rather than some other. Suppose we think of a person's life as like a path, with forks in the road at certain junctures, where the traveller must decide which way to take. Then we might say that the presumption in much popular Christian piety, where such prayers are part of everyday life, is that human intercession may influence which branch of the forking path is taken. Thus, Smith prays in the hope that God will save her spouse, and return her to full health. She prays in the hope that the fork in the path that is taken is the one that leads to this particular outcome. In such cases, prayer seems to be thought of in terms of a two-way contingency. Things could go one way or another, and Smith prays for one outcome, not the other, to obtain. [1]

There is much to be said for such prayer. And, although I do not think that this particular analysis of impetration is the correct one,[2] it is a common one; perhaps the most common among practising Christians today. For this reason, I shall call it the *default option on petitionary prayer*, or just *the default option*, since there seems to be a popular misunderstanding in Christianity that this particular way of construing impetration is not only the 'correct' analysis, but also that impetration (understood in this way) comprises the totality, or at least the most important way of thinking about prayer as a spiritual discipline. In other words, there seems to be a popular misunderstanding that conflates a particular way of understanding the nature of impetration with prayer *as such*, as though there were no other ways of thinking about prayer, especially impetratory prayer, and no other modes of praying besides impetration.[3]

In this chapter, I want to do two things. First, I want to explore one other way of thinking about prayer. Since I am interested only in prayer in Christianity, as a Christian philosophical theologian,

---

[1]In his classic treatment of petitionary prayer, Peter Geach speaks of this notion of forking paths as a 'two way contingency', thus: 'The upshot is that if we are to be justified in saying that a state of affairs S came about from somebody's impetratory prayer, then at the time of the prayer S must have had two-way contingency: it could have come about, and it also could not come about.' Geach, *God and the Soul* (London: Routledge & Kegan Paul, 1969), 89. A sophisticated recent treatment of petitionary prayer can be found in Scott A. Davison, *Petitionary Prayer: A Philosophical Investigation* (Oxford: Oxford University Press, 2017).

[2]For an argument for this conclusion, see Oliver D. Crisp, 'John Calvin and Petitioning God', in *Retrieving Doctrine*, ch. 7. See also, Paul Helm, 'Omnipotence and Change', *Philosophy* 51 (1976): 454–61, and Christopher Woznicki, 'Is Prayer Redundant? Calvin and the Early Reformers on the Problem of Petitionary Prayer', *The Journal of the Evangelical Theological Society* 60.2 (2017): 333–48.

[3]Compare Simon Tugwell, who writes: 'Originally there can be no doubt whatsoever that words for "prayer" meant "petition".' However, he opines, 'The history of the word "prayer" represents an outstanding triumph of the Humpty Dumpty school of philology, whose basic premise as enunciated by its founder is "When I use a word, it means just what It choose it to mean – neither more nor less."' Tugwell, 'Prayer, Humpty Dumpty and Thomas Aquinas', in Brian Davies, ed., *Language, Meaning, and God: Essays in Honor of Herbert McCabe* (London: Geoffrey Chapman, 1988), 24. We shall return to this matter in a later section.

I shall restrict myself to consideration of prayer in this particular tradition, although it may be that what I say here has application to other religious traditions as well, particular (though perhaps not exclusively) to members of other Abrahamic faiths. The alternative conception of prayer that I want to focus on is *prayer as complaint*. This is not necessarily antithetical to impetration, or inconsistent with the practice of impetration. In fact, it seems to me that in the biblical writings we find cases of prayer as complaint and prayer as petition side by side and without any evidence that this should be regarded as an embarrassment or as something incongruous, let alone inconsistent. This should not surprise us, since we commonly complain about something with one breath only to ask for something with the next. The child complains that she feels unloved at one moment, and the next is asking her parent when dinner will be served. These are not two inconsistent actions. Similar things could be said, the relevant changes having been made, concerning our prayers to God. We may complain and we may ask for something from God, and there may be good reasons to do both, either consecutively (as with the example of the ungrateful child) or concurrently – as when the child complains that she is hungry and asks for food in the same sentence. Nevertheless, prayer as complaint is different in important respects from prayer as petition, as we shall see.

This brings me to a second matter with which this chapter is concerned. This is that prayer as complaint fits better with an alternative analysis of impetration than the one just offered. On the face of it, one might think that one important reason for complaining is that the complainant wishes things were different with respect to some particular circumstance or situation. So, it appears that prayer as complaint would fit better with the default option of understanding prayer as impetration. However, my contention is that an analysis of prayer as complaint helps us to see that prayer as impetration need not be understood according to the default option, and that the default option has a harder time of providing a plausible understanding of prayer as complaint. It seems to me that the alternative account of prayer as impetration fits better with prayer as complaint, and may also be a better fit with other modes of prayer as well (such as mystical prayer, and prayer as meditation) though space constraints prevent the fuller exploration of this larger claim. If this is right, then it has important implications for how Christians think about prayer as well as the liturgical shape of prayers that are offered in the Christian churches.[4]

We proceed in three stages. In the first, I shall offer an account of prayer as complaint. Then, in a second section, I shall apply this to impetration showing how it fits better with my own characterization of impetration than with the default option. The third section considers two potential complications for this view concerning direct address to the Deity, and concerning atheistic prayers. Then, in a final section, I raise the issue of the deformation of prayer, which is a problem for the default option, but not for a view that thinks of prayer as principally a matter of alignment with God's will.

An Account of Prayer as Complaint

Let us begin with some brief remarks about prayer before turning to complaint as a mode of prayer. What is prayer? Although this may seem obvious, the nature of prayer is, in fact, disputed. For present purposes, I shall adopt a fairly minimalist approach to the notion of prayer, and admit within its bounds a range of *communicative acts directed towards God.*[5] This is not permissive enough for some, for it appears to exclude relevant communicative acts directed towards non-divine entities, such as saints or angels or even demons.[6] And it is not restrictive enough for others, for whom certain sorts of communicative act would not count as prayer even if they were directed to God (e.g. idle chatter).[7] However, rather than provide a

---

[4]An aside: Christopher Woznicki's recent paper 'Is Prayer Redundant? Calvin and the Early Reformers on the Problem of Petitionary Prayer', shows that this alternative way of thinking about impetration is in fact deeply rooted in Reformation theology. I direct interested readers to that essay for further development of this point.

[5]This follows Shieva Kleinschmidt's analysis in 'Atheistic Prayer', *Faith and Philosophy* 34.2 (2017): 152–75, to which this section is indebted.

[6]I presume that certain practitioners of the hermetic arts think they are communicating with demons, and some Christian exorcists use biblical passages like Matt. 18.18 as justification for addressing themselves to putative demonic entities in an attitude of prayer.

[7]Tugwell in 'Prayer, Humpty Dumpty and Thomas Aquinas' cites Hugh of St Victor as a theologian who thought that idle chatter was a mockery of prayer. See Tugwell, 'Prayer, Humpty Dumpty and Thomas Aquinas', 24, citing Hugh of St Victor, *De*

set of necessary and sufficient conditions for an act being a prayer, I shall simply stipulate that the sort of prayer in view in what follows is prayer that is a communicative act directed towards God. There may be other sorts of act that count as prayer that are not directed towards God (e.g. prayers to saints or to demons), and there may be other conditions necessary for a complete account of the nature of prayer from a Christian point of view (e.g. whether only certain sorts of communicative act count as prayers). But for present purposes, this rough-and-ready characterization will suffice. For I presume that complaint-prayers, like many other sorts of prayers in the Christian tradition, are normally communicative acts directed towards God. We shall see that there are objections that can be raised to the claim that all complaints, including all prayers of complaint, are other-directed. For now, it is important to be clear that the view I have in mind here, and that is the subject of the remainder of the chapter, is the one according to which complaint-prayers are *normally* communicative actions that are, indeed, other-directed and, specifically, are actions that are directed Godward.

With this in mind, we can turn to our target, namely prayer as complaint. The Bible is full of complaints. Many of these are in the form of prayers. Some of these are prayers that have been given a stable liturgical form in the life of the people of God in psalmody, as well as in other parts of Scripture (e.g. the book of Job). There are also many instances in Scripture of prayers or what seem like prayers – communicative acts directed at the Deity – that are what might be described as laments.[8] Are these the same sort of phenomenon?

Historically, these two sorts of prayer, that is, complaints and laments, are frequently conflated or, at least, are not clearly distinguished. We can see this in the literary trope of the *jeremiad*, which is often taken to include a component of complaint, including

---

virtue orandi, in J. P. Migne, ed., *Patrologiae Cursus Completus. Series Latina*, vol. 176 (1854), 981–2.

[8]See R. W. L. Moberly, *Old Testament Theology: Reading the Hebrew Bible as Christian Scripture* (Grand Rapids: Baker Academic, 2013). Moberly writes, 'the single most common type of psalm is not the praise but the lament.' 211. This is a common observation. Compare Gordon J. Wenham, *Psalms as Torah: Reading Biblical Song Ethically* (Grand Rapids: Baker Academic, 2012), 167.

the listing of various woes, as well as an element of lament.[9] Thus, in his little 1537 work, *Instruction in Faith*, John Calvin writes that 'Prayer is similar to a communication between God and us whereby we expound to him our desires, our joys, our sighs, in a word, all the thoughts of our hearts'. And later in the same chapter, he goes on to say, 'prayer has not been instituted in order to raise us arrogantly before God, nor to extol our dignity, but to the end that we confess with sighs our calamities, just as children expound with familiarity their complaints to their fathers.'[10] Here Calvin seems to think of prayer as a way of bringing complaints before God. But the language of 'sighing' and bringing before God our 'calamities' might just as easily refer to grievances expressed (though not necessarily fully articulated) as laments offered up to the Almighty.

Although complaints and laments have a close association in the tradition, it seems to me that 'prayers of complaint' is a more general term under which we might include prayers of lament as a species.[11] A complaint is an expression of dissatisfaction that normally includes a reason for the dissatisfaction stated in the form of some kind of grievance. We might say that a grievance is a complaint in which a reason is given for the dissatisfaction of the complainant. Sometimes the grievance of the complainant is expressed in the complaint; sometimes it is only implied or intimated elliptically, so to speak, in the way in which the complaint is articulated. But if the utterance really is an instance of a complaint, some grievance should be included (either expressed or intimated) in the utterance of the complainant. I suppose one might also complain by means of a gesture, or a sigh, or some other act that is not articulated in the

---

[9]In the literature on colonial New England, the jeremiad has become associated with a particular kind of homiletical form, in which the preacher bewailed the sins of the people and implored God to be merciful. As historian Harry Stout puts it, such sermons expressed 'the rhetoric of failure'. Harry S. Stout, *The New England Soul: Preaching and Religious Culture in Colonial New England*. 25th Anniversary Edition (New York: Oxford University Press, 2012 [1986]), 63.

[10]John Calvin, *Instruction in Faith* (1537), trans. Paul T. Fuhrmann (Philadelphia: Westminster Press, 1969), 57 and 58, respectively.

[11]Another species of complaint-prayer might be prayer as protest, which Michael C. Rea has explored in more detail in his essay, 'Protest, Worship, and the Deformation of Prayer', in Rea, *Essays in Analytic Theology*. Oxford Studies in Analytic Theology, 2 vols (Oxford: Oxford University Press, 2020). I will return to this later in the chapter.

form of speech. In that case the complaint would be only partially expressed by means of the speech act or the non-verbal gesture, and the context of the complaint would normally make clear the reason for the complaint and, therefore, the grievance of the complainant. (Scripture is not unaware of such elliptical prayer, of course. Paul speaks of it in Rom. 8.26-27.)

Two examples will make the point clearer. First, if someone complains to the manager of a swimming pool that there is too much chlorine in the water, the complainant has provided a reason for her dissatisfaction. This reason constitutes the substance of the grievance, which, in this case, is articulated by the complainant. The grievance is that the pool is unsuitable for bathing because of the ratio of chlorine to water in the pool, a matter which the complainant assumes the pool's management ought to address. But often, complaints are made without a grievance being clearly expressed. For instance, the common complaint 'You never listen to me!' is an expression of dissatisfaction with some circumstance, although the reason for the complaint is not wholly articulated. It may be that the complainant thinks that his interlocutor habitually does not give sufficient attention to reasons for a particular course of action that he suggests. (The context of the utterance usually provides sufficient information for this particular speech act, and the suppressed grievance, to be understood by the parties to the disagreement.) Stated in terms of a grievance, this may amount to the claim that 'my interlocutor does not give sufficient attention to reasons for a particular course of action that I suggest'. So even when a grievance is not stated, as in this second sort of complaint, this is usually because the complaint is elliptical. The reason for the complaint, though not stated, is implied or assumed. Where the grievance is not expressed, and not understood elliptically (or otherwise, by gesture or speech act, or whatever), the nature of the complaint is not clearly understood by those who are parties to the complaint.

The book of Job is perhaps the pre-eminent biblical example of a work in which complaint is a recurrent device in the narrative. Complaints where the grievance is expressed, or only implied or intimated, can be found throughout this work. Although Job's interlocutors all attempt to provide traditional justifications for the actions of God in the face of Job's complaints, it appears at the end of the work, when God speaks to Job out of the whirlwind in chapter 38, that none of these apologetic strategies have, in fact, been successful (Job 42.7).

What, then, of lament, which is also present in much of the biblical material? It seems to me that laments are best understood as a *kind* of complaint. Specifically, they are a passionate expression of grief or sorrow, often involving mourning over great loss or hardship. A lament may also involve expressing reasons for the anguish undergone by the one lamenting, for example Ps. 22, which speaks of the distress experienced by the psalmist because of 'a gang of evildoers' that has surrounded him. But sometimes reasons for the lament are not clearly expressed, as is the case in Psalm 130 with its famous opening line, 'Out of the depths I call to you, LORD!'

Even when some reason for the lament is given, it is not clear to me that these reasons include the expression of a grievance against God or against some other creature. A good biblical example of this can be found in Jer. 31.15: 'A voice is heard in Ramah, mourning and great weeping, Rachel weeping for her children and refusing to be comforted, because they are no more.' This is a clear example of what might be called a *reported lament*. In this case, Rachel is a figural proxy for the people of Ramah mourning for their dead children, and the prophet reports that lament in this powerful metaphor. The reason for the grief of figural Rachel is given in the prophetic gloss on her behalf, but is not articulated by her in the text. And, in addition to this, the reason the prophet gives for her lament does not constitute a grievance against God. Rather, it is an expression of great anguish in the face of tremendous suffering because of the loss of her children – what is, in effect, the destruction of the future of the community of Ramah.

Let us take another example. Psalm 88 opens with a complaint in the form of a lament rather than a complaint that includes a stated grievance: 'Lord, you are the God who saves me; day and night I cry out to you. May my prayer come before you; turn your ear to my cry' (Ps. 88.1-2). Such laments in psalmody often end with the expectation that God will hear the voice of the psalmist, as Gordon Wenham points out: 'Usually, laments end with a joyful assurance that God will indeed hear the prayer (e.g., Ps 6; 7; 13).' Nevertheless, 'In many of these laments it is not stated how God will answer the prayer. We are left to use our imagination as to how God will deal with the oppressors who are making life a misery for the psalmist.'[12] The resolution to the anguish experienced by the psalmist is often inferred or assumed in the resolution of the psalm. It is not always clearly stated.

To sum up, we may differentiate prayers of complaint and prayers of lament in this way: lament is a kind of complaint. The logical form of these two sorts of prayers are not always clearly distinguished in Scripture or the post-biblical tradition, and sometimes examples of such prayers are not fully articulated in speech. Nevertheless, it seems to me that a helpful way of making clear the difference between these two sorts of prayer is as follows:

COMPLAINT-PRAYER: an expression of dissatisfaction in a communicative act directed toward God that normally includes a reason for the dissatisfaction stated in the form of some kind of grievance.

LAMENT-PRAYER: an expression of grief or sorrow in a communicative act directed toward God, often involving mourning over great loss or hardship.

A further complication: recently Michael Rea has distinguished between what he calls *pious* and *impious protest* forms of prayer.[13] As I have already indicated, as I understand it, a protest prayer is another species of prayer as complaint. Once more, the words uttered by Job when faced with God speaking out of the whirlwind in the closing chapters of the book are a good example of such protest prayer. As Rea points out, God does not merely *permit* Job to say the things he does about God and his purposes; he seems to *validate* Job's protest:

> This is not to say that God endorses or agrees with Job's protest. Rather, the idea is simply that God accepts it and recognizes it as a reasonable response to Job's circumstances on the part of someone who loves goodness and justice but whose understanding of goodness, justice, and the relations between particular goods

---

[12]Wenham, *Psalms as Torah*, 167.
[13]See Michael C. Rea, *The Hiddenness of God* (Oxford: Oxford University Press, 2018), ch. 8, and Rea, 'Protest, Worship, and the Deformation of Prayer', in *Essays in Analytic Theology*.

and evils is occluded by familiar human limitations. I read this validation partly in God's explicit remark at the end of the book to the effect that Job alone among the speakers in the book has spoken rightly of God, but also in God's treatment of Job when God finally appears in response to Job's summons.[14]

Lament-prayer is not necessarily the same as protest prayer, though a lament may be a kind of protest (for instance, a lament-prayer that is also a protest against some egregious violence suffered by the person offering up the lament to God). I suggest that the difference lies in the fact that a lament as an expression of grief or sorrow need not include a clearly articulated reason for the lament, as with prayers that protest something that the one praying is suffering or enduring – presumably, as in the case of Job, something that either originates with God or could be prevented or stopped by God. Nevertheless, lament may be impious. The person whose existential angst yields an angry cry towards God may well be addressing God in an impious way. And, if Rea is right, it may also be that in some circumstances, like that reported in Job, God nevertheless validates such prayer even if it is uttered from a state of theological confusion.

Complaint and Intercession

With our distinction between COMPLAINT-PRAYER and LAMENT-PRAYER in place, we may turn to the relationship between prayer as complaint and prayer as intercession. On the face of it, prayer of complaint, like prayers of petition, seem to presume a kind of two-way contingency. In the case of petitionary prayer, some state of affairs, S, may obtain or may not obtain, and the petitioner prays either that S obtains or that S does not obtain. On this way of characterizing petitionary prayer, the 'success' of a given petition can be analysed in terms of a counterfactual dependence such that, as Davison puts it, 'a person's prayer for some event is answered if and only if had the person not prayed for it, the event in question would not have occurred'.[15] The case of complaint-prayers

---

[14]Rea, 'Protest, Worship, and the Deformation of Prayer', 196.
[15]Davison, *Petitionary Prayer*, 27.

is not *exactly* like this, of course. For the form of a complaint-prayer typically involves some state of affairs that *already obtains*, and that the complainant thinks God could have been prevented, but didn't prevent. Nevertheless, this way of thinking about both complaint-prayer and petitionary prayer depends upon the notion of a two-way contingency.

But suppose we think of petitionary prayer not as asking for God to bring about or prevent some state of affairs from obtaining, but rather as a way of aligning our fallen human wills with what God wills. D. Z. Phillips has something like this view in mind when he writes, 'the prayer of petition is best understood, not as an attempt at influencing the way things go, but as an expression of, and request for, devotion to God through the way things go.'[16] This strategy involves decoupling petitionary prayer from the notion of a two-way contingency. There are good reasons for considering this option, given the well-known problems with what I am calling the default option on intercessory prayer. For instance, suppose one is attracted to a traditional, orthodox account of the divine nature. Then, God is immutable in a strong sense (i.e. incapable of substantial change). He is also omniscient, and essentially loving. Finally, on at least one traditional (Pauline-Augustinian) way of thinking about these matters, God ordains all that comes to pass (e.g. Eph. 1; Rom. 9). But if that is true, then it is difficult to see how God's action can be affected by human petition. In fact, one might think that if God is essentially loving and all-knowing, then he has the knowledge and motivation to ensure that the right state of affairs obtains independent of any human petition. And if God is also strongly immutable, then what he has willed cannot be changed. Finally, if God ordains all that comes to pass, then there is no metaphysical wiggle room whereby creaturely agents may, through their petitions, change God's action in creation.

The notion that petitionary prayer does not depend on a two-way contingency because it is not concerned to change God but rather to change the petitioner, bringing her desires and will into alignment with God's desires and will faces other problems, of course. Chiefly, there is a worry about apparent redundancy. If petitioning God does

---

[16]D. Z. Phillips, *The Concept of Prayer* (London: Routledge & Kegan Paul, 1965), 120–1.

not bring about a change in God is such prayer redundant? I do not see why it must be. Consider the case of an addict who knows he needs to kick his habit or face multiple organ failure and death. He is checked into a rehabilitation clinic. Each day he is visited by the clinic's physician, and each day he petitions her. 'Please help me,' he says. 'I am helping you,' comes the reply. 'Please help me to have the strength to do what needs to be done in order to kick this habit.' 'I will help you,' the physician assures him. There is no expectation in these petitions that the state of affairs the addict is in will change so that he can return to his substance abuse. He acknowledges his own weakness, his desire for the wrong course of action, and his desire to desire the right course of action, which is in keeping with what the physician desires for the addict as well. Somehow, the addict needs to find the will to continue to desire to desire the right course of action, and the will to desire it too, in order that he may overcome his harmful desires and continue with the course of treatment that will return him to full health.

The story is only analogous to the idea of petitioning God as bringing one's will and desires into alignment with God's will and desires, but even this analogy helps us see how such an account is able to make sense of much in traditional ways of thinking about petitioning God. And, importantly, this story is consistent with the idea that the physician's will is immutable, that he has ordained a course of treatment that the patient must follow to recover, and that the physician knows exactly what the patient needs to reach that goal, and cares deeply for the patient's wellbeing. What is more, this story helps us see how in such a state of affairs the daily petitions of the addict are not redundant; they express his existential angst, and his need for reassurance and help in bringing about the appropriate course of action.

Now, suppose we transpose this sort of thinking about petitionary prayer as alignment to the divine will to the case of prayer as complaint. As with our petitioner, so here in the case of our complainer, the prayer in question is directed towards God without the supposition that some sort of two-way contingency is in play. The complainer, like the petitioner, is not attempting to change God's mind. Rather, knowing that God ordains what comes to pass, is immutable, omniscient and loving, the complainer addresses herself to God in the hope that God may help her to reconcile herself to the tragic and difficult circumstances in which she finds herself. In her current state of mind she is not reconciled to these circumstances; they are deeply troubling, causing great anguish. But she knows that 'all things work together for good for those who love God, who are called according to his purpose' (Rom. 8.28). And she knows this is true even if she cannot understand her present circumstances, or how it is that these circumstances do, in fact, ultimately work together for good.

This is not to trivialize the seriousness of a person's complaint or the circumstances that give rise to it. It is not to try to explain or explain away those circumstances either. Our task is merely to provide some theological account of such prayer and the circumstances that give rise to them. Consider these words penned by William Abraham in writing about the grief he endured upon the unexpected death of his son:

> Why did the Lord not grant our request for healing? Here the answer is simple: God does indeed know best. Our perspective and range of information is limited. To submit to the will of God is utterly apt and decisively correct. For me it makes no intellectual or theological sense whatsoever to get mad or angry at God. Of course, emotionally and psychologically it makes sense when we get angry at God in these circumstances. However, it makes no coherent or intellectual sense given what I believe about God; and I have not had the slightest temptation to do so.[17]

I am suggesting something similar with respect to both petitionary prayer and complaint-prayer. It may be emotionally and psychologically understandable that we get angry at God in certain circumstances, and complain to God – perhaps even rail against God. But given the sort of traditional, orthodox account of the divine nature, it makes little theological or intellectual sense to do so. Rather, what makes sense is to submit to the will of God even when we do not understand why God has permitted what has happened. My suggestion is that this way of thinking about petitionary prayer is not redundant, and may be extended to include complaint-prayers. In fact, it makes good sense to think

---

[17]William J. Abraham, *Among the Ashes: On Death, Grief, and Hope* (Grand Rapids: Eerdmans, 2017), 8.

of complaint-prayers in this manner, given that we often complain about things in more mundane circumstances even when we know that they are for our good, and that they may not be changed, but must be endured.

Two Potential Complications

Let us now turn to two further complications that may prove problematic for the account of prayer as complaint that I have outlined here. A first group of concerns have to do with the claim, central to the view as I have expressed it, that such prayer is other-directed. Recall that, as I have characterized these two closely related forms of prayer, COMPLAINT-PRAYER and LAMENT-PRAYER both include the notion that prayer is directed towards God. That is, both forms of prayer require that the person praying intentionally directs their remarks towards a particular divine entity. But this may be disputed.[18] There are at least two ways in which this might be questioned that are salient for our purposes.

The first of these involves a claim about the elliptical nature of much prayer, which we have already touched upon. The worry is this. If the prayer is not clearly articulated, or not even articulated in words at all as a groan or a sigh, yet the context in which the prayer is uttered makes it clear that the intention of the person praying is to express a complaint or a lament, is it clear that this is God-directed? It is feasible to utter a form of words that sounds like a complaint or lament without directly addressing oneself to another person in so doing. It is even possible to utter an exclamation that has no addressee, such as the case of a colleague alone in the next room who suddenly cries out, 'Why is life so hard? Tell me why?' But it seems to me that such cases are normally better described as verbal ejaculations or exclamations, rather than forms of address. If the person in question is offering a complaint-prayer or lament-prayer, rather than some verbal or non-verbal exclamation, an important factor in determining whether what is uttered or performed is indeed a prayer, has to do with intention and whether the speech and/or act is other-directed. So the solitary colleague who cries out

---

[18]See, for example, Kleinschmidt, 'Atheistic Prayer'.

in the adjacent room, 'Why is life so hard? Tell me why?' intends to complain all right. But absent reasons for thinking the colleague is addressing some invisible entity, there is no obvious intention to address his complaint *to a particular individual or group*. It is a kind of exclamation rather than a form of address, rather like the cry, 'That's it! I've had enough!' which, when uttered, is not usually directed at anyone in particular. Normally, when someone utters such a verbal ejaculation or exclamation, no response is expected because no one in particular is addressed. This is quite unlike an exclamation that is unambiguously other-directed, such as the person who addresses his spouse with the questions, 'Why life is so hard? Tell me why?' Of course, someone could offer a complaint-prayer to something other than God – to an idol, say, or some other putative deity, or intermediary like an angel or saint as we have already indicated in introducing this topic. But in these cases there is clearly intentionality, and the prayer in question is still other-directed even if it falls on deaf ears, so to speak.

In each of the cases just mentioned, context is important. The solitary colleague in the room next door who utters the exclamation about the difficulty of life is not normally disposed to address himself to invisible entities, and may well be under a lot of pressure with writing deadlines and teaching responsibilities. So it would seem reasonable to assume his exclamation is not other-directed but a kind of verbal ejaculation. However, if you know his wife is sitting with him in the next room or you know that your colleague does have a habit of addressing himself to invisible entities, then things are rather different and we would normally treat his exclamation differently – as a form of address that is, most probably, other-directed.

Now, if the context is one in which it seems reasonable to assume the person is praying, and the person intends to offer a prayer of complaint, the salient issue is whether an elliptical or inarticulate or non-verbal complaint can count as a form of address rather than as a mere verbal ejaculation or exclamation. That does not seem to be particularly implausible. There are many everyday cases of such forms of address, such as the groan of a teenager upon being asked to do her chores. In which case, this does not appear to be an insurmountable objection to our analysis.

The second, closely related way in which the claim that complaints and laments are God-directed might be disputed has to do with the notion that someone could offer up such prayers without necessarily directing them towards the Almighty. For instance, it would seem that an atheist can offer prayers, including prayers of complaint or lament. A particularly powerful example of this can be found in Elie Wiesel's book, *Night*. There, in describing the death marches the SS soldiers made the Jewish concentration camp prisoners endure, Wiesel writes of a prayer he offered in the hope that he would not abandon his father as had happened on the marches to another character in the narrative, the elderly Rabbi Eliahu. 'And in spite of myself, a prayer formed inside me', writes Wiesel, 'a prayer to this God in whom I no longer believed. "Oh God, Master of the Universe, give me the strength never to do what Rabbi Eliahu's son has done."'[19] The form of the prayer reported here is not a complaint or lament. It is a request. Nevertheless, it is a powerful example of a prayer offered by someone who is, for all practical purposes, an atheist. Whatever analysis we give of such examples, there does seem to be a plausible way in which prayers of this form do count as being other-directed even if the person uttering them claims to be an atheist.[20]

Now, clearly a person may use a form of words without intending to direct them to a particular addressee. Rather like the common distinction between mention and use,[21] the idea here is that a person might utter a particular form of words that are a prayer without necessarily intending them to be directed towards God. In such cases I am inclined to think that the person in question is doing something analogous to mentioning the prayer rather than using it. It might be thought that the case of Wiesel rather complicates matters. But if a person is a professed atheist and yet still utters the prayer, it is difficult not to treat this as at least a form of address – in this case, a form of address directed towards an entity that one hopes exists given one's parlous circumstances, even if one is normally inclined to think the entity in question does not, in fact,

---

[19]Elie Wiesel, *Night: A Memoir* (New York: Hill and Wang, 2006 [1958]), 90.
[20]Setting to one side ironic or insincere ways in which someone might utter such prayers.
[21]The distinction is this: mention of a thing does not entail its use. Thus, if in a dispute about expletives a friend utters a particular expletive as an example of what she is talking about, her mentioning of the purported expletive does not count as an instance of her using the expletive to punctuate her speech.

exist. If that much is true, then it is not clear that this objection amounts to very much either.

Coda

But does this reflect how Christians have thought about prayer as petition and as complaint? I think it does. In fact, it seems to me that the default option on impetration (and complaint) often leads to a kind of *deformation* of prayer, which is avoided on the analysis I have offered here. Let me explain.

Lauren Winner has recently called attention to ways in which Christian practices like prayer can become deformed. She writes, 'Not all damage, but some damage, belongs to the form of the thing damaged, and is characteristic of it. Another way of naming a thing's characteristic damage is to say that the thing has been "deformed": Deformities, after all, are exactly that – related to (or, more pointedly, away from) a particular form.'[22] The deformity I have in mind here is not the two-way contingency characterization of prayer that drives the default option. The notion of a two-way contingency is not a deformation as such, though I have suggested that it might involve a mistaken way of thinking about the form of prayer given certain traditional, orthodox claims about the divine nature. No, the deformation of prayer I have in mind is not about how we characterize impetration or complaint or any other form of prayer, but about what we think about the upshot of such prayer. In a similar fashion, there is a question about how a sausage machine works to produce sausages from the ground meat fed into it. We might wonder about the processes that go on inside the machine. But whatever those processes are, the question of the outputs the machine generates – the sausages themselves – is a different matter. And, really, in the case of the sausage machine we mostly want to know: Will this machine make delicious sausages or not? Just so, in the matter of prayer there is an important question about the process itself. What do we *mean* by impetration? What do we *mean* by complaint? What is *going on* when we pray in these ways? But

---

[22]Lauren F. Winner, *The Dangers of Christian Practice: On Wayward Gifts, Characteristic Damage, and Sin* (New Haven: Yale University Press, 2019), 5.

there is also a distinct question about the outputs of such praying. What do we think such prayer *does*? What does it produce?

One residual worry about the default option is that such a way of thinking reduces prayer to something *superstitious*, making of it a kind of magical formula or spell that ought to be efficacious given the right form of words.[23] That is surely a deformation of Christian practice in Winner's sense of the term. But God is not a Jinn, and prayer (whatever its particular form) is not an incantation. Although the two-way contingency approach to prayer need not end up in a deformation of this sort, it is certainly a real worry with such a conception of prayer – a kind of liability built into such a conception of prayer. One of the benefits of the alternative I have been discussing here is that it does not have this consequence. Rather, prayers of impetration or complaint that presume prayer is fundamentally about bringing my own will into alignment with God's will foster a sense of dependence on God that, I suggest, better reflects the overall narrative of Scripture and common Christian practice.

---

[23]This issue is raised by Phillips, *The Concept of Prayer*, ch. 6.

BIBLIOGRAPHY

Abraham, William J. *Among the Ashes: On Death, Grief, and Hope.* Grand Rapids: Eerdmans, 2017.

Adams, Marilyn McCord. *Christ and Horrors: The Coherence of Christology.* Current Issues in Theology. Cambridge: Cambridge University Press, 2006.

Alston, William P. 'The Indwelling of the Holy Spirit', in Thomas V. Morris, ed. *Philosophy and the Christian Faith.* Notre Dame: University of Notre Dame Press, 1988, 121–50.

Anderson, James N. and Manata, Paul. 'Determined to Come Most Freely: Some Challenges for Libertarian Calvinism', *Journal of Reformed Theology* 11 (2017): 272–97.

Anizor, Uche. *Trinity and Humanity: An Introduction to the Theology of Colin Gunton.* Milton Keynes: Paternoster, 2016.

Anselm of Canterbury. *Anselm: Basic Writings*, trans. Thomas Williams. Indianapolis: Hackett Publishing, 2007.

Anselm of Canterbury. *S. Anselmi, Cantuariensis Archepiscopi, Opera Omnia, Tomus Primus et Tomus Secundus*, ed. F. S. Schmit. Stutgart: Friedrich Frommann Verlag, 1984 [1968].

Aquinas, Thomas. *Summa Theologica, 5 Vols*, trans. Brothers of the English Dominican Province. New York: Benziger Brothers, 1948 [1911].

Arcadi, James M. *An Incarnational Model of the Eucharist.* Current Issues in Theology. Cambridge: Cambridge University Press, 2018.

Arcadi, James M. 'Kryptic or Cryptic? The Divine Preconscious Model of the Incarnation as a Concrete-Nature Christology', *Neue Zeitschrift für Systematische Theologie und Religionsphilosophie* 58.2 (2016): 229–43..

Arcadi, James M. 'Recent Philosophical Work on the Doctrine of the Eucharist', *Philosophy Compass* 11.7 (2016): 402–12.

Armstrong, Brian G. *Calvinism and the Amyraut Heresy: Protestant Scholasticism and Humanism in Seventeenth Century France.* Madison, WI: University of Wisconsin Press, 1969.

Augustine, Aurelius. *City of God*, trans. Henry Bettenson. Harmondsworth: Penguin, 1984.

Augustine, Aurelius. *Confessions*, trans. Thomas Williams. Indianapolis: Hackett, 2019.

Augustine, Aurelius. *Enchiridion*, trans. Ernest Evans. London: SPCK, 1953.

Ayres, Lewis. 'Review of Review of Colin E. Gunton, *The Promise of Trinitarian Theology* (Edinburgh: T&T Clark, 1991)', *Journal of Theological Studies* 43.2 (1992): 780–2.

Beatrice, Pier Franco. *The Transmission of Sin: Augustine and the Pre-Augustinian Sources*. New York: Oxford University Press, 2013.

Berkouwer, G. C. *Sin*. Grand Rapids: Eerdmans, 1971.

Blacketer, Raymond. 'Definite Atonement in Historical Perspective', in Charles E. Hill and Frank A. James III, eds *The Glory of The Atonement: Biblical, Theological and Practical Perspectives*. Downers Grove, IL: IVP Academic, 2004, 304–23.

Brümmer, Vincent. *What Are We Doing When We Pray? On Prayer and the Nature of Faith*. Aldershot: Ashgate, 2008.

Calvin, John. *Institutes of the Christian Religion*, ed. John T. McNeill, trans. Ford Lewis Battles. Philadelphia: Westminster Press, 1960 [1559].

Calvin, John. *Instruction in Faith* (1537), trans. Paul T. Fuhrmann. Philadelphia: Westminster Press, 1969.

Cassidy, Jame J. 'T. F. Torrance's Realistic Soteriology Objectivism and the Elimination of Dualisms: Union with Christ in Current Perspective', *Mid-America Journal of Theology* 19 (2008): 165–94.

Catechism of the Catholic Church. New York: Doubleday, 1995.

Clifford, Alan C. *Atonement and Justification: English Evangelical Theology 1640–1790. An Evaluation*. Oxford: Oxford University Press, 1990.

Coleman, Andrew M. *A Dictionary of Psychology*. Oxford: Oxford University Press, 2001.

Collins, Robin. 'Evolution and Original Sin', in Keith B. Miller, ed. *Perspectives on an Evolving Creation*. Grand Rapids: Eerdmans, 2003, 469–501.

Congdon, David. 'Apokatastasis and Apostolicity: A Response to Oliver Crisp on the Question of Barth's Universalism', *Scottish Journal of Theology* 67.4 (2014): 464–80.

Couenhoven, Jesse. *Stricken by Sin, Cured by Christ: Agency, Necessity, and Culpability in Augustinian Theology*. New York: Oxford University Press, 2013.

Crisp, Oliver D. *Analyzing Doctrine: Toward A Systematic Theology*. Waco: Baylor University Press, 2019.

Crisp, Oliver D. *Deviant Calvinism: Broadening Reformed Theology*. Minneapolis: Fortress Press, 2014.

Crisp, Oliver D. *Divinity and Humanity: The Incarnation Reconsidered.*
Current Issues in Theology. Cambridge: Cambridge University Press,
2007.

Crisp, Oliver D. *God, Creation, and Salvation: Studies in Reformed
Theology.* London: T&T Clark, 2020.

Crisp, Oliver D. *God Incarnate: Explorations in Christology.* London:
T&T Clark, 2009.

Crisp, Oliver D. *Jonathan Edwards Among the Theologians.* Grand
Rapids: Eerdmans, 2015.

Crisp, Oliver D. *Jonathan Edwards and the Metaphysics of Sin.* Aldershot:
Ashgate, 2005.

Crisp, Oliver D. 'Jonathan Edwards on God's Relation to Creation',
Jonathan Edwards Studies 8.1 (2018): 2–16.

Crisp, Oliver D. 'Meticulous Providence', in Oliver D. Crisp and
Fred Sanders, eds *Divine Action and Providence: Explorations in
Constructive Dogmatics.* Proceedings of the Seventh Los Angeles
Theology Conference, 2019. Grand Rapids: Zondervan Academic, 2019.

Crisp, Oliver D. 'On Original Sin', *International Journal of Systematic
Theology* 17.3 (2015): 252–66.

Crisp, Oliver D. 'On the Vicarious Humanity of Christ', *International
Journal of Systematic Theology* 21.3 (2019): 235–50.

Crisp, Oliver D. 'Original Sin and Atonement', in Thomas P. Flint
and Michael C. Rea, eds *The Oxford Handbook of Philosophical
Theology.* Oxford: Oxford University Press, 2009, 430–51.

Crisp, Oliver D. *Retrieving Doctrine: Essays in Reformed Theology.*
Downers Grove, IL: IVP Academic, 2011.

Crisp, Oliver D. *Revisioning Christology: Theology in the Reformed
Tradition.* Abingdon: Routledge, 2016 [2011].

Crisp, Oliver D. *Saving Calvinism: Expanding the Reformed Tradition.*
Downers Grove, IL: IVP Academic, 2016.

Crisp, Oliver D. *The Word Enfleshed: Exploring the Person and Work of
Christ.* Grand Rapids: Baker Academic, 2016.

Dabney, Robert. *Lectures in Theology.* Edinburgh: Banner of Truth, 1985
[1871].

Davenant, John A. 'Dissertation on the Death of Christ' in *An Exposition
of the Epistle of St Paul to the Colossians*, 2 vols. London: Hamilton,
Adams, and Co., 1832.

Davidson Ivor J. and Rae, Murray A. eds *The God of Salvation:
Soteriology in Theological Perspective.* Aldershot: Ashgate, 2011.

Davies, Brian. *Introduction to the Philosophy of Religion, Third Edition.*
Oxford: Oxford University Press, 2004 [1982].

Davison, Scott A. *Petitionary Prayer: A Philosophical Investigation.*
Oxford: Oxford University Press, 2017.

Edwards, Jonathan. *A Jonathan Edwards Reader*, eds John E. Smith, Harry S. Stout, and Kenneth P. Minkema. New Haven: Yale University Press, 1995.

Edwards, Jonathan. *Ethical Writings: The Works of Jonathan Edwards*, vol. 8, ed. Paul Ramsey. New Haven: Yale University Press, 1989.

Edwards, Jonathan. *Freedom of the Will, The Works of Jonathan Edwards*, vol. 1, ed. Paul Ramsey. New Haven: Yale University Press, 1957.

Edwards, Jonathan. *The 'Miscellanies': Nos. a–z, aa–zz, 1–500, The Works of Jonathan Edwards Vol. 13*, ed. Thomas A. Schafer. New Haven: Yale University Press, 1994.

Edwards, Jonathan. *Original Sin, The Works of Jonathan Edwards,* vol. 3, ed. Clyde A. Holbrook. New Haven: Yale University Press, 1970.

Edwards, Jonathan. *Religious Affections, The Works of Jonathan Edwards,* vol. 2 ed. John E. Smith. New Haven: Yale University Press, 1959.

Edwards, Jonathan. *Writings on the Trinity, Grace and Faith, The Works of Jonathan Edwards*, vol. 21, ed. Sang Hyun Lee. New Haven: Yale University Press, 2002.

Ferguson, John Pelagius. *A Historical and Theological Study*. Cambridge: W. Heffer and Sons, 1956.

Fergusson, David. *The Providence of God, A Polyphonic Approach*. Cambridge: Cambridge University Press, 2018.

Flint, Thomas P. *Divine Providence: The Molinist Account*. Ithaca: Cornell University Press, 1998.

Frankfurt, Harry J. *The Importance of What We Care About: Philosophical Essays*. Cambridge: Cambridge University Press, 1998.

Gattiss, Lee. *For Us and For Our Salvation: 'Limited Atonement' in the Bible, Doctrine, History, and Ministry*. Latimer Studies 78. London: The Latimer Trust, 2012.

Geach, P. T. *God and the Soul*. London: Routledge & Kegan Paul, 1969.

Gerrish, B. A. 'The Lord's Supper in the Reformed Confessions', *Theology Today* July (1966): 224–43.

Godfrey, Robert. 'Reformed Thought on the Extent of the Atonement to 1618', *Westminster Theological Journal* 37 (1975): 133–71.

Grant, W. Matthews. 'Divine Causality and Libertarian Freedom', in Kevin Time and Daniel Speak, eds *Free Will and Theism: Connections, Contingencies, and Concerns*. Oxford: Oxford University Press, 2016, 214–33.

Grant, W. Matthews. *Free Will and God's Universal Causality: The Dual Sources Account*. Bloomsbury Studies in Philosophy of Religion. London: Routledge, 2020.

Green, Bradley G. *Colin Gunton and the Failure of Augustine: The Theology of Colin Gunton in the Light of Augustine.* Cambridge: James Clarke & Co., 2012.

Gunton, Colin E. *Act and Being: Toward a Theology of the Divine Attributes.* Grand Rapids: Eerdmans, 2002.

Gunton, Colin E. *Christ and Creation. The Didsbury Lectures.* Grand Rapids: Eerdmans, 1992.

Gunton, Colin E. *Father, Son and Holy Spirit: Toward a Fully Trinitarian Theology.* London: T&T Clark, 2003.

Gunton, Colin E. *The Christian Faith: An Introduction to Christian Doctrine.* Oxford: Blackwell, 2002.

Gunton, Colin E. *Theology Through the Theologians: Selected Essays, 1972–1995.* London: T&T Clark/Continuum, 1996.

Gunton, Colin E. *The One, The Three and the Many: God, Creation and the Culture of Modernity. The Bampton Lectures 1992.* Cambridge: Cambridge University Press, 1993.

Gunton, Colin E. 'Two Dogmas Revisited: Edward Irving's Christology', *Scottish Journal of Theology* 41.3 (1988): 359–76.

Gunton, Colin E. *Yesterday and Today: A Study of Continuities in Christology.* London: Dartman, Longman, and Todd, 1983.

Habets, Myk. 'Reformed Theosis? A Response to Gannon Murphy', *Theology Today* 65 (2009): 489–98.

Habets, Myk. 'Spirit Christology: The Future of Christology?' in Myk Habets, ed. *Third Article Theology: A Pneumatological Dogmatics.* Minneapolis: Fortress Press, 2016, 207–32.

Habets, Myk. *Theosis in the Theology of Thomas Torrance.* Ashgate New Critical Thinking in Religion, Theology and Biblical Studies. Abingdon: Ashgate, 2009.

Habets, Myk and Grow, Robert, eds *Evangelical Calvinism: Essays Resourcing the Continuing Reformation of the Church.* Eugene: Wipf and Stock, 2012.

Habets, Myk and Grow, Robert. *Evangelical Calvinism, Vol. 2: Dogmatics and Devotion.* Eugene: Wipf and Stock, 2017.

Hallonsten, Gösta. 'Theosis in Recent Research: A Renewal of Interest and a Need for Clarity', in Michael J. Christensen and Jeffery A. Wittung, eds *Partakers of the Divine Nature: The History and Development of Deification in the Christian Tradition.* Grand Rapids: Baker Academic, 2007, 281–93.

Harding, Matthew S. 'Atonement Theory Revisited: Calvin, Beza, and Amyraut on the Extent of the Atonement', *Perichoresis* 11.1 (2013): 49–73.

Harvey, Lincoln, ed. *The Theology of Colin Gunton.* London: T&T Clark/Bloomsbury, 2010.

Haslanger, Sally. 'Persistence Through Time', in Michael J. Loux and Dean W. Zimmerman, eds *The Oxford Handbook of Metaphysics*. Oxford: Oxford University Press, 2003, 315–54.

Haykin, Michael A. G. and Jones, Mark, eds *Drawn into Controversie: Reformed Theological Diversity and Debates Within Seventeenth-Century British Puritanism. Reformed Historical Theology*, vol. 17. Göttingen: Vandenhoeck and Ruprecht, 2011.

Helm, Paul. 'Calvin, Indefinite Language, and Definite Atonement', in David Gibson and Jonathan Gibson, eds *From Heaven He Came and Sought Her: Definite Atonement in Historical, Biblical, Theological, and Pastoral Perspective*. Wheaton: Crossway, 2013, 97–120.

Helm, Paul. 'Omnipotence and Change', *Philosophy* 51 (1976): 454–61.

Helm, Paul. 'Regeneration and the Spirit', in Marc Cortez, Joshua R. Farris, and S. Mark Hamilton, eds *Being Saved: Explorations in Human Salvation*. London: SCM Press, 2019, 246–61.

Heppe, Heinrich. *Reformed Dogmatics*, trans. G. T. Thomson. London: Collins, 1950.

Hoekema, Anthony A. *Created in God's Image*. Grand Rapids: Eerdmans, 1986.

Holcomb, Justin S. and Johnson, David A. eds *Christian Theologies of the Sacraments: A Comparative Introduction*. New York: New York University Press, 2017.

Hudson, Hud. *The Fall and Hypertime*. Oxford: Oxford University Press, 2014.

Hugh of St Victor. *De virtue orandi* in J. P. Migne, ed. *Patrologiae Cursus Completus. Series Latina* 176 (1854): 981–2.

Hunsinger, George. *The Eucharist and Ecumenism: Let Us Keep the Feast*. Current Issues in Theology. Cambridge: Cambridge University Press, 2008.

Hunter, Justus H. *If Adam Had Not Sinned: The Reason for the Incarnation from Anselm to Scotus*. Washington, DC: Catholic University of America Press, 2020.

Hutchinson, George P. *The Problem of Original Sin in American Presbyterian Theology*. Biblical and Theological Studies Series. N.P.: Presbyterian and Reformed Co., 1972.

Jacobs, Alan. *Original Sin: A Cultural History*. San Francisco: HarperOne, 2008.

Johnson, Marcus Peter. *One with Christ: An Evangelical Theology of Salvation*. Wheaton: Crossway, 2013.

Jowers, Dennis, ed. *Four Views on Divine Providence*. Grand Rapids: Zondervan, 2011.

Kennedy, Kevin Dixon. *Union with Christ and the Extent of the Atonement in Calvin*. Studies in Biblical Literature. Bern: Peter Lang, 2002.

Kittle, Simon. 'Grace and Free Will: Quiescence and Control', *Journal of Analytic Theology* 3 (2015): 89–108.

Kleinschmidt, Shieva. 'Atheistic Prayer', *Faith and Philosophy* 34.2 (2017): 152–75.

Kroll, Kimberley. 'Indwelling without the Indwelling Holy Spirit: A Critique of Ray Yeo's Modified Account', *Journal of Analytic Theology* 7 (2019): 124–41.

Kroll, Kimberley. 'The Condescension of the Spirit: The Nature of the Relation of the Indwelling Holy Spirit', PhD dissertation, University of St Andrews, 2020.

Lampe, Geoffrey. *God as Spirit: The Bampton Lectures 1976.* Oxford: Oxford University Press, 1977.

Loke, Andrew Ter Ern. *A Kryptic Model of the Incarnation.* Ashgate New Critical Thinking in Religion, Theology and Biblical Studies. Aldershot: Ashgate, 2014.

Loke, Andrew Ter Ern. 'On the Divine Preconscious Model of the Incarnation and Concrete-Nature Christology: A Reply to James Arcadi', *Neue Zeitschrift für Systematische Theologie und Religionsphilosophie* 59.1 (2017): 26–33.

Loke, Andrew Ter Ern. 'Sanday's Christology Revisited', *Journal of Theological Studies* 63.1 (2012): 187–97.

Lombard, Peter. *The Sentences, Book 3: On the Incarnation of the Word,* trans. Guilo Silano. Toronto: Pontifical Institute of Medieval Studies, 2008.

Louth, Andrew. *Introducing Eastern Orthodox Theology.* Downers Grove, IL: IVP Academic, 2013.

Mackie, J. L. 'Clauses and Conditions', *American Philosophical Quarterly* 2 (1965): 245–64.

Macleod, Donald. 'Original Sin in Reformed Theology', in Hans Madueme and Michael Reeves, eds *Adam, the Fall, and Original Sin: Theological, Biblical, and Scientific Perspectives.* Grand Rapids: Baker Academic, 2014, 129–46.

Matava, R. J. *Divine Causality and Human Free Choice: Domingo Báñez, Physical Premotion and the Controversy De Auxiliis Revisited.* Studies in Intellectual History, vol. 252. Leiden: Brill, 2016.

McCall, Thomas H. *Against God and Nature: The Doctrine of Sin.* Foundations of Evangelical Theology. Wheaton: Crossway, 2019.

McCormack, Bruce. 'The One, The Three and The Many: In Memory of Colin Gunton', *Cultural Encounters* Summer (2005): 13–14.

McFarland, Ian A. *In Adam's Fall: A Meditation on the Christian Doctrine of Original Sin.* Oxford: Wiley-Blackwell, 2010.

McNall, Joshua A. *Free Corrector: Colin Gunton and the Legacy of Augustine.* Minneapolis: Fortress Press, 2015.

Milton, Anthony, ed. *The British Delegation and the Synod of Dort (1618–1619)*. Church of England Record Society, vol. 13. Woodbridge: Boydell Press, 2005.

Moberly, R. W. L. *Old Testament Theology: Reading the Hebrew Bible as Christian Scripture*. Grand Rapids: Baker Academic, 2013.

Molina, Louis de. *On Divine Foreknowledge: Part IV of the Concordia*, ed. and trans. Alfred J. Freddoso. Ithaca: Cornell University Press, 1988.

Molnar, Paul D. *Thomas F. Torrance: Theologian of the Trinity*. Aldershot: Ashgate, 2009.

Moore, Jonathan D. *English Hypothetical Universalism: John Preston and the Softening of Reformed Theology*. Grand Rapids: Eerdmans, 2007.

Morimoto, Anri. *Jonathan Edwards and the Catholic View of Salvation*. University Park: Pennsylvania State University Press, 1995.

Muller, Richard A. *Calvin and the Reformed Tradition: On the Work of Christ and the Order of Salvation*. Grand Rapids: Baker Academic, 2012.

Muller, Richard A. *Divine Will and Human Choice: Freedom, Contingency, and Necessity in Early Modern Reformed Thought*. Grand Rapids: Baker Academic, 2017.

Murray, John. *The Imputation of Adam's Sin*. Grand Rapids: Eerdmans, 1959.

Myers, Benjamin. 'The Patristic Doctrine of Atonement', in Oliver D. Crisp and Fred Sanders, eds *Locating Atonement: Explorations in Constructive Dogmatics*. Grand Rapids: Zondervan Academic, 2015, 71–88.

Nazianzus, Gregory. *Letter to Cledonius the Priest Against Apollinarius* in *On God and Christ: The Five Theological Orations and Two Letters to Cledonius*, trans. Frederick Williams and Lionel Wickham. Crestwood: St. Vladimir's Seminary Press, 2002.

Nimmo, Paul T. and Fergusson, David A. S., eds *The Cambridge Companion to Reformed Theology*. Cambridge: Cambridge University Press, 2016.

Ott, Ludwig. *Fundamentals of Catholic Dogma*, trans. John Bastible. Rockford, IL: Tan Books, 1955.

Owen, John. 'Pneumatalogia', in William Goold, ed. *The Works of John Owen*, vol. 3. Edinburgh: Banner of Truth, 1966 [1862].

Paul, L. A. *Transformative Experience*. Oxford: Oxford University Press, 2014.

Pelagius. *Pelagius's Commentary on St Paul's Epistle to the Romans*. Oxford Early Christian Studies Series, trans. Theodore de Bruyn. Oxford: Oxford University Press, 1993.

Peppiatt, Lucy. 'Life in the Spirit: Christ's and Ours', in Oliver D. Crisp and Fred Sanders, eds *The Christian Doctrine of Humanity*:

Explorations in Constructive Dogmatics. Grand Rapids: Zondervan Academic, 2018, 166–82.

Phillips, D. Z. *The Concept of Prayer*. London: Routledge & Kegan Paul, 1965.

Porter, Steven L. and Rickabaugh, Brandon. 'The Sanctifying Work of the Holy Spirit: Revisiting Alston's Interpersonal Model', *Journal of Analytic Theology* 6 (2018): 112–30.

Preciado, Michael Patrick A. *Reformed View of Freedom: The Compatibility of Guidance Control and Reformed Theology*. Eugene, OR: Pickwick Publications, 2019.

Rae, Murray. 'Gunton on Atonement', in Andrew Picard, Murray Rae, and Myk Habets, eds *T&T Clark Companion of Colin Gunton*. London: T&T Clark, 2021, ch. 6.

Rea, Michael C. 'Protest, Worship, and the Deformation of Prayer', in Michael C. Rea, ed. *Essays in Analytic Theology*, 2 vols. Oxford Studies in Analytic Theology. Oxford: Oxford University Press, 2020.

Rea, Michael C. *The Hiddenness of God*. Oxford: Oxford University Press, 2018.

Rea, Michael C. 'The Metaphysics of Original Sin', in Peter van Inwagen and Dean Zimmerman, eds *Persons: Human and Divine*. Oxford: Oxford University Press, 2007, 319–56.

Rees, B. R. ed. and trans. *The Letters of Pelagius and His Followers*. Woodbridge: Boydell Press, 1991.

Romanides, John S. *The Ancestral Sin*. Ridgewood, NJ: Zephyr Publishing, 1998.

Rogers, Katherin A. *Anselm on Freedom*. Oxford: Oxford University Press, 2008.

Rogers, Katherin A. *Freedom and Self-Creation: Anselmian Libertarianism*. Oxford: Oxford University Press, 2015.

Sanday, William. *Christology and Personality*. New York: Oxford University Press, 1911.

Sanday, William. *Christology and Personality, Containing I. Christologies Ancient and Modern II. Personality in Christ and in Ourselves*. Oxford: Oxford University Press, 1911.

Schaff, Philip. *Creeds of Christendom with a History and Critical Notes. Vol. 1. The History of the Creeds*. New York: Harper and Brothers, 1877.

Schmeman, Alexander. *The Eucharist*. Crestwood: St Vladimir's Seminary Press, 1988.

Shedd, William G. T. *A Critical and Doctrinal Commentary on the Epistle of St. Paul to The Romans*. Eugene, OR: Wipf and Stock, 2001 [1879].

Shuster, Marguerite. *The Fall and Sin: What We Have Become as Sinners*. Grand Rapids: Eerdmans, 2004.

Spence, Alan. *Incarnation and Inspiration: John Owen and the Coherence of Christology*. London: T&T Clark/Continuum, 2007.

Stephens, W. P. *Zwingli, An Introduction to His Thought*. Oxford: Oxford University Press, 1992.

Stewart, Kenneth J. *10 Myths About Calvinism: Recovering the Breadth of the Reformed Tradition*. Downers Grove: IVP Academic 2011.

Stout, Harry S. *The New England Soul: Preaching and Religious Culture in Colonial New England. 25th Anniversary Edition*. New York: Oxford University Press, 2012 [1986].

Strong, Augustus. *Systematic Theology [3 Vols. in 1]*. Valley Forge, PA: Judson Press, 1907.

Stump, J. B. and Meister, Chad, eds *Original Sin and the Fall: Five Views*. Downers Grove, IL: IVP Academic, 2020.

Stump, Eleonore. *Aquinas*. New York: Routledge 2003.

Stump, Eleonore. 'Augustine on Free Will', in Stump and Norman Kretzmann, eds *The Cambridge Companion to Augustine*. Cambridge: Cambridge University Press, 2001, 124–47.

Swinburne, Richard. *Responsibility and Atonement*. Oxford: Oxford University Press, 1989.

The Constitution of The Presbyterian Church (USA) Part I: Book of Confessions. Louisville: Office of the General Assembly, 2004.

Thomas, G. Michael. *The Extent of the Atonement: A Dilemma for Reformed Theology from Calvin to the Consensus (1536–1675)*. Studies in Christian History and Thought. Milton Keynes: Paternoster, 1997.

Timpe, Kevin. *Free Will in Philosophical Theology*. London: Bloomsbury Academic, 2014.

Timpe, Kevin. *Free Will: Sourcehood and Its Alternatives*, Second Edition. London: Bloomsbury Academic, 2013.

Torrance, T. F. *Atonement: The Person and Work of Christ*, ed. R. T. Walker. Downer Grove, IL: IVP Academic, 2009.

Torrance, T. F. *Incarnation*. Downers Grove, IL: IVP Academic, 2009.

Torrance, T. F. *Karl Barth: Biblical and Evangelical Theologian*. Edinburgh: T & T Clark, 1990.

Torrance, T. F. *Space, Time, and Resurrection*. Grand Rapids: Eerdmans, 1976.

Torrance, T. F. 'The Atonement. The Singularity of Christ and the Finality of the Cross: The Atonement and the Moral Order', in Nigel M. de S. Cameron, ed. *Universalism and the Doctrine of Hell*. Carlisle: Paternoster, and Grand Rapids: Baker, 1992, 225–56.

Torrance, T. F. 'The Goodness and Dignity of Man in the Christian Tradition', *Modern Theology* 4 (1988): 309–22.

Torrance, T. F. *The Mediation of Christ*. Colorado Springs: Helmers and Howard, 1992 [1984].

Torrance, T. F. *Theology in Reconstruction*. Grand Rapids: Eerdmans, 1996.

Torrance, T. F. 'Universalism or Election?' *Scottish Journal of Theology* 2 (1949): 310–18.

Tugwell, Simon. 'Prayer, Humpty Dumpty and Thomas Aquinas', in Brian Davies, ed. *Language, Meaning, and God: Essays in Honor of Herbert McCabe*. London: Geoffrey Chapman, 1988, 24–50.

van Asselt, Willem J., Bac, J. Martin, and te Velde, Roelf T., eds *Reformed Thought on Freedom: The Concept of Free Choice in Early Modern Reformed Theology*. Texts and Studies in Reformation and Post-Reformation Thought. Grand Rapids: Baker Academic, 2010.

van Driel, Edwin Christian. *Incarnation Anyway: Arguments for Supralapsarian Christology*. New York: Oxford University Press, 2008.

van Inwagen, Peter. *An Essay on Free Will*. Oxford: Oxford University Press, 1983.

van Kuiken, Jerome. *Christ's Humanity in Current and Ancient Controversy: Fallen or Not?* London: T&T Clark, 2017.

van Stam, F. P. *The Controversy Over the Theology of Saumur, 1635–1650: Disrupting Debates Among the Huguenots in Complicated Circumstances*. Amsterdam: APA-Holland University Press, 1988.

Vanhoozer, Kevin J. 'The Origin of Paul's Soteriology: Election, Incarnation, and Union with Christ in Ephesians 1:4 (with Special Reference to Evangelical Calvinism)', in Benjamin E. Reynolds, Brian Lugioyo, and Kevin J. Vanhoozer, eds *Reconsidering the Relationship between Biblical and Systematic Theology in the New Testament: Essays by Theologians and New Testament Scholars*. Tübingen: Mohr Siebeck, 2014, 177–211.

Visser, Sandra and Williams, Thomas. *Anselm*. Great Medieval Thinkers. Oxford: Oxford University Press, 2008.

Wenham, Gordon J. *Psalms as Torah: Reading Biblical Song Ethically*. Grand Rapids: Baker Academic, 2012.

Wesley, John. *John Wesley*, ed. Albert Outler. New York: Oxford University Press, 1964.

Wiesel, Elie. *Night: A Memoir*. New York: Hill and Wang, 2006 [1958].

Wiley, Tatha. *Original Sin: Origins, Development, Contemporary Meanings*. Mahwah, NJ: Paulist Press, 2002.

Williams, N. P. *The Ideas of the Fall and of Original Sin*. London: Longmans, Green, and Co., 1927.

Williams, Patricia A. *Doing Without Adam and Eve: Sociobiology and Original Sin*. Minneapolis: Augsburg Fortress, 2001.

Winner, Lauren F. *The Dangers of Christian Practice: On Wayward Gifts, Characteristic Damage, and Sin*. New Haven: Yale University Press, 2019.

Woznicki, Christopher G. 'Is Prayer Redundant? Calvin and the Early
    Reformers on the Problem of Petitionary Prayer', *The Journal of the
    Evangelical Theological Society* 60.2 (2017): 333–48.
Woznicki, Christopher G. 'Peter Martyr Vermigli's Account of Petitionary
    Prayer: A Reformation Alternative to Contemporary Two-Way
    Contingency Accounts', *Philosophia Christi* 20.1 (2018): 119–37.
Woznicki, Christopher G. 'The One and the Many: The Metaphysics of
    Human Nature in T. F. Torrance's Doctrine of Atonement', *Journal of
    Reformed Theology* 12 (2018): 103–26.
Yeo, Ray. 'Towards a Model of Indwelling: A Conversation with Jonathan
    Edwards and William Alston', *Journal of Analytic Theology* 2 (2014):
    210–37.
Zwingli, Ulrich. *On Providence and Other Essays*, ed. Samuel Macauley
    Jackson. Durham, NC: Labyrinth Press, 1983 [1922].

NAME INDEX

Abraham, William 194
Adams, Marilyn McCord 165, 170, 172–6
Alston, William 135, 149, 151
Amyraut, Moise, *see* Amyraldism
Anderson, James 14
Anselm of Canterbury 9–10, 13, 29–30, 83, 97, 118
Apostle Paul 97, 109, 120, 134, 138, 144, 174, 180, 188, 192
Aquinas, Thomas 139
Arcadi, James 53, 57–62, 165–77
Athanasius 83, 109, 118
Augustine of Hippo 27, 30–1, 33, 67, 106, 134–8, 167, 192

Baird, Samuel 38
Barth, Karl 74, 102, 109, 112, 132

Calvin, John 91, 138, 144, 147, 150, 168, 187
Cameron, John 89
Cappadocians 67–8
Cassidy, James 124–5
Cranmer, Thomas 169, 171

Dabney, Robert 38
Davenant, John 89, 94–5

Edwards, Jonathan 38, 40–1, 43, 135, 138–43, 145, 147–8, 152–5, 157–8

Farel, William 91
Fergusson, David 11–12
Frankfurt, Harry 147–8

Gerrish, Brian 165
Grant, W. Matthews 20–1, 23
Gunton, Colin E. 64–82

Habets, Myk 130
Hunsinger, George 165, 170–2, 174–5, 177

Ignatius of Antioch 83
Irenaeus 109, 118
Irving, Edward 73, 77

Jenson, Robert 67
John the Baptist 136, 158

Kant, Immanuel 24
Kroll, Kimberley 135

Lampe, Geoffrey 72–3
Landis, Robert 38
Loke, Andrew 53–63
Lombard, Peter 93–4, 98
Louth, Andrew 131
Luther, Martin 163

Macki, J. L. 18–19, 23
Manata, Paul 14
Mary, Mother of God 28, 115
Maximus the Confessor 79
Moore, Andrew 94

Muller, Richard 94
Myers, Benjamin 115

Owen, John 73

Paul, Laurie 134, 136
Pelagius 24, 47
Philips, D. Z. 192
Placaeus, Josue 45
Preston, John 89, 94–5

Rea, Michael 190–1

Sanday, William 54, 56–7
Sanders, Mister, *see* Winnie the Pooh
Schmemann, Alexander 171
Scotus, Duns 69
Shedd, William 38
Spence, Alan 81–2
Strong, Augustus 38
Stump, Eleonore 146–7, 149

Thornwell, James 38
Tibbs, Paraskevè 69

Tigger 42, *see also* Sanders, Mister
Torrance, Thomas F. 68, 101–2, 108–33, 136, 157–8

Ussher, James of Armagh 89, 94–5

Van Inwagen, Peter 6
van Kuiken, Jerome 114
Vermigli, Martin 171
von Harnack, Adolf 67

Weisel, Elie 197
Wenham, Gordon 189
Wesley, John 137–8
Winner, Lauren 198–9
Winnie the Pooh, *see* Tigger
Woznicki, Christopher 110, 116–17, 123

Yeo, Ray 135, 152–4, 157, 159

Zwingli, Huldrych 25, 28–32, 46–9, 163, 167–8

SUBJECT INDEX

abstract nature   58–9, 61–2,
    115–18, 121–2
adoptionism   60
Amyraldism   89–91, 94–6, 99
Anglican tradition   94–6,
    98–101, 103–4, 107–8, 111,
    163, 165, 176
Apollinarianism   59, 79
assumption, *see* Christology,
    vicarious humanity
atonement   87, 89–93, 95–100,
    103–11, 113–15, 118–19,
    121–2, 125–32, 143–4, 149,
    154, 157–8

Calvinism, *see* Kobayashi Maru;
    reformed tradition
Chalcedon   54, 60, 63, 81
Christology
    anhypostasia   73, 116
    dyothelitism (*see* Christology,
        two wills)
    fallen nature of Christ   66, 74,
        77, 84, 109, 114–15, 118,
        121–2, 129
    hypostatic union   53, 56, 71,
        121, 129–30, 172–8, 180–1
    incarnation   53–63, 68, 71–8,
        108, 113–15, 117–19, 121,
        123–5, 128–30, 132, 172,
        180
    kenosis   54, 63, 66, 70–1, 84
    monothelitism   79–80, 83
    Spirit Christology   66, 68,
        72–4, 76, 84, 153–4, 163

three-part Christology   55, 59,
    61–3, 173
two-minds   53–4, 56–7, 60,
    62
two-natures   26, 54, 71, 79,
    81–4
two wills   66, 79–81, 83–4
union with Christ   41–3,
    114–19, 122–4, 129–32,
    142, 152–8, 168, 170–2,
    174, 177–80
vicarious humanity   108–10,
    113–15, 118–21, 123–5,
    128–30, 132, 157–8
Word   56–63, 116–17, 172,
    176
communication idiomatum
    71–2
communion   44–5, 120–1, 140–1,
    148–9, 152–8, 163–9, 171,
    175, 181–7, 190
compatibilism   3, 7, 11, 13, 17,
    22
Composite Humanity   43–4
concrete nature, *see* particular
    nature
concurrence   4–5, 12, 17–23
consciousness   54–62
Constantinople III   79
Council of Trent   26

deification, *see* theosis
determinism   3–4, 6–7, 11–14,
    16, 18, 22, 95–6, 100,
    120

divine
  action 19–22, 36–7, 71–9,
    82, 95, 98, 119, 128, 140–3,
    147–8, 151–8, 192
  agency 6, 78–9, 143, 147,
    149, 154, 158, 176, 180
  life 20, 63, 126–30, 133,
    141–2, 149, 151, 154–7
  love 119, 126–7, 129, 139,
    155–6, 192, 194
  nature 54, 56–9, 79–80, 116,
    130, 173, 192, 198
  Preconscious Model 53–8, 63
  simplicity 63, 152
  Subconscious Model 54, 57
  will 53–9, 61–3, 185, 193,
    194, 199
divinization, see theosis

Eastern Orthodox tradition
    67–8, 112–13, 163, 171
election 43, 92–3, 95, 97–8, 100,
    104–5, 107, 111, 125–6,
    132
eucharist
  Canterbury parallelism 168–70
  consubstantiation 166, 179
  corporeal presence 166–9,
    171–3, 175–9, 181
  Genevan
    instrumentalism 168–70
  hypostatic impanation 165,
    172–6, 181
  instrumental impanation 165,
    174–6
  local presence 175–9
  memorialism 167–70
  no non-normal presence
    166–7, 172, 177–8
  pneumatic presence 166, 169,
    172, 177–8
  sacramental impanation 165
  Saint Andrean impanation
    176–80

transelementation 165,
    170–1, 174–5
transubstantiation 166, 171,
    179
Evangelical Calvinism 90, 102,
    108–11

faith 95, 98, 100–1, 103–8,
    122–5, 132–4, 157, 168,
    180
federalism 32–8, 42, 47–8
first-order desire 147–8

governance 5, 12

Holy Spirit 43, 66–8, 72–82,
    121–3, 134–8, 141–4,
    147–58, 163, 168–9, 171,
    176–7, 180
human
  agency 4, 9, 11, 13–18, 20,
    36, 45–6, 75, 79, 99, 101,
    120, 144–6, 149, 158, 192
  free choice (see human, free
    will)
  free will 3, 7–13, 15–23, 47,
    82, 145
  nature 30, 39–43, 54–60,
    70–6, 79–80, 97, 114–19,
    121–3, 128–30, 140–3, 145,
    158, 172–5, 177–9

identity 150
image 45, 119–21, 131–2, 143,
    148, 150, 158
incompatibilism 8–13
indwelling 67, 72, 75–6, 134,
    136, 140–1, 148–9, 151–5,
    158, 170
infusion 135–6, 138, 141,
    149–58

justification 109–10, 113, 115,
    121–6, 129, 132

Kobayashi Maru, *see* Calvinism

Libertarian Calvinism   3–5,
    11–14, 16–17, 20–3
libertarianism   2–4, 8–11, 14–15,
    17, 19
Lutheran tradition   163, 166

meticulous providence   4–5,
    11–14, 17, 19–20, 22–3,
    99
monergism   144, 148–51, 158
moral responsibility   3, 7–11,
    13, 15–18, 101, 105, 146–7
mysterianism   113, 127–8, 132

Nestorianism   59–60, 62, 79–82
Nicene   26

Occam's Razor   99
omnipresence   71, 163
omniscience   192–3

participation   42–3, 115–16,
    121–33, 142–3, 148–9,
    151, 154–8, 167, 171,
    174
particular nature   55–6, 58–63,
    115–18, 122, 125, 172
pelagianism, *see* Pelagius
perichoresis, *see* indwelling
person   5, 29, 33, 54, 56, 60,
    66–71, 73–84, 97, 104–5,
    114, 116–17, 119, 130, 132,
    140, 147–8, 150–2, 154,
    156, 172, 174, 179–80, 182,
    195–7
personhood, *see* person
prayer   80, 167, 182–91,
    193–9
    atheistic   185, 197
    complaint   184–99
    deformation   185, 198–9
    elliptical   188, 195–6

impetration (*see* prayer,
    intercession)
intercession   182–5, 191–4,
    199
lament   186–7, 189–91,
    195–7
petition (*see* prayer,
    intercession)
predestination, *see* determinism
preservation   5, 12

quiescence   147, 149, 158

reconciliation, *see* atonement
Reformed tradition   3–5, 11–14,
    17, 20–2, 24–5, 29–33, 38,
    45–6, 49, 64, 87, 92, 94,
    99, 101–2, 106–8, 111–13,
    119, 122, 130, 132, 135,
    139, 143–4, 149, 154, 157,
    163–70, 172–3, 176–9,
    181
regeneration   123, 134–41,
    143–5, 148–55, 157–8
relation   20–1, 45, 68–9, 71–2,
    77, 141, 150–1, 153, 156,
    170, 175, 179
representationalism, *see*
    federalism
resurrection   43, 119, 123, 129
Roman Catholic tradition   26,
    79, 163

salvation, *see* soteriology
Salvation Army   167
sanctification   114, 120, 122,
    136, 142
second-order desire   147–8
sensus divinitatis   138,
    140–1, 148, 151, 154,
    156, 158
sin   24–9, 74, 77, 99, 103–6,
    114–15, 125, 140, 144–5,
    147, 150–1, 155

culpability   26, 28–33, 35–6,
    45–7, 49, 114–15, 144–5,
    147–8, 180
guilt (*see* sin, culpability)
noetic effects   145, 147–8,
    151
original   24–9, 31–7, 39–42,
    44–8, 78, 114–15, 144
primal (*see* sin, original)
realism   33, 37–42, 44, 47–8
transmission of   25, 27, 32–9,
    41–5, 47–8
Society of Friends   167
soteriology   18, 27, 48, 92–8,
    100–7, 109–19, 124–9,
    131–3, 141–7, 151–9, 174
spiritual sense, *see sensus
    divinitatis*
substance dualism   55
sufficiency-efficiency
    distinction   93–5, 98, 100,
    126
Synod of Dort   87, 89

theistic personalism   63
theosis   112–13, 129–32,
    142–3, 148, 152, 154,
    156–8
Thomism   4, 17, 20, 68, 72, 141,
    146, 149
Trinity   26, 60, 65, 67–9, 75–6,
    78, 80, 83–4, 93, 104,
    129–30, 133, 155, 179
    bond of love   156
    social trinitarianism   67,
        83–4

universalism   102, 105, 109–13,
    125–7, 132, 157
    hopeful   110, 132
    hypothetical   94–109, 111,
        126
universal nature, *see* abstract
    nature

Westminster Confession   14, 24,
    29

SCRIPTURE INDEX

Genesis
2.17   32
50.20-21   18

Deuteronomy
32.4   35

Job   186, 188
38   189
42.7   189

Psalms   186
6   189
7   189
13   189
22   189
88   189
88.1-2   189
130   189

Jeremiah
31.15   189

Habakkuk
1.13   35, 103

Wisdom of Solomon
8.1   139

Matthew
26.36-35   80

Mark
14.32-42   80

Luke
22.19   163
22.39-46   80

John
3.16   94
6.63   163

Romans
8.23   109
8.26-27   188
8.28   194
9   97, 100, 192
11.29   97
13.13-14   134

1 Corinthians
11.27   180
11.29   180
15.22   98

2 Corinthians
5.21   109
15.14-15   98

Ephesians
1   192
1.4-5   100
2   144
2.1   144
2.8   100

Philippians
2   70
2.13   145

Colossians
1   94
1.20   98

1 Timothy
1.17   138
4.10   98

Titus
2.11   98

Hebrews
2.9   98
4.15   59, 61, 118

6.10   103
7.9-10   39

James
1.13   103

1 John
1.15   35
2.2   98
4.14   98